The Word of Wisdom
and the
Creation of Animals in Africa

Shelagh Ranger

James Clarke & Co

James Clarke & Co
P.O. Box 60
Cambridge
CB1 2NT

www.jamesclarke.co.uk
publishing@jamesclarke.co.uk

ISBN 978 0 227 67986 9

British Library Cataloguing in Publication Data
A catalogue record is available from the British Library

Contents

Great things did the Lord lead me into, and wonderful depths were opening unto me, beyond what can by words be declared; but as people come into subjection to the Spirit of God, and grow up in the image and power of the Almighty, they may receive the Word of Wisdom that opens all things, and come to know the hidden unity in the Eternal Being.

George Fox[1]

But gentle Reader as thou art a man, so thou must consider since Adam went out of Paradise, there was never any that was able perfectly to describe the universal condition of all sorts of beasts.

Conrad Gesner[2]

Noah, the world's second taxonomist (after Adam) had to decide who to allow on to his Ark. He took on board seven pairs of each of the biblical clean animals (ruminants, those who chew the cud and have cloven feet) and a pair of each of a selection of the unclean beasts (including, it seems, all the insects — those that 'walk on many feet'). His Ark is estimated by Biblical scholars to have been four hundred and fifty feet long. Nowadays it would have to be a lot bigger.

Steve Jones[3]

1. Quoted in John Punshon, *Portrait in Grey: A short history of the Quakers* (London: Quaker Home Service, 1984/1991) p. 44.
2. *Historiae Animalium*, 1551, quoted in Richard Mabey (ed), *The Oxford Book of Nature Writing* (Oxford University Press, 1997) p. 42.
3. *Almost Like a Whale: The Origin of Species Updated* (Transworld Doubleday, 1999), p. 51.

Acknowledgements

This book had its genesis somewhere between the ancient University of Oxford and the newly built Jesuit Library at Arrupe College in Zimbabwe. My initial inspiration to embark on an anthology of animals and nature in African religious thought came from the Revd. Professor Andrew Linzey, who held the world's first fellowship in theology and animal welfare at Mansfield College, Oxford. He encouraged me and provided invaluable scholarly criticism of my first draft, which I produced after spending some time in Zimbabwe in 1998. My husband was then a visiting professor at the University of Zimbabwe, and we were given a flat in Mount Pleasant within walking distance of Arrupe College, where Jesuit ordinands from all over Africa come for philosophical training. I was allowed access to their magnificent new library with all its international resources, which I explored over a period of more than three years.

On occasional visits home, enthusiastic support for the project was provided by friends and family, several of whom read early drafts of my ms. My brother, Professor Bryan Clarke, FRS, and my sister-in-law, Dr Ann Clarke, Senior Research Fellow at the Institute of Genetics, University of Nottingham, made detailed comments and encouraged me from a scientific point of view. They have been largely responsible for a recent initiative, known as the Frozen Ark, supported by the Natural History Museum and the Zoological Society of London, which aims to collect, preserve and store DNA and tissue samples from animals in danger of extinction, to ensure that the important genetic information of each animal is secured should they become extinct. Like many others, they are concerned about moral and ethical questions raised by recent scientific discoveries, which have hardly been addressed by traditional Christianity.

Encouragement also came from cousin Cherrie de Kisshazy, who as an animals rights activist had first put me in touch with Andrew Linzey. Dr John Reed, an old friend whom we had known at the

University College of Rhodesia & Nyasaland since 1958, encouraged me from the point of view of a retired professor of English language and literature with African experience, providing books and references, as well as useful comments and criticisms.

Wise advice about publishing was provided by Professor Jesse Mugambi in Nairobi and Irene Staunton in Harare. Among other academic friends in Africa who offered encouragement were Professor Mercy Amba-Oduyoye and the Rt Rev. Patrick Kalilombe, both of whom have generously contributed the foreword and the afterword. Dr. Yvonne Vera, Director of the Art Gallery in Bulawayo, and Pip Curling at the Zimbabwe Art Gallery in Harare, helped me in finding suitable illustrations. Many African authors and publishers were generously willing to grant me permission to quote their works free of charge. Every effort has been made to contact copyright-holders of selected excerpts and illustrations and to give them due acknowledgement.

Finally, I have to admit that this book would not have been possible without the inspiration provided by my husband, Professor Terence Ranger, who has written so much about the history of religion in Africa in a much more scholarly way. Needless to say, any historical errors or theological heresies are entirely my own.

Foreword
by Professor Patrick Kalilombe

The Word of Wisdom is, for me, a paradoxical achievement. It is at one and the same time vulnerable and yet powerfully explosive. Probably Shelagh Ranger would not want to consider herself a professional academic. And yet here she is, boldly entering the area of Theology and Religious Studies, precisely in the specialized category of 'Creation and Ecological Theology'. Here she summons and challenges African and other thinkers from the so-called 'Third World' to come along with her. The repeated calls she makes to them in this book remind one of Prophetess Deborah of old, that 'mother in Israel' (Judges 5:7), who took the initiative to rally the embattled troops of Israel (Judges 4:6-10). Deborah dared them to come out and do battle against formidable odds. Shelagh is encouraging African thinkers to claim a terrain where Western theological specialists, with their accustomed 'scientific' tools of investigation, have tended to dominate. The African thinkers should not think that they do not have the required weapons. On the contrary, they should seek to take the lead, for they do have the most appropriate tool: the 'Wisdom of Sheba'.

As I read the book, it seems to me that Shelagh is making several important points:

- The Theology of Creation and Ecology, which is developing fast these days, is a most important development in theological thinking. Its insights about the importance of human relations with animals and the rest of creation are peculiarly relevant to the needs of a new global theology.
- What she has identified as 'The Wisdom of Sheba' is the appropriate tool for articulating such a theology.
- This Wisdom of Sheba is a traditional heritage of Africa, so it is available to African theologians if only they open their eyes to discover it all around them, and learn to make use of it in their theologizing.

One may ask: But where is this Wisdom of Sheba to be found, and what kind of insights does it contain?

In answer, the book calls attention to several areas of the African heritage, old as well as contemporary. Shelagh has identified six such areas and has turned them into as many Sections of the book. In each Section she has collected concrete samples of 'literature' out of which the insights of this Wisdom can be teased. The large number of extracts included in the anthology, the wide variety of their provenance and the long span of time over which they are spread, are proof of extensive and careful research. And yet there is no pretension of presenting them as exhaustive. It is clear that the selection has been commanded by the compiler's understanding of what the Wisdom of Sheba is supposed to be. The introductions to each Section, where the selected extracts are presented and commented on, give the reader an idea of her interpretation and modes of discussion. The judgments as to how and what the selected texts exhibit as 'The Wisdom of Sheba' are evidently personal; they are not presented as prescriptive, but simply as suggestive and open to further discussion.

Nevertheless they are invaluable in that they suggest a number of ways for making sense of these widely differing types of literature, most of which would be resistant to the usual set of rules of academic interpretation. These ways have undoubtedly much in common with the manner the owners and users of these genres of popular folklore have traditionally been making sense of them. Those traditions are here being affirmed, valorized and vindicated.

I was suggesting that Shelagh's book is vulnerable and runs the risk of being dismissed by formal academics. Such people will object that the book is nothing but a collection of texts from all kinds of incompatible sources, and that out of them no demonstrably tight line of argument can be drawn. And indeed the selection is unashamedly eclectic and the conclusions sometimes arrived at in unconventional ways. Other scholars will take issue with the way the supernatural and the miraculous seem to be taken seriously. Angels and demons, spirits of the dead, animals, trees, and even natural features of the landscape converse and interact with ordinary people, arguing serious issues of human life and destiny. It is as if they all constitute one community and are responsible for and answerable to one another for the universe they all have a right to share. Is that not the stuff of children's fairy tales? What kind of 'Wisdom' could come out of such naive and imaginary material to enrich serious theological discussion?

Such objections would show that the point being made in this book has not been understood. What may sound shocking and unacceptable to some people is precisely what makes the book so powerful. This 'Wisdom of Sheba' is in line with a particular world-view according to which the whole of creation, with its diverse parts, belongs together as an organic community under their common Creator and Sustainer. It is like the way the various members of the human body relate to one another as inter-dependent, mutually complementary units in order to assure their common survival, growth and development.

In the same way the various components of the universe: the visible as well as the invisible, humankind as well as the animal world, other animate and inanimate beings, were created to function together in mutual service and care. Humanity, conscious of having been made in the image of the Creator, may consider itself as the head and/or heart of this universe. But that does not mean it is the sole repository of the art of successful global living: humanity should be ready to learn, through attentive and respectful observation, from the 'wisdom' exhibited in the rest of creation. Neither should the human species act as though the whole universe is just for its own selfish needs and interests, and permit itself to dominate, oppress and exploit at will the rest of creation. The other partners too have legitimate rights; and if these are not respected, the delicate balance of creation is destroyed. The resulting disaster punishes not only the injured members, but also ultimately the human community itself.

As the collection of extracts in the present anthology demonstrates, this is the world-view that has been characteristic of most human cultures, in the past as well as in our contemporary world. If I understand correctly, the central point being made by *The Word of Wisdom* is that, in the current ecological crisis, the insights of this world-view are sorely needed. I hope the African theologians who are being called upon will take the summons seriously and go to look with new eyes at the rich heritage of their ancestors. Who knows? What they may have tended to undervalue, due to their 'Western' education, might prove to be part of the salvation of the present world.

Rt. Rev. P.A.Kalilombe
Zomba
Malawi

Abbreviations

AAEC	Association of African Earthkeeping Churches
Acts	Acts of the Apostles in N.T.
AIC	African Independent (or Indigenous) Church.
ATR	African Traditional Religion
BCE	Before Common Era (equivalent of BC)
CE	Common Era (equivalent of AD)
c. or *ca.*	Circa (about)
Chron.	Book of Chronicles in O.T.
Deut.	Book of Deuteronomy in O.T.
Dr	Doctor
ed. eds.	Editor, editors
et al	with others
Exod.	Book of Exodus in O.T.
Ezek.	Book of Ezekiel in O.T.
Gen.	Book of Genesis in O.T.
Gr.	Greek
ibid.	in the same previously cited work
Jn.	Gospel of John in N.T.
Jub.	Book of Jubilees in Apocrypha
Lv.	Book of Leviticus in O.T.
LXX	Septuagint
Matt.	Gospel of Matthew
ms	manuscript
N.T.	New Testament
Num.	Book of Numbers in O.T.
O.T.	Old Testament
Pet.	Epistle of Peter in N.T.
pl.	plural
RC	Roman Catholic
Rev	Reverend (clerical title of a priest or minister)
Rev.	Book of Revelations in N.T.
Rt Rev.	Right Reverend (clerical title of a bishop)
SJ	Society of Jesus (JESUIT)
St	Saint
transl.	translation or translator
UN	United Nations
WCC	World Council of Churches
Zech.	Book of Zechariah in O.T.
Zirrcon	Zimbabwean Institute of Religious Research &Ecological Conservation

Introduction
and Historical Background

In introducing students of theology to Africa's traditional wisdom regarding God's Creation and the relationship that human beings have, or should have, with other animals, it is necessary to draw on the work of scholars in many different disciplines. The anthology is divided into Six Sections, relating to the main sources of wisdom: (1) African traditional religions (ATRs) south of the Sahara; (2) the religion of early civilizations in the Nile valley; (3) Jewish writings and pseudepigraphical scriptures found in Africa; (4) Christian writings, including extra-canonical gospels and epistles, written, translated or discovered in Africa; (5) Islamic texts, the oral traditions and writings of African Muslims; (6) recent writings and praxis of African theologians. In a concluding chapter attention is drawn to four topics that need further theological exploration, namely *Angelic Powers, Ancestral Spirits, Blood Sacrifice,* and *Language,* in the hope that readers will be encouraged to embark on academic research. To begin with, however, it may be helpful to provide some historical background as well as thoughts about why such research is needed today.

Our African Origins

A century and a half ago Charles Darwin came to the conclusion that it was 'somewhat more probable that our early progenitors lived on the African continent than elsewhere.'[1] His tentative theory, which shocked his contemporaries, has since been confirmed by excavations in Ethiopia.

Many nineteenth-century Christian missionaries refused to believe that the human race is descended from apes or that the seven days of Creation recorded in Genesis referred to millions of years.[2] Today Creationists and other fundamentalist Christians still insist on a literal interpretation of the Bible, but even those who accept Darwin's evolutionary theory, nevertheless regard the human species as uniquely superior, as Mary Midgley observes:

The meaning of kinship between humans and other animals depends on how those animals are conceived. And, as our imagery still shows, even today, at a deep imaginative level, people still tend to see animals as symbols of odious, anti-human qualities – wolf, pig, dog, cow, raven, rat, toad, jackal, snake – the list is endless. Nor are the images of our nearest relatives, the other primates much better. It is not surprising, then, that people who think that they are being asked to accept kinship with odious qualities resist the idea.[3]

Yet some of our African forebears were aware, long before Darwin, that humanity was a late arrival on earth and had not only much in common with other animal species but much to learn from them. African mythology suggests that animals have something, which has not always been heeded or has been lost sight of, to teach human beings. This primeval wisdom needs to be retrieved for the benefit of all God's creatures, including human beings, as Joseph Campbell is aware:

> The animal envoys of the Unseen Power no longer serve, as in primeval times, to teach and to guide mankind. Bears, lions, elephants, ibexes, and gazelles are in cages in our zoos. Man is no longer the newcomer in a world of unexplored plains and forests, and our immediate neighbors are not wild beasts but other human beings, contending for goods and space on a planet that is whirling without end around the fireball of a star. Neither in body nor in mind do we inhabit the world of those hunting races of the Paleolithic millennia, to whose lives and life ways we nevertheless owe the very forms of our bodies and structures of our minds. Memories of their animal envoys still must sleep, somehow, within us; for they wake a little and stir when we venture into the wilderness.[4]

Wilderness is a concept common to all the great religions of the world, including most African religions, as a place where human frailty is tested and where seekers meet God. It is also the place where other animals are encountered. The deserts and wild parts of Africa have long fascinated European explorers as places in which to discover unknown species, to study, dissect, analyse and photograph them – even to hunt them for 'sport'. But for Africans such places have had other significances. For early Christians in North Africa the desert wilderness was the site of the hermit and the monk; for adherents of Shona traditional religion the wilderness is a tract of 'sacred land' reserved from human exploitation; for members of some African Independent or Indigenous Churches (AICs)[5] wilderness is imaginatively constructed today in open spaces in the cities as a place where the Creator God may be worshipped and where the Holy Spirit can bring healing by vanquishing witches and demons.

Myths and Oral Traditions

The oral traditions of sub-Saharan Africa embody a wisdom which connects to the very earliest time, before Egyptian religion, before African Judaism, before African Christianity, and before African Islam. The myths, praise poems, prayers and folk stories about animals in Section One are drawn from a variety of sources, including African novelists, poets, mythologists, and theologians, as well as from the collections of expatriate scholars working in Africa. As Northrop Frye so eloquently expresses it:

> Man lives, not directly or nakedly in nature like the animals, but within a mythological universe, a body of assumptions and beliefs developed from his existential concerns. Most of this is held unconsciously, which means that our imaginations may recognize elements of it, when presented in art or literature, without consciously understanding what it is that we recognize.[6]

Music and poetry are Africa's traditional means of vernacular communication. Appreciation of the beauty and spiritual quality of animals, both wild and tame, is also expressed in painting and sculpture all over Africa. The stone sculptors in Zimbabwe today often depict spiritual animals that look unlike any known species, while rock paintings and etchings made hundreds, perhaps thousands, of years earlier by Bushmen (or San) often vividly portray recognizable animals. Some scholars think that some Bushmen images depict the vision of a shaman who is able to 'see' far beyond the reach of an ordinary person either by flying, in an 'out of body experience', or by taking the form of an animal.[7]

While the Genesis story has been interpreted by Europeans as giving human beings absolute authority, 'dominion', over our fellow creatures to use in any way we like, many African Creation myths provide an alternative world view more agreeable to those concerned about species now threatened with extinction. African myths also tell us much more than the Book of Genesis does about the origin and theological significance of the animal kingdom before the creation of mankind. Stories of Creation, the Fall, and a Tree of Life guarded by monsters, are found all over the world. Most academic theologians nowadays accept Karl Rahner's contention that 'the accounts in the first chapter of Genesis about the beginning of the history of the human race are not to be understood as an eyewitness report, . . . supplied by God as someone who was, as it were, involved in this primeval history.' If we know about our origins through revelation and tradition, such a tradition must appear in strange and varied mythological forms, and 'even the most abstract metaphysical language works with images, analogies and representations'.[8]

The function of myths in understanding or explaining human origins is different from, but not necessarily in opposition to, revelation. Indeed the vivid imagery of myth is often desirable and necessary for the sake of truth and is in fact a mode of knowing which surpasses all comprehension and expression, as Mary Midgley puts it:

> Myths play a crucial role in our imaginative and intellectual life by articulating the patterns that underlie our thought. They are the general background within which all detailed thought develops, and anyone who thinks he is free of them has simply not taken the trouble to become aware of that background. The way in which myths work is often very obscure to us. But, besides their value-implications – which are often very subtle – they also function as summaries of certain selected sets of facts.[9]

Yet in most Christian bible schools and seminaries the myths of African cultures, if they are considered at all, are not generally accorded the same weight as those of the Hebrews. University faculties of theology nowadays usually include a department of Comparative Religion, but this will seldom provide courses on African religions. Compared to those regarded as 'world religions' (Hindu, Muslim, Buddhist, etc.), the status of animals in Creation myths is not often a focus of academic research. What almost certainly will be studied, of course, is the status of women.

Natural Religion

In Europe three hundred years ago it was sometimes debated whether or not women had immortal souls. Although both women and 'heretics' were debarred from teaching, alternative views of Creation were put forward by proponents of Natural Religion, some of whom believed that because Adam and Eve had been created in the image of God, they did not need to be taught philosophy or theology, but possessed divine knowledge that they passed on to their descendants all over the world. To other Enlightenment thinkers Natural Religion meant the ability to arrive at truth by using the power of reason. Matthew Tindal expressed a view that present-day theologians might endorse:

> By *Natural Religion*, I understand the Belief of the Existence of a God, and the Sense and Practice of those Duties, which result from the Knowledge, we, by our Reason, have of him, and his

Perfections . . . and of the Relation we stand in to him, and to our Fellow-Creatures; so that the *Religion of Nature* takes in every Thing that is founded on Reason and Nature of Things.[10]

The Puritan divine, Richard Baxter (1615-91), while avowing that Christianity was the perfect religion, also recognized wisdom in other religions, even in that of the Greek philosophers:

And I find that the Idolatry of the wisest of them was not so foolish as that of the Vulgar; but they thought that the Universe was one animated world, and that the Universal Soul was the only Absolute Sovereign God, whom they described much like as Christians do: and that the Sun, and Stars, and Earth, and each particular Orb was an individual *Animal*, part of the Universal world, and besides the Universal, had each one a subordinate particular Soul, which they worshipped as a subordinate particular Deity, as some Christians do the Angels.[11]

Such views challenged the doctrines of the Church at the time of the European Enlightenment, but it was nearly three hundred years before African scholars dared to challenge European missionary doctrines. One of the first to do so was E. Bolanji Idowu, who lamented:

It has become increasingly clear, and disturbingly so, that the Church has been speaking in Africa and to Africans in strange or partially understood tongues. We must be thankful to God that in spite of man's weaknesses and short-sightedness, the miracle of grace has been taking place all over Africa. Nevertheless, we realize that both the tools and the method of evangelism as employed in this continent are now calling very loudly for a careful overhauling.[12]

Others make even more forceful criticisms. Hannah Kinoti begins by challenging the whole idea of the *Pax Britannica,* on which missionaries so heavily relied in British colonies. 'Pacification' was undertaken through a series of 'punitive expeditions' aimed at breaking the backbone and the soul of the natives, as she remembers:

These expeditions entailed shooting people – to demonstrate the power of the gun over spears, bows and arrows – burning villages, looting livestock and occupying land with utter disregard to its owners, who were then running away from gunfire. 'Pacification' further entailed a transformation of the society from the state of self-determination to the state of servitude in less than a decade.

In spite of such cruel treatment, she thinks 'the people were disposed to joy and forgiveness', even before missionaries began preaching Christianity, and asks:

Wherein lay the reason for this characteristic which is equally
evident in other African peoples? For these 'prehistoric' people
the reason must surely lie in the kind of upbringing of children
and the religio-cultural traditions that captured and stored the
ethos of a people more preoccupied with things lovely and
good. The Christian is enjoined to dwell on the positive: 'fill
your minds with those things that are true, noble, right, pure,
lovely, and honourable.' (Philippians 4:8)

Kinoti quotes an early Consolata missionary who recognized: 'The
Agikuyu do not possess books on ethics, psychology, or other high-
flown theories of modern science; but they possess a rich inheritance
of common-sense which is handed down in oral tradition from father
to son, told by grandfathers to the young people . . . in the form of
endless proverbs, parables and stories.'[13]

From a slightly different angle, another feminist theologian, Mercy
Amba-Oduyoye, challenges the imposition of a biblical culture on Africa:

Since the Bible depicts other peoples' cultures, and we know
from African culture that not everything in culture is liberating,
we come to the Bible with the same cautious approach we
have to culture. Any interpretation of the Bible is unacceptable
if it does harm to women, the vulnerable and the voiceless.
There are two sides to treating culture as a principle for
hermeneutics. Taking culture as a tool with which to understand
and interpret one's reality, and specifically the Bible, allows
one to take one's experience seriously and to connect it with
other realities.[14]

Such considerations are leading African theologians to rediscover their
traditional cultures and civilizations that once flourished in Africa.

Early Civilizations in the Nile Valley

After beginning in Section One with traditions and myths from sub-
Saharan Africa, we turn in Section Two to the religion of early Egyptian
and Nilotic civilizations. This sequence makes two important points.
The first is that Egyptian religion grew out of previous African rites
and traditions; the second is that the fully developed religion of the
Pharaohs was itself African. Moreover, Africans can be rightly proud
of the enormous contribution that Egypt made to western civilization.
Lionel Casson in his beautifully illustrated study, sums it up:

The Egyptians were political pioneers. So far as we know,
they were the first to create a unified state, to design
governmental machinery for administering hundreds of miles
and thousands of people, to plan and execute large projects.

They were also social pioneers. It was they who first worked out ways of gracious living, of enjoying leisure, of giving life an overlay of sophistication. It is in Egypt that we find the first houses which offer space and comfort, are handsomely decorated, and boast such amenities as baths and toilets. It is in Egypt that we first find serious attention given to the preparation of food, where the arts of cooking, baking, and brewing came to be developed and appreciated. It is Egypt that provides the earliest examples of dinner parties with their traditional features – elegant dress, efficient and courteous service, choice and abundant food, entertainment to amuse the guests. The ubiquitous tombs with their grave furniture and mummies give a wrong impression. The Egyptians were a worldly, materialistic people who, along with the sombre monuments to their dead and their gods, bequeathed to posterity the art of adding grace and refinement to daily living.[15]

More recently, John Iliffe adds an important further tribute to ancient Egyptian civilization, which contributed so much to the practice of the early Church if not to that of the later Holy Roman Empire:

Egypt had no powerful class or lineages collectively controlling property, which was held within the elementary family. Marriage was mainly monogamous, descent was largely bilateral from both father and mother, and women had an exceptionally high status with full rights to inherit property, preserve the dowry brought into marriage, and receive one third of jointly acquired property in case of divorce, which was easy and common.[16]

Egyptian civilization extended far to the South of the Third Cataract, where its roots may be found. In Nubia's richest agricultural region, black Nubians built Kerma, a huge walled city, with a ritual centre resembling an Egyptian temple. About 593 BCE, the capital of this ancient Nubian state moved still further south to Meroe, where it was to survive for almost another thousand years. Meroitic religion combined the Egyptian sun god Amen with local deities, such as the Lion god, Apedemak.[17] Rulers of Meroe called themselves Kings of Upper and Lower Egypt, but were chosen by the 'Queen Mother' in a manner wholly African. Meroe supplied gold, slaves, and tropical produce to the Mediterranean and Middle East. Its armies commanded cavalry using the first bridles, bits, and spurs found in Africa, and leaders were buried with their cherished horses.[18] By the second century BCE Nubians were apparently using twenty-three signs similar to Egyptian hieroglyphs to write the Meroitic language, although this has not yet been deciphered.[19] In Egypt two scripts were invented almost simultaneously: hieroglyphic script, the 'words of the god' with inherent magical power, was used for formal documents and inscriptions; while cursive script, used in daily life, was a greatly simplified version of hieroglyphic. Iliffe thinks that at this time probably no more than one in a hundred Egyptians was literate,[20] but this was probably a higher proportion than in Europe a thousand years later.

Thus the civilization of Egypt certainly interacted with, and developed from, the beliefs and practices of people living in sub-saharan Africa. According to Basil Davidson, kingdoms had emerged in what he calls 'inner Africa' before they did further north on the Nile. A classical Greek author, Diodorus of Sicily (*c. 50 BCE*), affirms that 'the Egyptians are colonists who were sent out by the Ethiopians'. Indeed:

> Archaeology has produced varied and no longer questioned evidence to show that the land of the blacks — of those whom the classical Greek authors called 'Ethiopians', not after the country we know as Ethiopia but after the Greek word for black persons, *aithiops* — were, in fact, the lands from which most of the inhabitants of Egypt had originally come.[21]

However, Davidson thinks the way Egyptian pharaohs were later made into gods was an aberration 'derived from the ambitions of an overweening priesthood', rather than from inner Africa, where kings were never accorded divine status. What was divine, in African belief, was their spiritual authority: 'kings would die, but that could not.'[22]

The Legacy of the Pharaohs

Not only did classical Greece adopt Egyptian philosophy and learning along with its pantheon of gods and sacrificial rites, but the influence of these beliefs and practices can be found in African Judaism and early Coptic Christianity. Hymns from the Pyramid Texts were described by James Henry Breasted in 1912 as, 'the oldest of all literary forms known to us'. They exhibit, 'an early poetic form, that of couplets displaying parallelism in arrangement of words and thought – the form which is familiar to all in the Hebrew psalms'.[23]

Martin Bernal suggests that the death and resurrection of Osiris, god of the Nile, every year was later understood by Egyptian Christians as a prefiguration of the sacrificial death and resurrection of Christ.[24] And, according to Ali Mazrui, the idea of a man being also a god was as familiar to ancient Egyptians as their centuries-old pyramids:

> After all, most pharaohs were both men and gods. But ah! there was something new. Jesus was not a pharaoh, at least not of this world. He was not even a priest in the usual

Egyptian sense of attachment to a temple and organised religion. Jesus was a common man. It was this notion of godliness without pomp, divinity without earthly royalty, which inspired some of the earliest Egyptian Christians into seeking the desert for solitude and humility. The neighbouring desert was a temptation of a different kind – a temptation away from temptation, beckoning the devout towards the life of self-denial. The splendour of the desert was a splendour of desolation, compatible with a view of a god who was also a common man, divine majesty in humble clothing, the grandeur of creation in the form of miles upon miles of emptiness.[25]

Egypt of the pharaohs was regarded by the Greeks as 'the fount and origin of wisdom, venerable in its beliefs and monuments, amazing in its mathematics and philosophy.' The names of nearly all the Greek gods were inherited from Egypt, and Homer believed that these gods flew south once a year to feast with the older gods of inland Africa.[26] The philosophy of ancient Egypt was taken up by Plato and his disciple, Aristotle. At the king of Macedonia's court school, Aristotle taught the young Alexander the Great. For the Greeks of the Classical Age, Egypt was where one went to learn history. Writers such as Herodotus of Halicarnassus (born around 490 BCE) took it for well-established fact that the Greeks had learned their civilization from the Egyptians. Yet, according to Davidson, the Greeks of the Classical Age also affirmed that pharaonic culture had derived from inner Africa, from the lands of the 'long-lived Ethiopians', as Herodotus called them, meaning not the people of the country we nowadays call Ethiopia but in general the country of the blacks.[27] Although the African roots of Western civilization's philosophy, art, and culture have not always been recognized, at the time of the Italian Renaissance it was generally acknowledged that 'Egypt was before Greece, the *Corpus Hermeticum* before the *Republic* and Hermes before Plato.' Indeed, it is thought that Plato's own Athenian academy was founded on the Egyptian model. Even the paraphernalia of European academic dress and graduation ceremonies can be traced back to sacred initiation rites in the temples of Egypt.[28]

Racism of Imperial Rome

Greek and Roman colonizers respected the wisdom of ancient Egypt and adopted their gods, while introducing rather different concepts of immortality. However, Brian P. Copenhaver notes the xenophobia and racism that later affected Roman attitudes to African wisdom:

Native Egyptian letters were still lively under the Ptolemies but soon took on Greek coloration. Roman xenophobia found a good target for its anxieties in Egypt, which became proverbial in Latin writing for opulence and degeneracy. Juvenal's abuse of Egyptian village religion — his fifteenth *Satire* — is the most celebrated example of this aspect of Roman racism:

> Who does not know what monsters lunatic Egypt
> Chooses to cherish? One part goes in for crocodile worship;
> One bows down to the ibis that feeds upon serpents; elsewhere
> A golden effigy shines, of a long-tailed holy monkey.[29]

Sadly, this negative Roman attitude was to become prevalent in European thought. Yet it was not until the Christian era that the systematic destruction of the ancient religion of the Nile Valley began. According to Mazrui, Christian rulers were nervous about the pre-Christian symbolism of the pyramids and the sphinx, often regarding them as potential signposts of subversion and sin. The iconoclasm begun by Christians was completed seven centuries later when Arab invaders imposed the monotheism of Islam, and in time 'Islamised Egypt was forced even further into an induced amnesia about its past.' Egyptians became not only Muslims, but also Arabs. Their African identity had been changed.[30]

Western scholars, while acknowledging Europe's debt to Pharaonic Egypt, have somehow managed to divorce Egyptian civilization from the rest of black Africa. Since the Islamic invasion in the seventh century, Egypt came to be seen as part of the Arab 'Middle East', and elaborate racial theories contributed to this view. Blumenbach, who in 1795 was the first to use the term 'Caucasian' to describe the superior 'white' race, included 'Semites' and 'Egyptians' in this category. His 'scientific' theories of the origins of mankind seemed to find support in both Scripture and Greek mythology. Because it was believed that Noah's Ark had landed on Mount Ararat in the Southern Caucasus, human origins were claimed to be 'Caucasian' and identified with Europeans:

> The Caucasus was the traditional site of the imprisonment and cruel punishment of Prometheus, who was considered the epitome of Europe. Not only was he the son of Iapetos, plausibly identified as the biblical Japhet, third son of Noah and the ancestor of the Europeans; but his heroic, beneficial and self-sacrificing action — of stealing fire for mankind — soon came to be seen as typically Aryan. Gobineau saw him as the ancestor of the principal white family and by the 20th century the ultra-Romantic Robert Graves was even suggesting that the name Prometheus meant 'swastika.'[31]

Although Semites had originally been included as part of the Caucasian 'race', Nazi ideology later introduced a more exclusive definition of Aryan to mean a Caucasian not of Jewish descent. However, in South Africa the policy of *apartheid* continued to classify 'white' Jews as Caucasian.[32]

African Jewry

Whether Noah's ark landed in Africa, in the Caucasus, or somewhere in between, there is a no doubt that Judaism itself has African roots. The Hebrew Bible records that Joseph, the youngest son of Jacob (Israel), when he was seventeen years old, was sold into slavery in Egypt. Through his ability to interpret dreams, he became the Pharoah's trusted servant and was eventually made governor of the whole land. When there was famine in Canaan, Joseph's brothers came in search of food, and at Joseph's invitation Jacob's entire family moved to Egypt, where they occupied the land of Ramases.[33] Joseph married an Egyptian woman, Asenath,[34] and before he died Jacob blessed his son Joseph with words that reflect a sense of God's presence in all of his Creation:

> blessings of grain and flowers,
> blessings of ancient mountains;
> bounty of the everlasting hills;
> may they descend on Joseph's head,
> on the brow of the dedicated one among his brothers.

Although the body of Jacob was embalmed and returned to the land of Canaan, Joseph continued to live in Egypt, and when he died his body was laid in a coffin there. The Egyptians mourned him for seventy days.[35] Thus Joseph's family, the children of Israel, were immigrants who had settled in Egypt and made it their home. To what extent Hebrews were distinguishable from other Semites at this time is debatable. According to Alfred Guillaume, the people known as Habiru (or 'Apiru) are almost certainly to be identified with the Arabs: 'If that be so, then the Hebrews of the Old Testament were Arabs, part of the ancient inhabitants of the Arabian peninsula.'[36] In those days Egyptians did not regard themselves as part of the Arab world as they do today, and the indigenous inhabitants of Egypt (the Copts) were Africans.

Over the centuries the numbers of Hebrews in Egypt grew until they were said to number more than the native Copts. According to the Biblical account, in an attempt to limit the birthrate, two Hebrew midwives, Shiphrah and Puah, were instructed to kill male babies, but being 'God-fearing: they disobeyed the command of the king of Egypt.' One baby of the tribe of Levi was hidden in the bullrushes and, after being found by a princess, he grew up as an Egyptian. According to St Luke, Moses was 'schooled in all the wisdom of Egypt'.[37] Whether or not one accepts the argument of Sigmund Freud that Moses merely adopted the monotheism introduced by the Pharaoh Akhenaton,[38] certainly when he led some Hebrew slaves into the wilderness about 1250 BCE, the revelation of God given to him on Mount Sinai could only be expressed in the theological language of Egypt.

The Israelites whom Moses led out of Egypt were a 'mixed crowd' that included other foreigners, particularly black slaves from Cush or Ethiopia. The only requirement was that they be circumcised.[39] Moses himself, after marrying first a Midianite, Zipporah, took a Cushite wife.[40] The name of Moses' great nephew, Phinehas the priest, indicates that he was Black.[41]

Not only were some of Moses' followers African or of mixed race, many later Hebrew scriptures can be shown to have African roots. John Romer suggests that passages in the Books of *Genesis*, *Exodus* and *Proverbs* could have been derived from ancient Egyptian texts. The story of a baby floating down the Nile in a reed basket, is a variant of a tale told of several ancient heroes. Precisely the same story is told of King Sargon who around 2500 BCE founded a new empire based upon southern Mesopotamia. Like King Sargon, baby Moses drifts in a basket caulked with pitch, a common commodity in Mesopotamia but a rare importation in ancient Egypt. Moses' name, however, is Egyptian enough, and one he shares with many famous pharaohs; Ra-moses or Ramesses, Thoth-Moses or Tuthmosis: Ramesses means 'born of the god Ra', Tuthmosis 'born of the god Thoth'. Romer regards the flight from Egypt, commemorated in the Jewish Passover, as a myth for which there is little historical basis although the stories of the plagues recorded in *Exodus* accurately describe 'a genuine ancient catastrophe', which could well have brought down the Pharaoh, not as a punishment for enslaving the Israelites, but 'as part of a contest between the two deities, Pharaoh and Jehovah.'[42]

After the settlement in Canaan, there was a continual exchange of people between these territories, and Hebrew communities along the banks of the Nile developed their own traditions. Following the destruction of the temple in Jerusalem, there were in fact more Jews outside Palestine than in their 'homeland'.[43] Most of the Jews who survived Nebuchadnezzar's conquest of Judah were deported to Babylon, and only after Cyrus permitted the exiled Jews to return in 539 BCE to begin the rebuilding of the Temple was there a slow growth in the number of Jews in Palestine.[44] Jewish colonists at Elephantine in upper Egypt had built a temple where other gods were worshipped alongside Yahweh. When this temple was destroyed in the fifth century BCE, they wrote to the Persian governors of Judah and Samaria to ask for assistance in rebuilding it. Later when the last Zadokite high priest of Jerusalem was deposed in 175 BCE, his son built another temple in Egypt at Leontopolis, and Josephus, the priest reporting this event, evidently did not regard Solomon's temple in Jerusalem as unique. Not only did Jewish communities in the Diaspora build other temples, there is evidence that they also possessed other Arks of the Covenant. Most famous of these is the one in Ethiopia, which is believed to have been transported from Jerusalem to Aksum by Menelik, the son of King Solomon and the Queen of Sheba.[45]

Ethiopian Jews, known as Falasha or *Beta Israel* (House of Israel), claim to be the descendants of the bodyguard provided by King Solomon for his son's journey from Jerusalem. So there were Jews in Ethiopia before it became a Christian kingdom in the fourth century C.E. It is estimated that there may have been as many as half a million Jews in Ethiopia before the Emperor Susneyos (encouraged by Portuguese Jesuits) launched a pogrom in the seventeenth century, when thousands were killed and their children sold as slaves. By 1984 they numbered fewer than thirty thousand, and in the famine year of 1985 some seven thousand Falashas were airlifted to Israel in the controversial 'Operation Moses'. Today, there may be more Falasha living unhappily in Israel than remain in Ethiopia.[46]

African Judaism has a long history not only along the Nile and in Ethiopia but in other parts of the continent as well. North African Jewry, having survived Roman persecution and Arab invasions, enjoyed the dawn of a 'golden age' in the ninth and tenth centuries. Jewish traders established prosperous communities as far west as Marrakech with centres of learning to rival the authority of the ancient Babylonian academies. The first complete commentary on the Talmud was written by a Tunisian rabbi, Hananel ben Hushi'el (c. 1007 CE), and North African scholars wrote treatises on medicine, philosophy, mathematics and poetry. No doubt treatises were written about Creation and animals, which would be relevant to our current concerns. Indeed, according to Eli Barnavi, there was 'virtually no intellectual, spiritual or artistic sphere which was not explored and revitalized by medieval North African Jewry.' These communities survived for over a thousand years until twentieth-century Zionism encouraged some of them to 'return' to the land of Israel.[47] One can only hope that they have not lost touch with their African heritage.

Surprisingly, Africans are converting to Judaism today. For example, in Uganda an African Jewish community, known as the *Abuyudaya* (sons of Judah) was founded less than a hundred years ago by a military leader, Semei Kakungulu, who felt betrayed by the British colonial power. At that time (1919) he had never met another Jew. It was not until 1926 when he went to Kampala that Kakungulu made friends with a Jewish trader named Joseph, who was amazed to hear of his conversion to Judaism. Joseph agreed to instruct the *Abuayudaya* in the current prayers and practices of Judaism, including the slaughtering ritual and all the festivals and feasts to be celebrated. He taught the elders of the community the Hebrew alphabet, but none of them remember where Joseph came from; some think it was Ethiopia and others Jerusalem. Before Joseph left, he presented Kakungulu with a large Bible written in Hebrew and English. The history of this movement has been written by Arye Oded, an Israeli Ambassador to Uganda.[48] Since Kakungulu's death in 1928, the *Abayudaya* have survived persecution by Christians and by Idi Amin, who declared Uganda an Islamic state in 1974. Their rural environment has been afflicted with drought, floods, and ensuing famine, which 'leave the entire region at the mercy of Mother Nature' as Kenneth Schultz and Matthew Meyer observed when they visited recently. 'Yet their apparent poverty does not seem to interfere with their ability to live what they consider to be full and Jewish lives.'[49]

The Wisdom of Sheba

The Hebrew Bible records that the Queen of Sheba travelled from the Horn of Africa to the court of King Solomon in Jerusalem nearly three thousand years ago 'to test him with hard questions.' Moreover, 'she told him all that was on her mind'.[50] This African Queen (known in Ethiopia as Makeda) was not only a very rich and influential woman; she was also a scholar. Having heard of Solomon's wisdom from a merchant named Tamrin, she decided to visit Jerusalem.

> She had become convinced that wisdom was better than gold
> or silver, that nothing under the heavens could be compared to
> it. It was sweeter than honey and made the heart rejoice more
> than wine. It was light to the eyes, a shield for the breast and a
> helmet for the head. It could make the ears hear and the heart
> understand. No kingdom could stand without it.[51]

The wisdom that she and Solomon shared has become legendary amongst Christians in Africa, and is widely respected in the Muslim world. According to the Koran, when Solomon reviewed his army of birds, the Hoopoe (or Lapwing) brought him news of Sheba, where the Queen (whose Arabic name is Bilqis) and her people worshipped the sun. Solomon wrote her a letter, which the bird delivered, and she sent tribute before visiting Jerusalem and being converted to Islam.[52]

Queen Bilqis has been accorded a significance by Muslim theologians denied her by Christians outside Africa. For Muhyi-D-Din Ibn'Arabi she symbolizes the nature of woman in complement to the nature of man, represented by King Solomon. 'That magical and mysterious feminine nature that Bilqis represents is expressed by the Arab legend that her father was not human, but a *jinn*, a being from the subtle world.'[53]

Although archaeologists have located the kingdom of Saba or Sheba somewhere in Arabia,[54] Ethiopians claim Makeda as their queen; they have a tradition that she bore a son to Solomon, named Menelik, who later became king, thus establishing what they regard as the true dynasty of David for their country. According to the Ethiopian national epic, the *Kebra Nagast* (Glory of Kings), when young Menelik visited his father, Solomon cried, 'Behold, my father David has renewed his youth and has risen from the dead.' Therefore, before returning home to Africa, the young prince is anointed by Zadok the Priest and given the name David. He is warned of dreadful punishments that await his people if he fails to obey the ways of God.

> The land will be cursed, along with the cattle, all the herds and the flocks of sheep, even the children of his own body. Famine and pestilence will come upon his kingdom. The heavens will turn to brass and the earth to iron. The rain will be black, and dust will fall from heaven.

But Zadok also recites the blessings that will come if he obeys. Solomon blesses David and tells him that the Ark of Zion will be his guide, unaware that the young men chosen to accompany him are contriving to steal the Ark and carry it with them. When they set off, the people of the city begin to wail and weep. The animals too are in distress, the dogs howling and the asses screaming. Everyone is in tears. Solomon is dismayed to hear their anguish. He is trembling himself, and his tears fall on the ground as he cries out that he is lost. His glory is gone and the crown of his splendour has fallen. The majesty of his city has been taken away. When the young David (Menelik) realizes the Ark is with him, he 'jumps and skips like a lamb or a kid that has been fed on the milk of its mother, just as his grandfather David had danced before the Ark.'[55]

Drumming and dancing have always been an important part of worship in the Ethiopian Orthodox Church. The scholarly musicians and cantors (*däbtäras*) claim to have inherited this role from the Levites in Jerusalem. As Francisco Alvares reported in the sixteenth century, 'on this account they are more honoured than all the rest of the clergy.'[56] *Däbtäras* are more educated than village priests and are respected not only because they traditionally dance and sing at major feasts, but also because they have inherited the wisdom of Solomon and much of his magic powers. They inscribe parchment scrolls as talismans, which many Ethiopians wear.[57]

At Aksum the Ark (*Tabot*) containing the Old Law is identified with Mary of Zion who 'held the New Law in the person of Christ.' When Iyasu was consecrated Emperor in the 'Year of Creation' (7191 in the Ethiopian calendar, or 1691CE), in accordance with custom, he entered the sanctuary in the church of St Mary of Zion, kissed the *Tabot* and sat on the throne to receive the sacrament of the body and blood of Christ from the priests. The Ark spoke to him, offering wisdom and wise counsel, in exchange for which the Emperor placed his soul and body in the care of the Ark. The *Kebra Negast* (Book of the Glory of Kings) which records these events is believed to be a translation of a document found before 325 C.E. amongst the treasures St Sophia of Constantinople, but written in its present form during the reign of Iyasu.[58] The Church of St Mary of Zion at Aksum has become the true Jerusalem (or Zion) for both Jews and Christians, with profound theological implications, as Adrian Hastings explains:

> Zion is the Ark of the Covenant installed securely in Aksum. It is, by extension, the *tabot*, upon which every mass is celebrated. It is, by another extension, the Cathedral of Aksum itself. Again, it is another name for Mary, whose equivalence with the Ark of the Covenant goes back to the Gospel of Luke. It is, by the politically most important extension, Ethiopia.[59]

Hellenization and the Coptic Church

When Egypt was conquered by Alexander the Great in 332 BCE, the 'country of the Pharaohs was then exposed to the intensive influence of Greek colonization, called Hellenization.' The native Copts gradually accepted the Greek language and Alexandria became 'a cultural center even more important than Athens.' Although conquered by Rome three hundred years later, it remained a Greek city.[60]

The Hebrew scriptures were translated into Greek (the *Septuagint*) and leaders of the large Jewish community in Alexandria adapted their Hebraic monotheism to Greek philosophy. This Hellenized Judaism in turn profoundly influenced early Christian theology, particularly through the Jewish philosopher, Philo, who lived until 40 CE.[61]

> [His]writings are now recognized as essential for understanding the formative period of both Judaism and Christianity. They show the Judaism of this epoch to have been lively, diverse,

and speculative, open to a range of influences from the surrounding world, yet concerned to preserve and reinterpret its traditions in the face of outside threats. The adoption of these works by the Church reveals how deeply the new religion remained rooted in the soil of Judaism.[62]

There is an ancient tradition, recorded by Eusebius, that St. Mark established the Church of Alexandria, which was at that time by far the most important centre of the Jewish diaspora in the Mediterranean world. By the third century most, if not all, of the books of the New Testament as well as the Old Testament scriptures had been translated into Coptic. As Adrian Hastings maintains:

> In undeniable fashion, fourth-century Egyptian Christianity was to be paradigmatic for the Africa of the future. Starting as a religion of the urban imperial civilization with its Greek language drawn from outside Africa, it had crossed the culture and language gap to appeal to the native African. It had done so by taking his language seriously.[63]

The African Church flourished in spite of persecution. Indeed there were so many Christian martyrs in Egypt that 'a new chronology was started, beginning with the *Era martyrum*, i.e. the reign of Diocletian 283 CE. The Coptic Church continued to use this chronology even when other Churches began counting the years from the birth of Christ.'[64] In the face of persecution early Christians fled to the desert. It is often assumed that the Church began among Jewish communities who recognized Jesus as the promised Messiah. But many converts were Copts who had never been Jews and knew little of Old Testament prophesies. Their reflections on the significance of the dual identity of Jesus (human and divine) was a result of their Egyptian inheritance, which profoundly influenced the formulation of Christian doctrine.

The Coptic Church was a missionary church. Christianity reached Aksum (Ethiopia) in the fourth century, and Egyptian traders brought Christianity to Nubia by at least the fifth century. According to St Luke, an Ethiopian eunuch was one of the first African converts baptized by Philip on his way home to the court of Queen Candace.[65] The three Nubian kingdoms of Nobatia, Alwa and Makuria, remained Christian for nearly a thousand years. Bishops came from Alexandria, and events were dated by the Coptic era of the martyrs. The liturgical language was Greek; only slowly were parts of the liturgy and Bible translated into Nubian, written in the Coptic form of the Greek alphabet. Nubian Christianity did not adapt as fully to the local culture as did Ethiopian Christianity, which was more isolated from external influence. Nubian paintings, for example, always depicted Christ and the saints with white faces, a distinction not drawn in Ethiopian art. Yet Iliffe attributes the different fates of the two Churches more to their different relationships with Islam.[66]

Although the Coptic Church in Egypt was almost wiped out by militant Islam, and still suffers persecution to this day, it has survived and even sends missionaries to other parts of Africa.[67] According to Anthony O'Mahony, some 15,000 Egyptian Christians convert to Islam each year, mainly for reasons of divorce which can be obtained in a relatively easy fashion from Shari'a courts, but which is nearly impossible by Coptic canonical law. There has, however, been a Coptic revival in the last century, based on ancient monastic and ecclesial traditions, including more frequent celebration of the Eucharist. Like other Eastern Orthodox churches, the Coptic Church elects its own Pope, and in 1971 adopted procedures more democratic than those of papal elections in Rome. A list of nine candidates was printed in the daily press, before Pope Shenouda was elected the 117th Patriarch in the line of succession to the throne of St Mark.[68] In Egypt today Christians number perhaps only one in twelve, but the Coptic Church remains the largest denomination of Christians resident in the Arab world.[69]

The austere archaism of the Coptic rite, with melodies that may go back to the time of the Pharaohs, has been contrasted with the liturgical splendours of more recent Greek, Syrian, Maronite and Armenian communities in Alexandria. In Ethiopia the Coptic tradition was continued, but Irenée-Henri Dalmais thinks that when control by Alexandria extended no further than the appointment of the *Abuna* (bishop) the Ethiopian Church 'gave rein to an enthusiastic and fanciful piety, nourished on judaizing and apocalyptical legends, that was very different from Coptic austerity.'[70]

Monasticism

When the early Christians fled to the desert, communities of hermits were formed. The 'Desert Fathers' lived with the wild animals and developed a theology of respect for Creation. They practiced extreme asceticism and provided the model for Christian monasticism, which later carried the gospel message around the world. Antony and Pachomius, Coptic speakers in the African countryside, inspired one of the most important spiritual and institutional developments not only for the Egyptian, Nubian and Ethiopian Churches, but for the whole of Christendom.[71] Pilgrims came from all over the Christian world to see, to imitate and often to join them. One Desert Father, St Moses, is described as a tall black man, who had formerly been a captain of a band of robbers, but who after his conversion became not only an illustrious penitent, but so eminent in all virtue and sanctity as to be raised to the dignity of a priest, and superior of the holy monastery of Scete, and after his death to be enrolled amongst the Saints.[72]

An early Byzantine text states that this tall Ethiopian 'whose body was black had a soul more radiantly bright than the splendour of the sun.'[73] Today the Coptic Orthodox Liturgy of St Mark today still venerates 'St Moses the Black' and 'John the Black' among the heavenly hosts, yet they are virtually unknown in the Western Church. By the beginning of the sixth century the monastic order of Pachomius, established in Egypt in 323 CE, appeared in Ethiopia when Abba Aragawi and his eight companions built their first monastery in Tigray. Popularly venerated in Ethiopia as 'The Nine Saints', their monasteries remained 'for more than a millenium the most decisive institutions for the passing on of the tradition and ministry of the Church.' Monks undertook the laborious work of copying and translating scriptures. Manuscripts like *The Rule of Pachomious* and the *Life of Anthony* were translated into Ge'ez (Ethiopic), as was the *Shepherd of Hermas*, which became part of the Ethiopian canon of holy scripture.[74] Apart from sacred scriptures and lives of the saints, Ethiopian monks also translated into Ge'ez other books brought from Egypt, including biblical exegesis, service books, and homilies by the early church fathers, such as John Chrysostom, Athanasius of Alexandria, Severus of Antioch and Cyril of Alexandria.[75]

Monasticism is an important part of Ethiopian piety, where fasting and self-denial are regarded as a necessary discipline for the laity as much as for the clergy.

African Art and Celtic Illumination

Following early trade routes, monasticism spread from Africa as far west as Ireland, bringing not only the gospel but Christian art, which was to inspire the illuminators of manuscripts and other Celtic craftsmen. St Columba's *Cathach*, for example, shows a fish or dolphin motif familiar in Coptic Egypt, and the interlace ornament in the Book of Durrow was probably inspired by fifth and sixth century Coptic manuscripts and textiles displaying a similar ribbon interlace.[76]

The art of Coptic Egypt and the eastern Mediterranean may have its roots in black Africa, as suggested by Jacques Mercier's study of the talismanic scrolls of Ethiopia. Similar images found in West Africa may have been derived from Islamic talisman art. Ethiopian scrolls and a range of objects from the Sahel are usually thought to represent the art of the African edges of Mediterranean civilization. But the cultural current could have moved equally well the other way, from south to north. Drawing attention to the geometrism and frontality characteristic of West African masks and of Ethiopian drawings, with the focus on the eyes, which is almost absent from Mediterranean art, he asks: 'Could Ethiopia, then, be to black Africa and to the Christian culture of the Mediterranean as Ireland was to that same Christian culture and the Celtic world?'[77]

Carthage

Before reaching Ireland, Christianity spread westward along the north African coast to Carthage in what is now Tunisia. Founded by Phoenician merchants, Carthage had grown by the seventh century into a rich and powerful city which, with Utica, eventually broke away from Tyre and founded an empire of its own. After Alexander's death in 323 BCE, Carthage rivalled Rome for what McEvedy calls 'the hegemony of the classical world.' Eventually in 202 BCE, a Carthaginian army with eighty war elephants was defeated by Roman legions supported by Numidian cavalry. However, the Romans 'didn't annex Carthage immediately after their victory, they simply enlarged the new Berber kingdom of Numidia at Carthage's expense.'[78] In spite of this defeat, Carthage remained an important centre, and the Christian theological school later established there under Tertullian and Cyprian became for the Latin West what the School of Alexandria was for the Greek East.

During the first centuries of the Church at least two African popes, Victor I in 189 and Gelasius, in 492 were elected to the Roman Papacy.[79] However, compared with Alexandria and Carthage, Rome was an 'obscure Church', which according to Frend, 'never produced a theological school of its own, and down to the time of Leo, elected no bishop who could claim world authority.'[80] For at least four centuries Christianity was more African than Roman in orientation and in leadership, according to Theodor Mommsen: 'In the evolution of Christianity it is Africa that plays the most important role. Originating in Syria, Christianity achieved the status of a world religion only in and by way of Africa.'[81]

African scholars mastered the language and thought of imperial Rome while, paradoxically, until the middle of the third century Christian communities in Rome were still using Greek. It was in Africa that Tertullian hammered out for the Latin church the doctrines of the Trinity and of Christology. Noel King thinks Tertullian made use of local Berber wisdom and may have owed something to the old Carthaginians who brought similar doctrines from Phoenicia. Certainly,

'Some of the most influential early translations of the Bible into Latin were made in Roman Africa and helped to shape the thinking of the Latin Fathers from Tertullian to Augustine, and hence to influence the whole of Western Christianity.'[82] They may have used the same Latin translations, but these two African theologians had what have been described as diametrically opposed views of the church. Eduardo Hoornaert contrasts Tertullian's *Testimonio*, in defence of a church in which 'the poor evangelize the poor', with Augustine's *De Catechizandis Rudibus,* written two hundred years later. Augustine's view of the *rudes*, the uneducated who need to be catechized, is 'world's apart' from that of Tertullian.[83]

Whatever their differences, it was African scholarship and the theological schools of Alexandria and Carthage that ultimately defined Christian doctrine not only for Africa but for the whole of Christendom in the first centuries of the Church. Thereafter the monastic movement, begun by 'Desert Fathers' in Egypt, spread these doctrines all over the world. Why then did the Church at Carthage not survive? In a document prepared by the Vatican for a Special Assembly of African Bishops in 1990, its collapse was attributed to the Arab Muslim invasion of the seventh century, which culminated in the capture of Carthage in 698 CE. This document also mentions, as secondary causes, the exclusive use of Latin and the North African Church's failure to make translations into the local vernacular or to use 'elements of the native culture' to create a national church, as had been done in Egypt and Ethiopia. It admits that 'if the Bible and the Liturgy had been translated into the Berber language, it is quite possible that Christianity would have survived in North Africa, in spite of Islam, as it did in Egypt and the Middle East.'[84]

Others hold imperial Rome more directly responsible for the destruction of Carthage. Nelson Mandela speaking to African heads of state, identified its fall to Roman imperialism, the first stage in a willful destruction by Europe of Africa's ancient civilizations and cultures. He went on to express his hope that the time had come for a long-awaited *African Renaissance:*

> In the distant days of antiquity, a Roman sentenced this African city of Tunis to death: *Carthago delenda est;* 'Carthage must be destroyed.' And Carthage was destroyed. Today we wander among its ruins. Only our imagination and historical records enable us to experience its magnificence; only our African being makes it possible for us to hear the piteous cries of the victims of the vengeance of the Roman Empire. . . . But the ancient pride of the peoples of our continent asserted itself and gave us hope.[85]

For seven centuries Carthage had been the centre of Western Christian civilization, and only after its destruction was the Church of Rome able to assume primacy of the Western Church.

Christian Kingdoms

(a) Nubia

Before spreading West, along the North African coast to Carthage and into Europe, Christianity had been established much further south. Christian kingdoms in Nubia (biblical Kush or Ethiopia, present-day Sudan) flourished for over a thousand years up to about 1250 CE. Excavations have uncovered murals depicting black bishops of the tenth century, and books in Greek, Coptic and Old Nubian have been found there. Although the last of these Christian kingdoms was eventually overthrown by Arab invaders, an Arab document of the 1360s records that the Kingdom of Makuria was by then 'well-peopled with Christians from Nubia.'[86] The Bible had been translated into the Nubian language, but the church could not survive for long without clergy. Gradually the church buildings were turned into mosques.[87] Biblical scholars identify the 'Ethiopian eunuch' who was baptized by St Philip as a court official returning to the ancient African kingdom of Cush, which was ruled by a Queen mother, Candace, at Meroe in Nubia. J. Daniel Hays has identified several other Black Africans in the early church, including one of the five prophets and teachers in the Church at Antioch listed in *Acts*, Simeon, called *Niger*.[88]

(b) Abyssinia

Unlike Nubia, the Christian kingdom in Ethiopia (formerly known as Abyssinia) survived until the twentieth century. Abyssinia is said to have been evangelized by the apostle Matthew during the reign of King Aeglippus. The *Apostolic History* attributed to Abdia, bishop of Babylon, records that 'Matthew presided there twenty-three years, ordained clergy, and founded churches; baptized the king, queen, prince, and princess Ephigenia, who vowed chastity.'[89] There is no doubt that this Christian Kingdom dates back at least to the fourth century when Athanasius consecrated Frumentius as the first *Abuna* (bishop) of Aksum. For more than 1600 years the *Abuna* was a Copt appointed by the Patriarch in Alexandria.

The Solomonic dynasty of Aksum, which originally ruled the Amhara, a *Ge'ez* speaking people of the mountains, flourished from the first to the sixth century CE and through a series of wars extended the boundaries of the kingdom. According to Donald Levine, at two different periods Ethiopians crossed the Red Sea to become masters of Yemen. 'Of more enduring importance, they consolidated a monarchical tradition and a Christian culture that would survive transplantation to the south despite the destruction of Aksum as a political centre.'[90] By the ninth century the kingdom's core was no longer in Tigray but further south where the indigenous Cushitic people spoke Agaw languages. In 1137 an Agaw prince seized the throne and created the Zagwe dynasty which ruled until 1270.[91]

Ethiopians venerate their first Zagwe King, Lalibela, as a saint. Not long after his birth in Roha (the old name for Lalibela), his mother saw a dense swarm of bees surrounding him in his crib and, recalling an old belief that the animal world could foretell the future of important personages, she cried out 'Lalibela' – meaning, literally, 'the bees recognize his sovereignty'. When he grew up the reigning monarch tried to poison him. While his life hung in the balance, God took him up to heaven and there revealed that Lalibela would survive, and would become King; in return, however, he was to build eleven churches in the new capital named after him, following a master-plan revealed by the Almighty. As soon as he had ascended the throne, Lalibela set about fulfilling this task.[92]

These amazing monolithic churches, entirely hewn from the rock, are designed to represent the whole landscape of the Holy Land, complete with the River Jordan. Built between the eighth and thirteenth centuries, the work was accomplished, according to tradition, by human hands during the day and by angels at night. Because Islamic dominance in the region made it impossible for Christians to travel to the Holy Land, pilgrimages to these ancient churches and to local monasteries became an important part of Ethiopian piety.[93] Although isolated, renewed contacts were made with the rest of Christendom when in about 1187 an Ethiopian monastery and a chapel in the Holy Sepulchre there were built in Jerusalem.[94]

The Zagwe Dynasty was overthrown in 1270 CE by a pretender from Amhara, who took the name of Tesfa Iyesus (Hope of Jesus), claiming descent from the ancient rulers of Aksum and from King Solomon and the Queen of Sheba.[95] Thereafter kings continued to be crowned in Aksum, although it was at the monastery of Dabra Mitmaq in Shoa , a good 400 miles to the south, that in 1449 the Emperor Zara Ya' Iqob assembled a Church council to settle the problem of the Sabbath, which had become a cause of schism.[96] He also instituted drastic reforms intended to abolish sorcery and idolatry:

> Zara Yaqob was convinced that Ethiopian Christians had been contaminated by the pagan cults that surrounded them. Parish priests usually shared the life of the people they

served, and maintained the faith by not demanding too much
from converts who had been raised to believe in spirits
inhabiting mountains, trees, rivers, and lakes. But the *Lives*
of Ethiopian Saints are filled with dramatic accounts of stern
holy men who took a more vigorous line, denouncing pagan
cults and fighting with sorcerers and magicians. In his battle
to defeat paganism in the provinces of Shawa and Amhara,
Zara Yaqob employed holy men from the monastery of Debra
Libanos. If he learned that people were returning to the old
ways, sacrificing cows and sheep to serpent gods that lived
in trees, he would arrange for churches to be built where
the sacred trees had stood, and would send priests from
Debra Libanos to serve in them.[97]

There was a good deal of resistance to the emperor's reforms, and
his 'stern holy men' were able to overcome neither the practice of
animal sacrifice nor the popular belief in magic amongst Christians.
Douglas O'Hanlon, reckons that magic has three sources: Egyptian,
Jewish, and the practice of 'prehistoric inhabitants' of the country. A
distinction is made between black and white magic. Christians
associated black magic with the Falashas, with devil-worshipping sects
and with pagan magicians. White magic is thought to have begun with
Moses, and to have been continued by the prophets and Solomon.
Christ Himself is the greatest of all magicians. One book of prayers,
the Bandlet of Righteousness (*Lefafa Sedek*), O'Hanlon suggests is
similar to the Egyptian *Book of the Dead*. It contains all three sources
of Abyssinian magic and, while many of the stories are Jewish, the
beliefs expressed are Egyptian. In the *Lefafa Sedek* the Virgin Mary
plays the part which Isis plays in the *Book of the Dead*:

> According to Abyssinian tradition magical powers were
> bestowed on the Virgin by Christ himself. These were used for
> the benefit of all lovers of our Lord and of herself, both dead
> and living. Several of the magical prayers she is supposed to
> have made are written out in full. Throughout the book she
> presents a persistent request to Christ to reveal to her His secret
> name. A parallel is found in the Egyptian legend of Ra and Isis.
> Ra possessed 'many names' which were unknown even to the
> gods.[98]

Hastings thinks that the Catholicism of fifteenth or sixteenth century
Portugal or Spain had a good deal in common with African religion.
Many pre-Christian beliefs and practices had been absorbed into the
popular Christianity of late medieval Europe, much as they were in
Africa:

There was a vast multiplicity of local saints and protective relics and holy places to turn to, but especially and increasingly Mary, mostly a very localized Mary, Mary of somewhere. Mary alone was always kind, never associated with punishment. Evil too was often highly localized in witch and diabolical possession. The physical and the spiritual were inextricably woven together so that miracles and prodigies of all sorts could be expected and revered. There was a profound 'sense of divine participation in the landscape', whereby nature was invested with a kind of innate sensitivity to the sacred – a sort of animism, if one dare use the word, as much Iberian as African.[99]

When the Portuguese sent an embassy to Ethiopia in 1520, Father Francisco Alvares was much impressed with the piety of the people. He made a very detailed report on both state and church, then ruled by a Christian emperor whom Alvares called 'the Prester John'.[100] This was the culmination of a long search to locate the 'Prester John of the Indies', a priest king thought to rule the caravan cities of Central Asia, the Christians of St Thomas in South India, and the African kingdoms of Nubia and Ethiopia. In the twelfth century a letter written in Latin was circulated in Europe, announcing that Prester John possessed the highest crown on earth along with gold, silver, precious stones and strong fortresses. He claimed to rule over forty-two kings, all of them 'valiant and true Christians, who had sworn an oath to conquer the Holy Sepulchre and the entire Promised Land.' The letter also described fabulous African wildlife, but European princes were more interested in his oath than his 'descriptions of unicorns, phoenixes and other wonderful creatures who lived in the kingdom, or the rivers of precious stones, miraculous fountains, and robes woven by salamanders that could pass through flames as if through water. An ally who ruled beyond the Muslim powers of Egypt and the Levant and who could help to encircle the armies of the infidel might secure the prize for which Crusaders were struggling.'[101] Although such hopes were not realized, and although Prester John is dismissed by modern historians as a medieval legend, there is according to Greenfield, ample evidence that all the Indian Ocean coastlands, now occupied by Somali tribesmen, were once part of, or allied to, the Empire of Ethiopia.[102]

By the seventeenth century Ethiopia was enjoying something of a cultural renaissance. The Spanish Jesuit, Manoel de Almeida (who arrived in 1624), made detailed observations of the landscape and people, as well as the great variety of animals. He was impressed not only by the scholarship of Ethiopians, but by their material wealth, and particularly their magnificent horses. He found plenty of wildlife because 'the ordinary people are not much given to hunting'. Almeida's book is a valuable record of the environment and customs of Ethiopia at that time. It describes the Emperor's 'submission to Rome' in 1622 as the greatest achievement of Pedro Páez S.J., but records that ten years later, because of incessant riots, Susneyos was forced to issue 'a proclamation restoring the old religion and directing that the churches should again be occupied by the Monophysite clergy'.[103] As already noted, Susneyos had been encouraged by the Jesuits to launch a pogrom against his Jewish subjects, which no doubt contributed to his downfall.[104] But today the Ethiopian Orthodox Tewahedo Church with 9377 monasteries claims thirty million members,[105] who proudly trace their religious descent back to Solomon. The Ethiopian Church is important theologically, because 'it became more than any other surviving Church the heir and continuer of the original tradition of Jewish Christianity.'[106]

(c) Kongo

More than a millennium after the foundation of the kingdoms of East Africa, Afonso of the Kongo established another Christian kingdom with his son, Bishop Henrique, when in 1526 they outlined a programme of evangelization to be carried to the provinces of his realm. Links with Rome were maintained for over three hundred years, and over four hundred Capuchin friars were brought in as missionaries.[107]

Afonso had been baptized before he became king in 1506, and remained a committed Roman Catholic until his death in 1543. Hastings regards the sheer length of his rule and his unfaltering Christian commitment as quite exceptional. He was 'the one African figure of the sixteenth century who continues to bestride his age as a colossus'. Although missionary policy at that time was to train native priests, and Afonso sent a considerable number of young men to Lisbon to be educated and ordained, the shortage of priests was acute:

> In the early years of Afonso's rule quite a few were sent out from Portugal, but the conditions of life, the high mortality, and — perhaps most of all — the absence of an even moderately workable pastoral model for a few, wholly unprepared, priests to cope with a huge, profoundly pagan yet now nominally Christian society, ensured discouragement, withdrawal, or – alternatively – transference to a life of concubinage and slave-trading.[108]

To understand why the Eastern Orthodox Kingdom of Abyssinia survived better than the Roman Catholic Kingdom of the Kongo was able to do, one needs to remember not only the history of the Church's involvement in the slave trade, to which we shall return, but also the decisive schism between East and West at Chalcedon and, prior to that, the canonization of scripture.

Sacred Scriptures

Judaism, Christianity and Islam are often referred to as the religions of the Book. However, there is an important distinction to be made between the translation of their sacred texts:

> A sacred book is normally written with at least the concentration of poetry, so that, like poetry, it is closely involved with the conditions of its language. The Koran, for instance, is so interwoven with the special characteristics of the Arabic language that in practice Arabic has had to go everywhere the Islamic religion has gone. Jewish commentary and scholarship, whether Talmudic or Kabbalistic in direction, have always, inevitably, dealt with the purely linguistic features of the Hebrew text of the Old Testament. In contrast, while Christian scholarship is naturally no less aware of the importance of language, Christianity as a religion has been from the beginning dependent on translation.[109]

Jewish communities in Egypt were writing, translating, and preserving manuscripts that did not find their way into the Hebrew Bible, but are still regarded as sacred scripture in Africa.

The Hebrew Bible is itself a selection from a variety of ancient manuscripts, which were only put together fifty years after the Second Temple was destroyed by the Romans in 70 CE. Some writings not included in the Hebrew Bible were included in the Greek *Septuagint* and the Latin *Vulgate,* becoming known as deuterocanonical. One of these, *Ecclesiasticus* or the 'Wisdom of Jesus Ben Sirach', was translated from Hebrew into Greek in Egypt (*ca.* 132 BCE). In his Foreword, the translator comments:

> the fact is that you cannot find an equivalent for things originally written in Hebrew when you come to translate them into another language; what is more, you will find on examination that the Law itself, the Prophets and other books differ considerably in translation from what appears in the original text.

The Hebrew text of Ben Sirach, known to St Jerome and the rabbis but having been lost until 1896, was not included in the Hebrew Bible, and only the Greek translation was recognized by the Church as canonical.[110]

Before the end of the third century nearly all the books of the Bible had been translated into Coptic, and by the fifth century the New

Testament had been translated from Greek into Ethiopic (*Ge'ez*). The Ethiopians already had the Old Testament, probably translated direct from Hebrew. In addition, the Ethiopian Orthodox Church has preserved in *Ge'ez* translations of scriptures not included in the Hebrew Bible. Their O.T. canon of forty-six books includes *1 Enoch* (known as *Ethiopic Enoch*, because it has been preserved in its entirety only in Ethiopia), the *Book of Jubilees, Maccabees 3 Esdras, 4 Esdras, Tobit, Judith, Wisdom of Solomon, Sirach, Baruch, Epistle of Jeremiah, History of Susanna, Bel and the Dragon,* and *Song of the Three Children.* The Ethiopic N.T. canon has until recently always included the *Sinodos*, a collection of documents describing the early history of the Church, which O'Hanlon describes as their 'Corpus Juris Ecclesiastici'.[111] Excerpts from the Ethiopic scriptures in Sections Three and Four make it plain that God's promised redemption of Creation is intended as much for other animal species as for human beings.

In the West, works outside both the Hebrew and Roman canons of scripture are usually referred to as *pseudepigrapha,* although many scholars today are not happy with the term because some books of the Bible equally fit this definition and, on the grounds of character and content alone, it is not really possible to draw a sharp distinction between the non-canonical and the Hebrew Bible and the New Testament. With the closing of the Christian canons, other writings were denounced as heretical, but they were not completely suppressed, and, as J. R. Porter points out, 'many of these works remained influential in the West throughout the Middle Ages. It was the Reformation that brought about their neglect. Only in the last century were these works rediscovered and their true significance appreciated.'[112]

Jewish scholars, including Abraham Neuman, now regard writings that were excluded from the Hebrew canon to be among 'the most fascinating and historically illuminating books of the apocryphal series.' He recognizes that in many cases only the Christian Church saved them from oblivion and regards it as 'an act of redemption to reclaim these works for the Jewish people.' He is, however, aware that the Church, while saving ancient Jewish manuscripts, also sought to assimilate them to its own religious pattern through forced interpretations, occasional mistranslations and not infrequently, through Christological interpolations. In this manner the meaning and significance of important parts of the apocrypha appear out of focus.[113]

Apart from Jewish O.T. manuscripts, 'apocryphal' Christian gospels survived in Africa alone. Their exclusion from the Church's canon impoverished theology in the West, while continuing to inspire African

Christians. Linwood Urban thinks the discovery of a *Gospel of Thomas* in the Gnostic library at Nag Hammadi in 1945-6 challenges our previous reliance on the New Testament as 'the premier source for the origins of Christianity.'[114] This Gospel is a collection of traditional wisdom, including sayings, parables, prophesies, and proverbs attributed to Jesus. The only complete version known to exist is now conserved in the Coptic Museum of Old Cairo.[115] But it is only one of fifty-two Coptic translations, made about 1,500 years ago of still more ancient manuscripts, including the *Testimony of Truth*, which tells the story of the Garden of Eden from the viewpoint of the serpent.[116] A Valentinian *Gospel of Philip* claims that there were two trees in Paradise, and Adam's mistake was to eat from the one which produced animals, so that he begot animals and his children began to worship animals.[117]

Four other Jewish-Christian Gospels written in the early centuries of the Christian era: the *Gospel of the Nazarenes*, the *Gospel of the Ebionites*, the *Gospel of the Hebrews*, and the *Gospel of the Egyptians*, were quoted by Christian writers such as Justin Martyr (*c.* 100-165), Clement of Alexandria (*c.* 150-215) and Origen (*c.* 185-254), but since their time, none of the original manuscripts has survived.[118] Many second-century apocryphal texts show a recognition of goodness in the natural world at variance with 'gnostic' teaching of that time. For example, the *Protoevangelium of James* shows not only animals but inanimate nature responding to holiness. When as a child John the Baptist fled the soldiers of King Herod with his mother, Elizabeth, she appealed to the mountains for help, which 'opened to hide her and her son.' Many regard this as one of the most important of the apocryphal gospels, which was translated into Syriac, Ethiopic, Georgian, Sahidic, Old Church Slavonic, and Armenian. It was rejected in the West because it referred to Joseph's first marriage and as a result, no Latin translation has survived.[119] The term *Protevangelium*, according to Cameron, implies that most of the events recorded in this 'initial gospel' of James occurred prior to those recorded in the gospels of the New Testament.[120]

Of course, the early church had no 'New Testament' and did not use the name 'Old Testament' for the Jewish books. Stories were handed on orally, and only later written down. It was some 350 years before the books included in the New Testament were finally selected from other books thought to be apostolic. Owen Chadwick points out that 'there were some differences of opinion' between East and West about the Gospel of John, the Epistle to the Hebrews, and the Revelation. However, in 400 CE the East accepted the

Revelation and the West accepted Hebrews and the New Testament was agreed.'[121]

Rome's canonization of some biblical texts and rejection of others as apocryphal was of little concern to Coptic and Ethiopian Christians, who by this time had become separated from imperial 'orthodoxy' on account of their supposed adherence to the Monophysite heresy.

Chalcedon

The Emperor-theologian Justinian's attempts to impose unity on the Church meeting at Chalcedon was not successful. In 543 CE the Empress Theodora sent Jacob Baradai into Syria, resulting in the formation of a Syrian Church at Antioch which rejected the 'orthodox' faith as defined at Chalcedon, and adopted the ambiguous formula: 'There is only one nature in the Word of God made flesh'. This church was called Monophysite or 'Jacobite', after Jacob Baradai.

The Monophysite doctrine was supported by St Cyril and welcomed at Alexandria, where there was growing discontent with the Byzantine emperor's attempts to impose a patriarch of his own choosing. The Alexandrian see commanded wide popular support in Ethiopia, Syria, and other parts of the Byzantine empire. Religious dissent was fired by ethnic feelings of resentment at Greek dominance. The church of Alexandria became split between the native Coptic-speaking Egyptians, who adhered to Monophysite teaching, and the Hellenized Greek-speaking Egyptians, known as Melchite, who accepted Chalcedonian 'orthodoxy.' Eventually two patriarchs occupied the Alexandrian see, and as long as Egypt remained under Byzantine rule, the Melchite patriarch resided in the city of Alexandria, while the Coptic Monophysite patriarch had to operate from a monastery in the desert.[122] Meanwhile, the faith of the Ethiopian Church remained pre-Chalcedonian, which Hastings thinks was 'substantially no different from that of Rome or Constantinople'.[123]

Although efforts have been made to heal the rift caused by the Council of Chalcedon, nationalism has continued to influence the spread of Christianity in Africa. A Christian nationalist movement called Ethiopianism developed at the end of the nineteenth century.[124] This gave birth to a variety of AICs, which are today the fastest growing Christian communities in Africa. Some of them have creatively drawn on ancient Coptic and Ethiopic texts to supplement Bibles provided by European missionaries (see Section Four). Not only has Bible reading inspired African Christians to set up their own independent churches, it has even inspired others to return to the tenets of Judaism, repudiating Christian missionary teaching altogether.[125]

Slavery and European Missionary Expansion

Long before the Atlantic slave trade, the ancient civilizations of Africa, like those of the Middle East and Europe, were to a certain extent dependent on the institution of slavery. The pyramids and the great monuments of Egypt on which Pharaohs recorded their ancient wisdom probably could not have been built without human slaves, assisted by large numbers of draught animals, although this is disputed.[126] When Solomon was building his temple and palace in Jerusalem, he

> took a count of all the aliens resident in the land of Israel and found there were 153,600. He impressed 70,000 of these for carrying loads, 80,000 for quarrying in the hill country and 3,600 overseers in charge of them.'[127]

Similarly, the Greek and Roman world adopted not only much of Egypt's religion, philosophy, mathematics, engineering, artistic and administrative skills, it also adopted the institution of slavery. Later the Islamic world flourished upon slavery; slaves were integral to its domestic, military, naval, and commercial life. A Muslim was allowed only four wives but any number of slave concubines. In Africa, when a king became a Muslim, the number of his wives went down, but that of his concubines went up.[128]

When Europeans first began to trade with West Africa, as well as gold and ivory, captive slaves could be purchased without much difficulty. In Benin, however, traders found that objection was taken to the enslavement of people who were within the protection of the *Oba*, a monarch whose power derived from God. By custom and moral law, Africans thought that slaves ought to be captured from neighbouring peoples rather than from amongst one's fellow countrymen. This rule of the *Oba* was similar to the ones Popes in Rome had tried to impose on Venetian, Genoese, Pisan and Florentine merchants who enslaved their own people:

> Where possible the European merchants who dealt in chattel slaves were accustomed to buy infidels or Jews: otherwise they simply did as the Benin traders would do in somewhat later times. They bought 'believers'. They sold their 'fellow-natives'. Papal records show the Vatican repeatedly inveighing against this practice. All the great city states of medieval Italy appear to have dealt in Christian slaves. . . . European slaves were being carried in European ships to the Sultanate of Egypt despite all ecclesiastical rebukes and threats.[129]

Of course at this time, the Vatican was not inveighing against the institution of slavery as such, but only against the enslaving of European Christians. Slavery was tolerated in spite of Augustine's teaching that

'God did not want a rational being, made in his image, to have dominion over any except irrational creatures; not man over man, but over the beasts.' Unlike man's dominion over woman, his dominion over other men was thought to violate their original equality; hence 'such a condition as slavery could only have arisen as a result of sin.'[130] Nevertheless, Aristotle's concept of the 'natural slave' became very popular:

> The natural slave is one who is capable of belonging to another, which is why he does so belong, and who shares in (*koinônein*) reason (*logos*) to the extent of appreciating it (*aisthanesthai*), but not having it (*ekhein*). The other animals do not obey reason by appreciating it, but obey only their passions. And the use made of them differs little, since bodily help for basic necessities comes equally from slaves and tame animals.[131]

The Roman Church's crusade against 'paganism' legitimated slavery. The concept of *terra nullius* (no-man's land) was invoked to dispossess non-Christians of their goods, to invade and conquer their lands, to expel them, or subjugate them in perpetual servitude. *Romanus Pontifex* (1455) is one of a number of papal bulls that stipulate Portuguese rights, privileges, and obligations in the colonization of newly discovered countries. It decrees that, as non-Christian peoples have no ownership rights to the land on which they are living, when Christian Europeans meet the local king or chief and his advisers, they should present to them a Christian interpretation of history, closely following the Old and New Testaments. If the natives fail to accept the 'truth', it is not only legal but also an act of faith and a religious duty for the colonizers to kill them. The philosophical system underlying the *Romanus Pontifex* is Aristotelian, as V. Y. Mudimbe explains:

> The basis for the '*terra nullius*' concept – that is, the concept of the European right of sovereignty outside of Europe, and ultimately the right of colonization and the practice of slavery, was said to spring from 'Natural Law'. Thus, just as in a forest where there are stronger and weaker essences, the latter living and developing under the protection of the former, the human 'races' would observe the same rule. It would be the 'mission' of the stronger race to help their inferior 'brethren' to grow up; and in any case, according to the doctrine, it was up to the most advanced race to make sure that all goods made by God for the whole of humankind should be exploited. In 1526, Francisco de Vitoria justified colonial conquests on the basis of Christian trade rights, explaining that it was God's intent that all nations should trade with each other. His contemporary,

Sepulveda, invoking Aristotle's lesson, maintained that natives were meant by God to be dominated. In sum, from a Christian point of view, to oppose the process of colonization or that of slavery could only be morally wrong.[132]

From the fifteenth century onwards, Christian missionaries accompanied European economic expansion in sub-Saharan Africa. European traders discovered the riches of the West African kingdoms, including works of art wrought in gold and ivory. Some of the first treasures to reach European collections were ivories brought to Portugal in the last years of the fifteenth century by Portuguese traders who commissioned Sapi and Benin artists to make chalices, saltcellars and spoons, and to carve ivory tusks (*oliphants*) with African animals and the coats of arms of the Portuguese aristocracy. These Afro-Portuguese ivories are rare and precious not only as works of art, but as the only surviving African documents of this earliest contact with Europe. At that time the exchange between Africans and Europeans was untroubled by the racist ideology that later followed. According to Susan Vogel, 'Renaissance Europe and traditional Africa were more alike than either is like our twentieth century.' Many, if not most, Europeans, then lived in thatched houses. 'Religion permeated both worlds. Neither society relied on writing to reach the people. In Europe literacy was very limited, so Christianity was taught and its power was preserved through images . . . images and emblems of the holy figures were thought to have a power of their own. Much African art is associated with spirits, gods or ancestors, and certain sculptures and objects are believed to be numinous.' In this period, Vogel believes that Europeans and Africans probably did not perceive each other as fundamentally different.[133] Basil Davidson quotes a Dutchman writing around 1600, who found the people of Benin to be 'hospitable and honest partners', who 'are in no way inferior to the Dutch in cleanliness. They wash and scrub their houses so well that they are as polished as a looking glass.' In fact this European found Benin city more impressive than Amsterdam:

> You enter by a great broad street, not paved, which seems to be seven or eight times broader than the Warmoes-street in Amsterdam. This street goes right through, not bending; and the place where I was lodged with Mattheus Cornelison was at least a quarter of an hour's going from the gate, and yet I could not see the other end of it.
>
> The houses in the town stand in good order, one close and even with the next as our Dutch houses are ... while the king's palace is very large.[134]

Therefore, in the initial missionary expansion of the sixteenth century, there was no sense that Africans were inferior to Europeans, and new converts were readily ordained to the Catholic priesthood in the kingdom of the Kongo, as already noted. Nevertheless, when Africa came to replace Europe as a source of slaves, the Church's toleration of, and participation in, the slave trade increased. In Luanda, for instance, the trade became an important source of income for the diocese. According to Joseph Miller, by the latter part of the eighteenth-century, the number of Luanda slaves had declined noticeably. Although all sectors of the population, including the Catholic religious orders, still owned slaves in the 1760s the city's population numbered only about twice as many slaves as free subjects of any complexion.[135]

This history, still vividly remembered in Africa, is largely forgotten in Europe today. A recent *Lineament,* issued by the Vatican, avoids reflecting on the long-term effects this exploitation of their labour and natural resources has had on generations of Africans, but instead boasts that:

> A certain number of Episcopal Sees were erected during this period, and one of the first fruits of that missionary endeavor was the consecration in Rome, by Pope Leo X in 1518, of Don Henrique, the son of Don Alfonso I, King of the Congo, as Titular Bishop of Utica. Don Henrique thus became the first native Bishop of Black Africa.[136]

In calling Henrique the 'first native Bishop of Black Africa', the Vatican overlooked Eastern Orthodox bishops of the previous millennium in Nubia and Ethiopia. However, this omission was corrected at an assembly of African bishops a few years later when Pope John Paul II recalled the words of his predecessor, Pope Paul VI.[137] On this occasion, the Pope not only remembered Nubia, he reminded those present that the African Church had considerable influence on the spread and development of Christianity, particularly through the monastic movement. Although it makes no mention of slavery, this statement deserves to be quoted in full:

> We think of the Christian Churches of Africa whose origins go back to the times of the Apostles and are traditionally associated with the name and teaching of Mark the Evangelist. We think of their countless Saints, Martyrs, Confessors, and Virgins, and recall the fact that from the second to the fourth centuries Christian life in the North of Africa was most vigorous and had a leading place in theological study and literary production. The names of the great doctors and writers come to mind, men like Origen, Saint Athanasius, and Saint Cyril, leaders of

the Alexandrian school, and at the other end of the North African coastline, Tertullian, Saint Cyprian and above all Saint Augustine, one of the most brilliant lights of the Christian world. We shall mention the great Saints of the desert, Paul, Anthony, and Pachomius, the first founders of the monastic life, which later spread through their example in both the East and the West. And among many others we want also to mention Saint Frumentius, known by the name of Abba Salama, who was consecrated Bishop by Saint Athanasius and became the first Apostle of Ethiopia. During these first centuries of the Church in Africa, certain women also bore their own witness to Christ. Among them Saints Perpetua and Felicitas, Saint Monica and Saint Thecla are particularly deserving of mention.

These noble examples, as also the saintly African Popes, Victor I, Melchiades and Gelasius I, belong to the common heritage of the Church, and the Christian writers of Africa remain today a basic source for deepening our knowledge of the history of salvation in the light of the word of God. In recalling the ancient glories of Christian Africa, we wish to express our profound respect for the Churches with which we are not in full communion: the Greek Church of the Patriarchate of Alexandria, the Coptic Church of Egypt and the Church of Ethiopia, which share with the Catholic Church a common origin and the doctrinal and spiritual heritage of the great Fathers and Saints, not only of their own land, but of all the early Church. They have labored much and suffered much to keep the Christian name alive in Africa through all the vicissitudes of history. These Churches continue to give evidence down to our own times of the Christian vitality which flows from their Apostolic origins. This is especially true in Egypt, in Ethiopia and, until the seventeenth century, in Nubia. At that time a new phase of evangelization was beginning on the rest of the Continent.[138]

African Islam

Just as Judaism and Christianity can claim to have African roots, so can Islam. The Prophet Muhammad said of Abyssinia (Ethiopia) that it was 'a land of sincerity in religion' where, before the Hijrah, some eighty of his followers, including the Prophet's daughter Ruqayyah and her husband, Uthman, had taken refuge.[139]

Muhammad was born at Mecca (*c.* 571 CE), of the aristocratic tribe of Quraish. Because his father, Abdullah, died before the Prophet was born, and his mother, Amina, soon after, he was brought up in Mecca by his grandfather,

> a kindly, generous, and stout-hearted man who lived and died a pagan. When he was about forty years old Muhammad began to receive revelations: the angel Gabriel gave him words to recite. Only later were these revelations gathered together and written down by his followers.[140]

Muslims venerate these writings (known as the Koran) as the Word of God, while also respecting the Torah and other holy books contained in the Hebrew Bible. In the beginning the Prophet was not hostile to Christianity nor to Judaism, and sought only to reform their teaching. The Koran recognizes the Virgin birth of Jesus, who is revered as a prophet. 'Orthodox' Muslims however, regard Muhammed as the last and greatest of the prophets and reject the Christian doctrine of the Incarnation.

The black stone at Mecca is believed to have been placed there by Abraham, and the *Ka'ba*, which houses it, was modelled on the Temple of Solomon. The view held by both Muslims and Jews that the *Ka'ba* was the sacred house of Abraham, may be traced back to the Book of Jubilees. There is however, another tradition that the Quraysh, who controlled the sanctuary before Muhammad's revelations, wanted to build a more permanent structure on the pattern of a church. When a ship from Byzantium, on its way to Ethiopia, was wrecked off the Arabian coast, the marble, timber and iron it was carrying, was put to this use.

> Apparently, a Christian craftsman named Pachomius built the roof and decorated the Ka'ba with images of the prophets, including, Abraham, Mary and Jesus. After he established Muslim rule in the city, Muhammad allowed the portraits of Jesus and Mary to remain in the Ka'ba, and they did so until the fire that destroyed them in the twelfth century.[141]

Because the first followers of Muhammad had taken refuge in Abyssinia, the Koran forbade *jihad* against the Ethiopians, calling them 'a humble people of priests and monks.'

Arab forces invaded Nubia however, in 641 CE. Having met fierce resistance from Nubian bowmen, they made a treaty in 652 CE with the kingdom of Makuria, which undertook to deliver 360 slaves a year in return for peace.[142] According to Sulayman Nyang, this Baqt treaty, remained the foundation of Muslim-Nubian relations for over six centuries, but Muslim traders gradually penetrated the country, and their growing numbers resulted in an eventual takeover by Islamic forces.[143] Thus, according to Hastings, at times violently but more often quietly enough, did Islam advance while Christianity, like an ill-adapted dinosaur, declined and expired in place after place, crushed essentially by its own limitations, its fossilized traditions, and the lack of a truly viable, self-renewing structure.'[144]

By 705 CE North Africa had become part of the Islamic world, and from the Maghrib al-Aqsa (the far West), Spain was conquered by 'the Moors'. The North African scholar and reformer, Ibn Tumart, born *ca.* 1080 CE in the mountainous district of Sus, southwest of Morocco, studied in Tunisia and Egypt. After a profound religious experience in 1121, he proclaimed himself the *Mahdi* (Saviour), preaching the unity of God and insisting that creatures cannot know the Creator nor understand His works. Tumart's successors united the entire Mediterranean coast of Africa, so that for five hundred years, from the tenth century onwards, large portions of Spain were ruled by two African Muslim dynasties, the Almoravids followed by the Almohades.[145]

By the tenth century CE, Muslim Arabs had established coastal centres around the Horn of Africa, which facilitated a stream of Arab immigrants into Somali territory. Some of these settlers became founders of Muslim lineages, while Islamized Somali tribesmen moved south, 'displacing indigenous Bantu cultivators and Bushmanoid hunting fishing people' and establishing their presence 'in the vast area of the Horn which they have occupied ever since.'[146]

Meanwhile, from the North African coast, Islam spread rapidly south across the Sahara in a way that Judaism and Christianity had failed to do. According to Sulayman Nyang,

> The Berbers seemed to have been chosen by history to carry the banner of Islam into West Africa, because of their geographical location and their historical role as middle-men between Arabs and black Africans.[147]

The Sanhaja Berbers made use of the camel, an animal first brought to Egypt by Persians in the sixth century BCE. Camel drivers in the desert found deposits of rock salt which they exchanged on the banks of the Senegal for gold dust on a pound-for-pound basis. Eventually these prosperous merchants brought back reports of the Soninke kingdom of Ghana, and, through contact with Berbers, many West African kingdoms were Islamicized long before Christian missionaries arrived on the scene. Colin McEvedy notes that later chronicles often describe the founders of these kingdoms as 'white', meaning Berber or Arab, although there can be no doubt that the common people and all later kings were entirely black (Negroes or Nilo-Saharans like the Songhay). In fact, while acknowledging the Prophet's authority, these kingdoms retained much of their traditional beliefs and practices. As McEvedy remarks, 'Islam by this time had long since ceased to be run from Arabia, in fact had almost ceased to be run at all', and the spiritual supremacy of the caliphs of Baghdad was not enforced.[148]

Thus, over a thousand years ago, rulers of powerful West African kingdoms became Muslim. Mali controlled the rich trade of the Sudan region, much as ancient Ghana had done, but its empire was larger. By the early fourteenth century it stretched over 1,000 miles from the Atlantic to the Middle Niger. When its Emperor Mansa Musa made a pilgrimage to Mecca in 1324-25 CE, he is said to have taken an army of as many as 100,000 men and so much gold that his power and wealth became famous throughout Europe and the Middle East.[149]

A Muslim university was founded at Timbuktu long before Christian missionaries began to establish schools and colleges in Africa. African scholars mastered the Arabic script and were able to record not only their reflections on the Koran, but the myths and legends of their vernacular traditions. The influence of African scholarship, philosophy, and traditional wisdom on Islam in the Arab world is not widely appreciated today, although there have been movements towards what Ali Mazrui calls the 'dis-Arabisation of Islam'. He regards the Ahmadiyya sect, founded by Mirza Ghulam Ahmad in India under the British Raj, is 'one of the best organised movements in Muslim Africa'. Doctrinally the movement upholds the Prophet Muhammad of Arabia as the most important of God's prophets, but Mirza Ghulam Ahmad is regarded as another prophet in East and West Africa. This is a major departure from mainstream Islam, which insists that Muhammad was both the greatest and the last of all the prophets.[150]

While Arabian Islam has been increasingly iconoclastic, in many African societies Muslims have been able to retain or adapt traditional images, ideas and practices, thereby making Islam more accessible to ordinary people. The written and oral literature of both East and West Africa gives testimony to this ecumenical spirit.

Muslim slaves from Africa were transported to the British colonies and other parts of the world, taking their brand of African Islam with them. More recently African migrants have introduced Islam into the American consciousness and made converts. According to Sulayman Nyang, the three most widely celebrated events among African Muslims in the United States are *Eid el-Fitr, Eid el-Adha,* and *Mawlad el-Nabi.* These feasts usually involve the sacrifice of a lamb (or other animal) which is shared with friends and neighbours, particularly at *Mawlad el-Nabi* when African brotherhoods organize lectures and chant their traditional *qasida.*[151]

Literature and Oracy

One significant difference between Islam and missionary Christianity, already noted, is in the use of language. Whereas Christian liturgies and scriptures are translated into the vernacular, Muslim converts are expected to say their prayers and hear the Koran read in Arabic. Moreover, even in those countries where Christians speak Arabic, the two faiths have distinctive vocabularies which inhibit dialogue, as Kenneth Cragg explains:

> It is true that pivotal words in the two faiths like *Allah* (God), *Injil* (Gospel), *Rasul* (Apostle), *Kitab* (Book), *Iman* (faith), *Rahmah* (mercy), *Tawbah* (repentance) and many more were common to both. But their usage differed sharply and some Muslims were disposed to demand, or assume, that only their Muslim import should properly enjoy currency.[152]

He describes how Constance Padwick, having observed this language gap in Egypt, set out to study Islam as it is lived in the daily recitations of Sufi liturgies and prayer manuals. Undeterred by critics who found these manuals somewhat naive or superstitious, even tending to the magical in recital or invocation, she was able to appreciate their focus on the divine 'presentness'. By rhythmic recital of the Names, low chanting and swaying, with concerted and often vigorous ejaculation, all the energies of voice and body are concentrated, so as to 'preoccupy' the soul with God:

> Askings terminate in the presence of His goodness, and needs pass away as the soul finds her stay in Him. The need of the creature is not sufficed by the whole of created things: it is necessary that its infinite need be met by an infinite generosity and power, by none other than the Truth Himself, praised and exalted be He.[153]

Clearly Padwick was ahead of her time in her appreciation of the value of oracy. Oral literature is now recognized as a subject for serious academic study.

The Arabic language has been an important vehicle of communication both orally and in writing, with its distinctive script. The popular Western conception that sub-Saharan Africa was without literacy until the coming of European missionaries is without foundation. For centuries Arabic scribes had produced huge numbers of manuscripts, including religious treatises, historical chronicles, and poetry, which can be found in West Africa and on the east coast, as well as in the Nile valley and on the north coast. Ruth Finnegan, however, reminds us that, although there was often some lively interaction between written and popular (oral) literature, there was nothing approaching mass literacy:

A poem first composed and written down, for instance, may pass into the oral tradition and be transmitted by word of mouth, parallel to the written form; oral compositions, on the other hand, are sometimes preserved by being written down. In short, the border-line between oral and written in these areas is often by no means clear-cut.[154]

Finnegan instances the traditional Swahili *tenzi,* long religious poems recalling deeds of Muslim heroes. Their emphasis is strongly Islamic, and they conventionally open with praise of God and his prophet. Nowadays *tenzi* appear in the vernacular press, written in Roman as distinct from the traditional Arabic Swahili script, and they may even have a Christian, rather than an Islamic, message.[155]

Apart from Swahili, many other African language groups had adopted a written form using the Arabic script, including Hausa, Fulani, Mandingo, Kanuri, and Songhai. Finnegan reminds us however, that the vast majority of those peoples had no access to the written word:

> In so far as the writings of the scholars reached them at all, it could only be by *oral* transmission. Swahili religious poems were publicly intoned for the enlightenment of the masses. Fulani poems were declaimed aloud, and Hausa compositions were memorized as oral forms and sung by beggars or chanted on the streets at night (or, nowadays, on the radio).[156]

One of the main sources for the study of African ideas about animals and Creation is this African literature, both written and oral, which goes back over four thousand years, and uses several different scripts. While Egyptians and Nubians undoubtedly developed writing skills, their culture was orally transmitted in legends, fables, and proverbs, some of which derived from other parts of Africa and later appeared in Hebrew scriptures. As Northrop Frye points out:

> The best-known purveyors of fables, Aesop and Phaedrus, were both slaves. The fable is not very prominent in the Old Testament, except that the Book of Job is an enormous expansion of one, but it comes into its own, as a vehicle of instruction, in the parables of Jesus. The proverb, on the other hand, is the kernel of wisdom literature, which consists largely of collections of proverbs. . . .
>
> All the Near Eastern civilizations seem to have cultivated the proverb a good deal: the Egyptians, with their rigidly stratified society, were especially fond of it. Some ancient Egyptian proverbial material reappears in the Book of Proverbs, where it is already centuries old.[157]

The literature of sub-Saharan Africa, as well as that of pre-Christian Egypt and the Nile valley, provides many stories of animals and Creation, yet Ethiopia's literary heritage, with its own peculiar script, is regarded by Claude Sumner as unique:

> In Ethiopia as elsewhere in Africa there is a very rich traditional thought. It is a popular philosophy, a wisdom, the product, not of the speculation of one man who makes up a whole system, but of the experience of a whole people. This experience is transmitted from father to son, from one generation to another, from one village to another, from one century to another. It is a river which collects the water flowing from all sides and from above, but this river always advances in the same direction: the living stream of tradition. Such a literature exists everywhere in Africa, but whereas in other African countries it is purely oral, in Ethiopia it is also written. Partly translation of Greek or Arabic originals, it . . . bears a typically Ethiopian stamp.[158]

Stories of Alexander the Great are part of the literary heritage of Ethiopia. Sir Ernest Budge thinks that the first history of this great conqueror was made in Egypt, where Alexander was claimed to be the son of an Egyptian king, Nectanebus, who had assumed the form of the god Ammon to consort with Alexander's mother, Olympias, wife of Philip of Macedon. Alexander was therefore accorded not only African but divine parentage. In Ethiopia translators endowed him with Christian virtues, making him an example for monks and nuns in his chastity, almsgiving and wisdom.[159] *The Alexander Book in Ethiopia* also tells of his encounter with the *Brahmans* of India, who were evidently regarded as true worshipers of the God of Abraham, being 'the remnant' of the children of Seth, the son of Adam, who somehow survived the Flood.

Ethiopic texts are often significantly different from their Greek or Roman counterparts. *The Book of the Philosophers,* translated into Ge'ez by Abba Mikael (*c.*1510-1522), is wholly original in its adaptation of the Greek text and in places, as Claude Sumner puts it, 'one seems to be listening to an Oriental monk speaking through the mouth of Socrates'.[160] These philosophical texts have not yet been widely translated into modern languages, nor made available to students in other parts of Africa. Oral traditions, on the other hand, are more easily passed on from one generation to the next. They are also more suitable for adaptation to the philosophical needs of the modern world, as we shall see in Section Six.

In taking up the oral literature of Africa, we may be surprised to discover the extent to which not only academic philosophy but also the popular folklore of Europe and America is already indebted to it. Alice Werner thinks it 'quite likely that our Aesop's Fables originated in Africa'. They may be traced back to Luqman, the Arab fabulist spoken of with approval by Muhammad in the thirty-first chapter of the Koran, who is said to have been an 'Ethiopian' (*i.e.* a black) slave. Known in Greece as *Aithiops*, this name was turned into Aesop. The Uncle Remus stories with their remarkable animals, became popular in the West over fifty years ago, and folklore students now recognize that they originally came from Africa, brought by the Negro slaves. While most slaves came from the Congo, Werner notes that some were imported from the East Coast. In Cuba there were slaves from Mombassa, and many cargoes of slaves were smuggled from Havana into the southern states after the trade had been declared illegal.

> This perhaps explains why the African hare (Kalulu of the Nyanja, Sungura of the Swahili) should be such a prominent figure in Negro folklore, while his place is taken on the Congo (where it appears there are no hares) by the little antelope known as the water chevrotain. The slaves of the British West Indies were chiefly West Africans (Yorubas, Ibos, Fantis, etc.), and their 'Nancy' stories are mostly concerned with the spider (Anansi).[161]

As we shall see in Section One, African myths present a view of humanity's fall from grace in terms rather different from those found in the Genesis stories.[162] As a result, black theology offers a more liberating approach to the doctrine of Original Sin than Scholastic or Calvinist theology has been able to do. This early African 'liberation' theology crossed the Atlantic with the slave trade and found expression in Afro-American Christianity. Peter J. Paris finds many continuities among slave communities in the Americas with their roots on the African continent.[163]

> Interestingly, unlike much of the Protestant theology taught the slaves by the slave-holders' preachers, the slaves lent little importance to the doctrine of original sin. In the words of Genovese, 'sin meant wrong-doing – injustice to others and violation of accepted moral codes.'. . . Not only did this view of wrongdoing fit their traditional African understanding, which had no sense of 'original fault' affecting the whole of creation, Africans in the diaspora responded to their oppression by making the quest for freedom their paramount goal.[164]

Slaves who never learnt to read or write may nevertheless have been the legitimate guardians of traditional wisdom. Although underappreciated by academic theologians, their wisdom inspires poets and novelists like Alice Walker. She writes of 'black women whose spirituality was so intense, so deep, so *unconscious* that they were themselves unaware of the richness they held.' They were not respected, and as slaves their bodies were abused by men, but she regards them as saints and asks: 'Who were these "Saints"? These crazy loony women? Some of them without a doubt were our mothers and grandmothers.' [165]

Mission Christianity

There have been two main periods of Christianity in Africa: the first dating from the very early Coptic church in North Africa, Nubia and Ethiopia; the second dating from the arrival of European missionaries. I have included texts from the first period but not from the second, largely because Coptic Christianity was in touch with African traditions and African Judaism in a way that the later missionary Christianity was not. This is very clear in the case of Ethiopia. Not only is the Queen of Sheba a central figure in Ethiopian mythology, so that Ethiopians make a specific claim to be possessed of her wisdom, they also lay claim to other varieties of African wisdom which are illustrated in this book. Ethiopian religion is marked by the influence of Egyptian ideas; it stems from African Judaism, it operates in an African language, and much of its rich traditional thought has been recorded in writing.

Coptic and Ethiopic Christianity has many similarities with African traditional ideas. It offers commentaries on and versions of the Genesis story, which amount to alternative myths of Creation. It allots great significance to animals as possessors of primal speech, as part of a continuum with humanity, and as participants in redemption.

By contrast, later mission Christianity – which has brought many benefits to Africa – lacked any connection with earlier African traditions. Dismissing every alternative African myth of Creation as superstitious nonsense, it nevertheless insisted on the literal truth of the myth of Genesis. It taught that human beings had a right to dominate and exploit the animal kingdom. It taught that God desired humanity to transform nature. The argument of this book is that contemporary African theologians need to go back beyond the teachings of mission Christianity to make connection again with the ancient wisdom of Africa. So there are no texts here from the official teaching of mission Christianity. Instead there are in Section Six extracts from the work of contemporary African theologians, many of whom were educated in mission schools, but who increasingly draw upon the varied cultural and religious traditions of their ancestors in making the Gospel message their own. One of the first to do so was a Roman Catholic bishop, Patrick Kalilombe, who asked over twenty years ago:

What would happen if African traditional religions were to be assessed by African Christians themselves? Perhaps the main lines of enquiry would shift. . . . I would have to return in spirit to where my people were. So we would not be talking any more about the customs and beliefs of those 'pagans' in the bush of Africa: I could not have the heart to speak of my own ancestors and religion in this contemptuous way. We are dealing with a concrete people now: my father and mother, my uncles and aunts, my brothers and sisters, my relatives, friends and neighbours, a lot of people who mean a lot to me and whom I cannot handle as if they were mere objects of curiosity and detached study. And especially, I would remember that I am looking at a venerable and sacred tradition handed over by generations of ancestors. These beliefs and customs will command my respect and careful consideration, even when I may not share them. I cannot act as if these are childish superstitions or mere primitive mumbo-jumbo, for I feel with my whole person the seriousness of the problems, questionings, preoccupations, hopes, fears, desires and joys from which these religious attitudes spring. I have no right to look down on my father's culture or to offer simplistic solutions to questions I know to be very complex.[166]

Although no excerpts from the writings of European missionaries are included, it may be worth recalling some of their heroic endeavours and some of their unfortunate mistakes. By the nineteenth century they were undoubtedly opposed to the slave trade, but they certainly regarded Africans as a lower order of humanity, an inferior race, who would ultimately benefit from contact with European civilization. Missionary societies enthusiastically supported colonial rule. As John Philip expressed it in 1828, British missionaries who ventured beyond the borders of what was then the Cape colony, were not only 'everywhere scattering the seeds of civilization, social order, and happiness', they were also 'by the most unexceptionable means, extending British interests, British influence, and the British empire'.[167]

David Livingstone's intuition that Africa was the scene of the mythical Garden of Eden[168] was not shared by most missionaries, who thought that Africans were mere slaves of nature and had to be taught how to dominate and exploit it. Missionary societies did not think it necessary to send their most learned clergy to Africa. John Venn, President of the Church Missionary Society, expressed the view regarding candidates that a 'missionary, dwelling among savages rude and illiterate, does not require the same kind of talents, manners or learning as are necessary in an officiating minister in England.'[169]

Even before Darwin published his *On the Origin of Species by Means of Natural Selection* in 1859 and his *The Descent of Man* in 1871, the idea of inferior races who were closer to animal species was generally accepted in Europe and America, where Christian missionaries were recruited. In the nineteenth century, animal welfare was sometimes promoted by comparing them with 'inferior races of mankind' who bore 'great resemblance, not only in looks, but in manners and intellect, to the monkey tribe.' The Rev. J.G. Wood regularly portrayed dogs and horses as morally superior to natives and savages, and many of his contemporaries compared their domestic pets favourably with Hottentots and Bushmen. Darwin himself writes:

> He who has seen a savage in his native land will not feel much shame, if forced to acknowledge that the blood of some more humble creature flows in his veins. For my own part I would as soon be descended from that heroic little monkey who braved his dreaded enemy in order to save the life of his keeper. . . as from a savage who delights to torture his enemies, offers up bloody sacrifices, practises infanticide without remorse, treats his wives like his slaves, knows no decency, and is haunted by the grossest superstitions.[170]

Such views, which had justified centuries of slavery, continued to justify colonial rule. All over Africa, hospitals and clinics were established by selfless missionary doctors. Albert Schweitzer, who brought the enlightenment of medical science as well as the Gospel of Jesus Christ to the darkness of Lambarene, learnt 'reverence for life' in Africa. His diary reveals that he saw the old 'natives' to whom he talked about 'the ultimate things of life' as 'deeper than we are', yet still like children, living in fear and ignorance. He valiantly attempted to defend them against their European detractors, who asked:

> What does the forest dweller understand of Christianity, and how does he understand – or misunderstand – it? In Europe I met the objection again and again that Christianity is something too high for primitive man, and it used to disturb me; now, as a result of my experience, I can boldly declare, 'No; it is not.'[171]

Schweitzer was unusually enlightened when compared with contemporary Roman Catholic missionaries. Aylward Shorter describes their view of African culture, which only began to be transformed after the Second Vatican Council:

> All was under the sway of the Devil and even the good actions of pagans were mortal sins. The world, especially the pagan world, was wholly evil. One African missionary society, for

example, enjoined a daily prayer to Our Lady on its members,
for the salvation of the Muslims 'and other infidels of Africa'.
One line went: 'have mercy on these unfortunate creatures
who are continually falling into Hell in spite of the merits of
your Son Jesus Christ'.[172]

Therefore the Church of Rome continued to support Belgian rule in
the Congo as well as Portuguese settlement in East and West Africa.
In 1927 colonial occupation was justified by a Belgian Jesuit, who
argued that the riches of God's Creation are intended for the benefit
of all humanity and should not be left in the hands of 'retarded people'
or 'indigenous despots' in Africa. Colonialism, he believed, had ended
the horrors of cannibalism, slavery and human sacrifice.[173]

Although in the sixteenth century Rome was happy to ordain African
converts to the priesthood in the Kongo, four hundred years later many
missionary societies were sadly reluctant to do so. The Jesuits in Rhodesia,
for example, ignored Pope Benedict XV's directive, and by 1955 had
ordained only twelve Africans to the priesthood.[174] Today Jesuits admit
that the missionary support of colonialism and neo-colonialism continues:

> It is no secret that, at least with regard to Cameroon, the Congo,
> Oubangui-Chari (today's Central African Republic), Gabon, and
> other colonial territories of equatorial or West Africa, the
> European missionaries enthusiastically collaborated with the
> colonial powers. . . . That mentality and practice, despite the
> undeniable progress in spiritual independence achieved by the
> heralds of the Gospel, have not disappeared. In the 1970s a
> scandal provoked considerable controversy in the United States:
> Republican Senator Mark Hatfield of Oregon, CIA director
> William Colby, and presidential adviser Philip Buchan admitted
> in writing that the use of missionaries as informants to the
> American administration was widespread. In December 1975
> President Gerald Ford and Mr. Colby even declared that they
> had no intention of renouncing this practice or of ceasing to
> distribute secret CIA funds for this purpose.[175]

The attitude of foreign missionaries, who continued to treat converts
and even their African catechists and staff as children, incapable of
running their own affairs, let alone developing their own theology, has
led to numerous AICs being formed, which are now Africa's fastest
growing body of Christian believers. Two main areas of theological
conflict or debate between traditionalists (ATRs), adherents of mission
churches, and the AICs, are worth noting, namely (a) the traditional
ceremonies known as 'rain-making' and (b) the diagnosis and healing
of diseases afflicting both humans and other animals.

Rain-making

David Livingstone had discovered that rain-making was one thing the Bakwena people of Botswana, among whom he settled, were most reluctant to relinquish. It was 'one of the most deeply-rooted articles of faith in this country'. He recorded a conversation between a missionary medical doctor and an obstinate 'Rain Doctor', who refused to pray in the name of Jesus Christ:

> God told us differently. He made black men first, and did not love us as he did the white men. He made you beautiful, and gave you clothing, and guns, and gunpowder, and horses, and wagons, and many other things about which we know nothing. But towards us he had no heart. He gave us nothing except the assegai, and cattle, and rainmaking; and he did not give us hearts like yours. . . . God has given us one little thing, which you know nothing of. He has given us the knowledge of certain medicines by which we can make rain. *We* do not despise those things which you possess, though we are ignorant of them. We don't understand your book, yet we don't despise it. *You* ought not to despise our little knowledge, though you are ignorant of it.[176]

Although sometimes encountering hostility, missionaries were often initially welcomed. Even before German colonial occupation, the Wafipa in southwest Tanganyika, for example, had been prepared by their indigenous prophets for the arrival of white men who would 'teach them about God'. However, when they arrived, the Berlin Mission soon became embattled with ATRs. Unaware of the way in which the Nyakyusa see the Creator manifesting His power through the provision of rain or the infliction of pestilence and plague, the missionaries tried without success to explain plague and drought in scientific terms. Their Christian faith could offer no spiritual protection against such plagues, nor was it able to ensure rain. Indeed, as W. B. Anderson comments, 'the extraordinary thing is the way that the mission continued in the spiritual struggle where their ignorance was such a great disadvantage to them', and he tells an amusing story:

> A rainmaker in Berega district of eastern Tanzania got up in church and denounced the trickery of rainmaking, saying that he would become a Christian. He would leave rainmaking, he said, since rain came only from God. An uproar broke out in the congregation. The Christians said that the rainmaker could become a Christian if he liked, but they would not allow him to stop making rain! Christianity in East Africa has opposed

African ways, but it has often retained old African beliefs beneath the surface.[177]

Even today, Churches in Central Africa cannot compete with territorial cults that enforce directives with regard to a community's use of its environment while conducting rituals to counteract droughts, floods, blights, pests and epidemic diseases afflicting cattle.[178] Kwesi Dickson points out that there are many continuities in African thought with the religion of the Old Testament. The prophet Elijah's sacrifice on Mount Carmel, for example, ended a three year drought.[179]

Rain-making is seen by most African societies as an essential concern of the Creator. Drought is a constant threat, and most Africans find the plight of their fellow creatures without water quite heart-rending, as Smith Mbedzi so eloquently expresses:

> The land belongs to the Creator and all its people and everything that belongs to it. There was a time when I was through, I travelled to Beit Bridge, which is my home, during the drought period, when you seemed to see impala and kudus really desperate. And I said within myself, because I was travelling alone, 'God, don't destroy'; even the trees were falling. I said, 'Mwari, don't destroy your creation because of the evils of mankind. Better destroy mankind and leave those others. It was a pathetic story. Because the kudu when it sees you would try to run away but it couldn't, just gets to the fence there to throw itself to the fence and then it falls down. But that was because of the evil of man, who is the super-natural creature of God.[180]

Thus, in spite of Christian missionary teaching, Africans continue to pray for rain and to articulate their concern for ecology in a traditional religious idiom.

Healing God's Creation

Although Western education has sometimes been despised or resented by Africans, missionary medical care, particularly for the victims of epidemics that were unknown before the arrival of European colonialists, was welcomed.[181] The years of conquest were 'a time of disastrous population loss over large parts of the continent'.

Steven Feierman studied traditional public health practices, cast in African thought idioms, as they operated in Tanzania before the eco-crisis at the end of the nineteenth century. He found that there had been a system by which a triad of healing specialists, chiefs and patriarchs identified the causes of disease, and regulated the use of irrigation channels, the burial of the dead, and the location of sites for human waste. But when diseases like influenza, rinderpest and lungsickness entered Africa for the first time, knowledge and power were separated:

> The local African authorities who had the knowledge necessary for preserving population in their particular environment lost power. And the conquerors, who had sufficient power to change basic living conditions, had not yet begun to understand the environment or the nature of local economies.[182]

Therefore devastating epidemics that afflicted both human and animal populations gave rise to new religious movements, combining traditional and Christian explanations or remedies. These often proved equally unacceptable to the mission churches and the colonial powers, who ruthlessly tried to suppress them.

The largest AIC in Francophone Africa today is known as the Church of Jesus Christ on Earth through the Prophet Simon Kimbangu. Simon had been an evangelist in the Baptist Church in the Kongo, but the Baptists had refused to recognize his healing ministry. He was reputed to have raised a dead child to life, and crowds flocked to his home village of Nkamba. In 1921 he was arrested, and after being sentenced to death and to 120 lashes, Simon spent the next thirty years in prison, remaining there until he died in 1951 at the age of sixty-two. The church, under the leadership of Simon's son, was finally granted toleration on the eve of political independence in 1960. In 1979 it was among the first AICs to be granted membership of the World Council of Churches.[183]

According to Philomena Mwaura, many African Christians, in spite of a mission education, 'still maintain their traditional beliefs and practices during important or critical stages of life; for example, birth, initiation, marriage, death and when faced with mysterious and incurable sickness, suffering and other anxieties of daily living.' Western remedies are seen as directed to 'different parts of the same person, the body and the soul.' This dualistic view is incompatible with the African world view, which in its approach to health has not been taken seriously by missionaries, often being totally ignored. 'Most mainstream Churches today still deny the reality of witchcraft, a denial that has alienated the church from a crucial area of pastoral care.' It is Mwaura's contention that 'any kind of medical treatment which is unrelated to the supernatural and the community has limited chances of success in Africa even if half the patients profess to be Christians'.[184]

Perhaps the first Jesuit missionaries in Ethiopia in the sixteenth century were more tolerant of the traditional healing practices than modern medical missionaries. Having spent most of his life in Africa, first as a missionary with the 'White Fathers' and then as a respected academic theologian, Aylward Shorter may be unusual in that he promotes a more holistic approach to healing based on African traditional understanding of the relationship between spiritual and physical disease. Shorter also thinks Christians today desperately need to rediscover faith in an organic link between human beings and God's other creatures. He draws attention to the way modern industrialized society abuses nature, and suggests that society must acquire a sacramental cast of mind.

> Medicine is the produce of the earth, and healing necessarily includes being at rights with the physical environment. Through such a reconciliation human nature is set at rights with the world of the Spirit. Jesus used the whole of nature as a parable of the transcendent wholeness he proclaimed, and he revealed that the physical world shares in this same destiny of positiveness and goodness, growing towards it in the power of the Spirit.[185]

Shorter admires the organic universe of the Kimbu people, who have integrated 'a sky-centered theology and an older earth-centered one'. The sun at its zenith occupies a position above the sacred hill of the chiefdom, and the high-flying birds are symbols of transcendence, while the great carnivores stand for beauty and power. That is why chiefs wear the skins of lions and leopards and the feathers of eagles. But other creatures each have their symbolic importance, even 'the friendly python which lurks among the rocks, a symbol of ancestral spirits whose graves are its home'.[186]

Such an organic cosmology appeals to African theologians like Hannah Kinoti who perceives that: 'Traditional society was much pre-occupied with the issue of well-being as evidence by the numerous ceremonies and rituals which were concerned with the health of human beings, their animals and that of the produce of their fields'.[187]

Global Theology

At the 1974 Roman Synod, Cardinal Joseph-Albert Malula of Zaire announced, 'In the past, foreign missionaries Christianized Africa. Today, the Christians of Africa are invited to Africanize Christianity'.[188] This invitation is being taken up not only by academic theologians, but by ordinary African Christians concerned about the salvation of other animal species. They would agree with Andrew Linzey and Dan Cohn-Sherbok that: 'Far from being another moral issue (although animal rights is at least that), the place and status of animals, once perceived theologically, raise interesting, even fundamental, questions for our thinking about God'.[189]

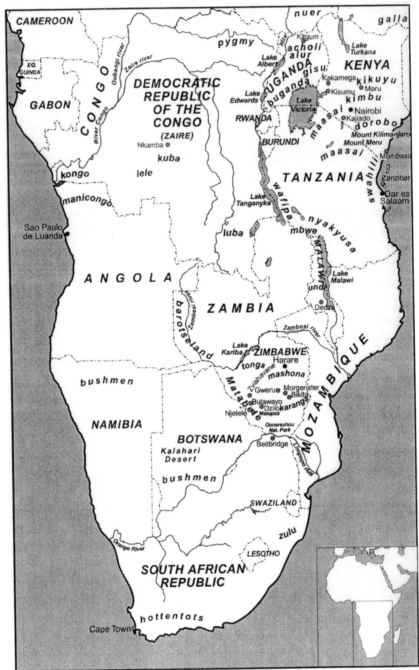

Map of sub-Saharan Africa from Cameroon to South African Republic

Traditional Religions
South of the Sahara

List of Excerpts

Traditional Religions
South of the Sahara

In this Section we draw largely on the work of scholars who have recorded the myths, stories, prayers and rituals of African societies south of the Sahara. These oral traditions often recognize the power of the Word in Creation much as the biblical account does. In most African accounts of Creation the supreme being is said to have formed the universe out of chaos by naming all things in it. While mankind sometimes has a part to play in Creation, the mere uttering of human words is seldom thought to have the same efficacy as the Word of God.[1] The Word of God, therefore, was widely known to be the chief agent of Creation.[2]

The pygmy people in equatorial Africa understood the Creator to be both eternal and without physical form, as can be seen from one simple prayer recorded by Ninian Smart and Richard D. Hecht, which they think 'contradicts many of the erroneous ideas about the deities of small-scale traditional peoples; the High-God cannot be rendered in a totemic or human form. The real being of God is related to word and not form.'

A Pygmy Prayer

In the beginning was God,
Today is God
Tomorrow will be God.
Who can make an image of God?
He has no body.
He is as a word
which comes out of your mouth.
That word! It is no more,
It is past, and still it lives!
So is God.[3]

African myths about the creation of the world often emphasize the relationship God intended humans to have with other species, perhaps more than the Genesis story does.[4] In Africa the 'Original Sin' of humankind was seen not as the eating of forbidden fruit but as the killing of one's fellow creatures. This is simply expressed in a story of the Borana people collected by Alex Chima:

Man and Elephant in the Garden

God created man and an elephant. These he put in a beautiful garden and he walked with them every day. There was pure drinking water in a flowing river. But the elephant started muddying the waters. He would listen to neither God nor man who told him not to. In the end, man killed the elephant. God, though, was upset at this act and drove man out of the garden. Hence the Borana now live in a ceaseless search for water in drought-stricken lands, semi-nomads in a semi-desert.[5]

This suggests that in the eyes of God elephants have just as much right to 'muddy the waters' as human beings. Wendy James records a myth common to the Uduk and Komo in which the 'Mother' leading the Great Dance at Creation takes the form of an elephant. At that time human beings were not yet upright: they were 'hoofed creatures' who could not speak properly who 'grew feet while we were still speaking gibberish'. Only later, when hostilities broke out, did humans become physically differentiated from other hoofed creatures.[6]

A Lozi story from Zambia teaches that animals are equally beloved children of the Creator, who did not intend them to be hunted and eaten. Here mankind is blamed for the origin of hunting and predation.

Why do you Kill?

Nyambe lived with his wife, Nasilele, long, long ago. It was he who made the forest and the river and the plain; it was he who made all the animals, the birds and the fishes; and he made also Kamunu and his wife. Kamunu distinguished himself quickly from the other animals. When Nyambe carved a piece of wood, Kamunu also carved his own. When Nyambe forged iron, the man also forged iron. Nyambe was amazed, and he began to fear man. Then man forged himself a lance, and one day he killed the male child of the big red antelope. He killed other animals as well, and ate them. Nyambe scolded him, saying: 'You man, your way of acting is bad. Why do you kill? These are your brothers. Do not eat them: you are all my children together.' Then Nyambe chased the man away, and sent him far off. . . .[7]

The Maasai tell a story of how their beloved cattle came down from heaven, which also explains why Dorobo hunters are blamed for the limited number of domestic cattle given by the Creator. Although wildlife has always been, and is still, abundant in Maasailand, traditionally the Maasai permit only an occasional lion hunt when their livestock are endangered by predators. Naomi Kipury, who grew up in a village of Kajiado district and recorded stories with the help of her mother, claims that her people love wild animals; children sing songs for them, and the role of animals in the social life of the people is deeply appreciated. Maasai despise the Dorobo hunters 'because of what is seen as an abnormal desire to kill domestic as well as wild animals and destroy what, in the Maasai mind, should be left to exist for its own aesthetic value'.[8]

The Love of Cattle

In the beginning, the Maasai did not have any cattle. One day God called Maasinta, who was the first Maasai, and said to him: 'I want you to make a large enclosure, and when you have done so, come back and inform me.' Maasinta went and did as he was instructed, and came back to report what he had done. Next, God said to him: 'Tomorrow, very early in the morning, I want you to go and stand against the outside wall of the house for I will give you something called cattle. But when you see or hear anything do not be surprised. Keep very silent.'

Very early next morning, Maasinta went to wait for what was to be given him. He soon heard the sound of thunder and God released a long leather thong from heaven to earth. Cattle descended down this thong into the enclosure. The surface of the earth shook so vigorously that his house almost fell over. Maasinta was gripped with fear, but did not make any move or sound. While the cattle were still descending, the Dorobo, who was a house-mate of Maasinta, woke up from his sleep. He went outside and on seeing the countless cattle coming down the strap, he was so surprised that he said: 'Ayieyieyie . . . !', an exclamation of utter shock. On hearing this, God took back the thong and the cattle stopped descending. God then said to Maasinta, thinking he was the one who had spoken: 'Is it that these cattle are enough for you? I will never again do this to you, so you had better love these cattle in the same way I love you.' That is why the Maasai love cattle very much.

How about the Dorobo? Maasinta was very upset with him for having cut God's thong. He cursed him thus: 'Dorobo, are you the one who cut God's thong? May you remain as poor as you have always been. You and your offspring will forever remain my servants. Let it be that you will live off animals in the wild. May the milk of my cattle be poison if you ever taste it.' This is why up to this day the Dorobo still live in the forest and they are never given milk.[9]

A myth from Malawi depicts animals as being surprised by some strange new creatures caught by the chameleon, who accidentally discover fire, which threatens the environment and causes the Creator to abandon the earth.

Cruelty of Humans

In the beginning there were no people, only god (Mulungu) and animals (nyama). There was peace and contentment in the world, and god lived on earth. One day the horned chameleon (kalilombe) went fishing in the river with a basket trap (mono) made of bamboo. The next morning he collected the fish, and took them back to the village to eat. The next day, when he inspected the trap, he found nothing. To his chagrin an otter (katumbwi) had entered the trap, and taken his fish. The following morning however, much to his surprise, he found that he had trapped two small unknown creatures. The chameleon did not know what to do, so he took them to god (Mulungu). He asked Mulungu what he should do with them. Mulungu replied that he should put them on land, so that they would grow. And this he did, and in time they became two full-grown human beings, male and female. All the animals and birds came to observe these two curious beings, and to watch what they did.

One day, quite by accident the humans made fire by rubbing two sticks together. They soon set the woodlands ablaze, and the animals had to run to escape the flames. The humans caught a buffalo (njati) by means of fire, and they roasted it on the fire for meat. Every day they set fires, and killed some animal and ate it. Mulungu complained to the chameleon about this state of affairs, for humans were burning the woodland, and killing all the animals. All the animals, in fact, had retreated into the woodlands to get as far away from the humans as they could. The chameleon had climbed into the trees, but Mulungu was old and unable to get away from the earth. He called the spider (tandaubwe) to help. The spider spun a web ladder, and Mulungu went with the spider on high. Thus Mulungu left the earth because of cruelty of humans towards the animals, proclaiming that when humans die they would also go on high.[10]

Another version of this myth was collected by Matthew Schoffeleers, according to which the *Maravi* (Malawi) people together with all the animals descended in a shower of rain and lived in peace with *Chiuta* (the Creator) until man invented fire, setting the grass ablaze. This made the animals flee, full of rage against man. Schoffeleers regards this myth as 'an impressive theological reflection on the movement of the seasons, on agriculture and hunting' as well as on other important facets of life.

A Shower of Rain

In the beginning there were Chiuta-God and the earth. Chiuta lived above in the sky, and below him was the earth, waterless and without life. One day, clouds began to cover the sky; lightning flared and peals of thunder were heard. Then the sky opened and from it Chiuta-God, the first human pair and all the animals descended in a shower of rain. They alighted on a flat-topped hill by the name of Kaphiri-Ktiwa, in the mountains of Dzala-Nyama. After their descent the soft surface hardened and turned into rock. On this rock the imprints of their feet as well as the spoors of many animals can still be seen. There can be seen two pairs of human feet: the man's larger than the woman's. There are also imprints of a hoe, a winnowing basket, and a mortar. Plants and trees grew up, yielding abundant food. God, men and animals lived together in happiness and peace.

One day, man accidentally invented fire by playing with two twirling sticks, one soft, the other hard. They warned him to stop, but he did not want to listen. In the end the grass was set alight, and there was great confusion. Among the animals, the dog and the goat fled to man for safety; but the elephant, the lion and their companions ran away, full of rage against man. The chameleon escaped by climbing a tree. He called out to God to follow him, but Chiuta-God replied that he was too old to climb. In the end the spider spun a thread lifting him up on high. Thus God was driven from the earth by the wickedness of man. As he ascended, he pronounced that henceforth man must die and join him in the sky.[11]

The name of God, *Chiuta*, means 'great bow' (*uta*, the hunting bow, *chi*, a prefix for large size or greatness), who is seen in the rainbow, drawn across the sky by the Creator and whose 'power is manifested in thunder, lightning and the rain'. Schoffeleers suggests that, although the Creator has departed, the great dance performed by the *nyau* societies, as first witnessed by Foà in 1894 CE, dramatizes hope for a truce between mankind and other animals:

The Great Dance

The Great Spirit of Men sends a message to the Great Spirit of the Forests in his domains. He tells Him that men are dancing every night by the light of the moon, that the earth is rejoicing, and that merriment and drunkenness reign supreme. He adds that He wants a truce of a few days with his enemy. Men will lay down their arms, and the animals must pull in their horns and take off their claws. He invites the visitors from the forest to mix with men, and to drink and dance with them to the sound of drums and by the light of the nocturnal luminary. The Spirit of the Forests accepts the invitation, and for the duration of the feast he sends every day a few of his subjects.[12]

A less hopeful view is expressed by Dr O. Imasogie, writing about the Nigerian understanding of the earth. Although it is a reality created by God, and the arena on which man is to live out his life in preparation for a fuller life in heaven, the earth is not as God originally intended.

The Earth a Battleground

In the various myths of creation and man's alienation from God, it is implied that the consequences of man's disobedience affect the earth also. Consequently, the earth has become the battleground where evil forces are ranged against man. There is no hope of the earth ever becoming anything other than what it is now. There is no general eschatology in which both man and his earth may be transformed. The earth is destined to remain as it is now.[13]

Perceptions obviously vary enormously across the continent. While fire however, is greatly feared in most African societies, rain is regarded as a great blessing, a gift of the Creator. Rain shrines are to be found everywhere, usually in sacred mountains. According to Brian Morris, in the pre-colonial period almost every mountain and large hill in Malawi had a rain shrine. At the main one at Msinja in the Dedza district, the central figure was a woman, known as *mangadzi* or *chauta* (of the hunting or rain bow), a correlate of *Chiuta* (the Creator God). According to Patrick Kalilombe, she was also known as *Makewana* (mother of children), the one responsible for the sustenance and wellbeing of the people.[14] Rain is therefore closely associated with fertility.

The Mother and the Serpent

As the wife of god [she] was unmarried, or broke her marriage ties when she assumed the role of mangadzi. *She was tended by a group of unmarried girls* (matsano) *who were also known as* akazi a chauta *(wives of god). Neither the* makewana *nor the* matsano *had sexual relations with human males. Only* thunga *(sacred serpent) or* nsato *(python), considered to be an epiphany or manifestation of the supreme spirit* (chiuta) *in the form of a snake, would visit the* makewana *on specified ritual occasions.* Thunga, . . . *was believed by the Chewa to be a kind of spirit entity that manifested itself as a huge snake. . . . It habitually lived in the mountains, or in some deep sacred pool, and it was seen as moving from place to place, and as controlling the rains.* Thunga *was associated with mountains and hills throughout the central region. At Msinja, the serpent spirit* thunga *was symbolized by one of the shrine officials Kamundi, who was of the Mbewe clan. It was Kamundi who made offerings to the spirit house, and was responsible for the ritual making of fire by means of fire sticks (*wopeka moto*). . . .*

Kamundi was the most important ritual official at the shrine. . . . He was the male consort of Makewana, who was essentially a prophetess or spirit-medium, not a goddess. She lived alone, unmarried, and largely hidden from ordinary people. She neither cultivated the ground, nor partook of meat or beer. . . . Only Kamundi, representing the snake, Thunga, entered her hut, to perform ritual intercourse. . . . This act has been interpreted as symbolizing the union of the sky (chiuta) *and the earth,* mangadzi *representing the earth (*dziko la pansi*) as a mother.*[15]

Rain-making rituals continue to be observed today in many parts of the continent, even by Christians, and the rain shrines in the Matopos hills in Zimbabwe attract pilgrims from all over southern Africa. According to Robert Tredgold, the rain ceremony has roots far back in the past, when it was performed solely by women:

> The dancers were young girls about twelve years old who wore a small apron when they danced; old women danced, too. They danced to the music of drums and women clapped their hands, whistles were not allowed. All the men had to go away when the dance was on. As they danced, they threw water up into the air.[16]

Today many of the shrines are controlled by men. Sitwanyana Ncube, chief priest at the Njelele rain shrine, told Ranger 'the shrine was responsible for everything, animals, grass, trees and people.' He had spent 'three months living with a lion, leopard, baboon, snake in Sihazabana cave', where he was taught the traditions of the shrine: 'I was talking directly to a snake which is the one which showed me all the caves'.[17]

A Creation myth collected by Herbert Aschwanden tells how Musikavanhu (an emissary from Mwali, the Creator) fell from the heavens to land softly on a white stone, from which he heard God's voice. This place became the stone of the pool (*mabwe adziva*, today called Matopos). The perennial pools in the shrine caves are identified with the uterus and amniotic fluid of a pregnant woman, and as the source of all life not only for humans, but also for animals and crops. 'When people in the Matopos pray for fertility the seed is sprinkled with water from the cave. It is water of life, they say, for it comes from the rock, and so from God'.[18]

The voice of God is heard not only in the Matopos hills; Oliver Zvabva, a Zimbabwean student, describes a cave far away on the frontier with Mozambique where the voice of *Dzivaguru*, eastern Zimbabwe's High God, is heard.

Paradise in a Cave
The structures inside the cave are very symbolic and have a bearing on agricultural fertility. In the cave is a stream which has its source in the cave, which flows into a ninga *or bottomless pit; a Baobab tree; a dome-shaped pillar;* mipfura *trees with bee-hives; two expansive rock* dwalas, *one close to the entrance and the other at the far back of the cave. . . .*

In the cave, scenery is attractive, full of life: biological as well as social. It has an independent existence, hence paradisial – like Adam in the Garden of Eden, the people are seen living in a paradise of their own.[19]

The Bible records that the Creator spoke with Adam and Eve in the Garden of Eden; thereafter He spoke with Moses on the mountain top, but Moses had to hide himself in a cave. The prophet Elijah also heard the voice of God in a cave.[20] There are other parallels, and biblical scholars may be interested in the extent to which African myths add to the Hebrew Creation story recorded in Genesis without contradicting it. A Kuba myth from Zaire depicts the Creator ruling over chaos, and bringing forth first the sun, moon and stars, before plants, animals and people. The order reflects that given in the Book of Genesis, except that the Kuba think woman was created before man.

Woman of the Waters
Darkness was over the earth which was nothing but water. Mbombo, the White Giant, ruled over this chaos. One day he felt a terrible pain in his stomach, and out came the Sun, the

Moon and the Stars. The Sun shone fiercely and the water steamed up in clouds. Gradually, the dry hills appeared. Mbombo again brought up things from his stomach: this time it was the forest, trees, animals and people. The first woman appeared, the leopard, the eagle, the first falling star, the monkey Fumu, the first man. Then the first tools appeared too: the anvil, the razor, medicines.

The Woman of the Waters, whose name was Nchienge, lived in the east. She gave birth to a son, Woto, and a daughter, Labama. Woto became the first king of the Bushongo (Bakuba) and moved westward with his children, who were still white. He dyed their skins black because they had to live in the forest as hunters and white men are too visible for the game. He put a medicine on their tongues so that they could suddenly speak the Kuba language. He married his sister but he decreed that only kings should have the privilege of living with their own sisters. Ordinary people had to mix with other clans to make the nation more extensive. King Woto had a niece who gave birth to a lamb; this was the first appearance of sheep. Only the royal family may own them; so precious are they that they are almost human. Woto found the monkey Fumu licking palm-wine and so this delicacy was discovered. He also found a pair of goats who agreed to stay with people if they would protect them against the leopard. Since then, men have made war against the leopard. Woto could make the banana trees grow by blowing his horn; he could make the bamboo speak at night. He could even call the crocodiles from the depth of the river.[21]

Alice Werner thinks much African folklore is inspired by sympathy with the underdog, and a feeling that 'the weak things of the world' have been chosen 'to confound the things which are mighty'. She relates a *Chinamwanga* story from northern Nyasaland:

The Shrew-Mouse

A Namwanga man one day went hunting with his dogs, and came upon a shrew (umulumba) by the roadside. It said to him, 'Master, help me across this swollen stream' (i.e., the path, which for him was just as impassable). He refused, and was going on, but the little creature entreated him again: 'Do help me across this swollen stream, and I will help you across yours.' The man turned back, picked it up and carried it across, 'very reluctantly.' (Why? Is there a feeling against touching a shrew, as Africans certainly shrink from touching a chameleon or some kinds of lizards?) It then disappeared from his sight, and he went on with his dogs and killed some guinea-fowl. Then, as it came on to rain, he took refuge in one of the little watch-huts put up in the gardens for those whose business it is to drive away monkeys by day and wild pigs by night. The shrew, which had followed him unseen, was hidden in the thatch. Presently a lion came along, and thus addressed the hunter: 'Give your guinea-fowl to the dogs, let them eat them, you eat the dogs, and then I'll eat you!'

The man was terrified, and could neither speak nor move. The lion roared out the same words a second time. Then came a little voice out of the thatch. 'Just so. Give the guinea-fowl to the dogs, let them eat them, you eat the dogs, the lion will eat you, and I'll eat the lion. 'The lion ran way without looking behind him.[22]

Stories that instill a respect for small creatures are plentiful in West Africa, and those who live underground are often thought to represent the spirits of buried ancestors, or even the Earth goddess. Studying the Akan of Ghana, Robert B. Fisher found that the land belongs to the ancestors and the living are merely its custodians, who may receive instruction from animals regarding the wishes of the ancestors.

Ananse the Spider

The common mother of the clan rose out of a cave deep in the earth. Interestingly enough, the trickster animal of the folktales, often called the wayward son of God, is the owner of mystical knowledge having to do with the riches of the earth. Among the Akan, I think that Kwaku Ananse is not only sometimes the manifestation of Onyame, but he is the link between the living and the ancestors with their knowledge of culture and life. The ground-dwelling spider comes out of its burrow, where it has lived in close proximity to the ancestors. Like the crab, another symbol of earth and sea, digging out of the sand, the spider crawls out with a message from the ancestors.[23]

Another aspect of the close relationship between human beings and other species in some African societies, known as totemism, is a topic often neglected by academic theologians, although much discussed by social anthropologists and psychoanalysts. A totem is usually an animal or other creature regarded as the ancestor of the clan. Clan members are expected to respect it, to protect it, and

never to eat it. The totem animal in turn is expected to protect its
fellow clanspeople from harm.

Although baboons are generally feared and despised as dangerous
thieves, in Zimbabwe those whose totem is *Soko* (baboon) sing their
praises in this hymn, collected by A.C. Hodza and translated by George
Fortune.

Chipuka Chinenge Munhu

Vene vamasango.
Vanayisi vemvura.
Vawisi vezviwizi namadora.
Vana vaMakudzagwara,
Vana uneyaneya kumisana.
Maresvausu
Mutanda usina makwati.
Matarira.
Mahomuhomu.
Utezutezu mumiti;
Mujiri uwakawaka
Zhizha nechirimo
hunongovd
Chipuka chinenge munhu
Muzivi wamatunduru namatamba. . . .
Zvikomana zvine vhudzi risingapumhwi,
Muviri ukaziva mvura yonaya.

Animal Almost Human

Masters of the forests.
Those who make the rain to fall.
And those who make all kinds of caterpillars come.
Sons of the Leader of big groups.
Their young clinging to their backs.
Those of the long faces.
Smooth as a log without any bark.
Watchmen.
Those of the gruff voices.
Swaying to and fro in the trees;
Swarming here and there in the fields.
In the rains and just before searching for food.
Animal almost human
Knowing where the wild plums and loquats are.
Fellows with unkempt hair,
Their body knows water only when it rains.[24]

The belief in a close relationship between animals of a particular species and people born with that totem is sometimes explained by saying that the original ancestor of the clan was born as twin to the animal concerned. According to Roy Willis, twins have a spiritual significance for the Nuer of the southern Sudan, who make effective pedagogical use of such a myth in remembering ancestors who were founders of descent lines:

> To found a new line is to break the social structure, to innovate: it is a historic event. And this even though, or rather because, the innovation is assimilated into the existing segmentary structure, so it is both the same and not the same after the event. A human twin-birth is conceptualized in the same pattern of split unity: twins have two physical bodies but they are one social person (*ran*) according to Nuer. Like a historical event, their birth is a sign of the intervention of *Kwoth* (spirit). Because of this, and to distinguish them from ordinary men, Nuer call human twins birds, because birds are the creatures closest to the primary abode of Spirit, which is the sky.

When the Nuer explain a totem relation between social groups and animal species by saying that an ancestor was born as twin to an animal, they are asserting their social identity, expressed in terms of the reciprocal relation between group and species; they are remembering the historic event of lineage foundation, expressed in an image of human-animal twin-birth which is a 'mythical charter' for the totem relation. Perhaps something similar may be observed in European heraldry, where animal emblems were frequently adopted by the landed gentry and aristocrats as symbols of their unique ancestry in order to distinguish one clan from another.

The wisdom of the ancestors handed down to the elders of the clan may sometimes be modified to suit local conditions. Bernardo Bernardi found that the oral traditions of the Meru, passed on by the elders, did not usually refer to Creation, which was simply stated as a work of God. Therefore he regards the following entertaining narrative, dictated by an elder of the Imenti, as a 'typical mythopoetical amalgamation'.

In the Beginning

We lived at Mbwa, but God created us. At that time we did not cultivate, which means that we did not need to eat or to wear clothes. God created first a boy. Having created him, God asked him: 'Are you pleased now?' 'No, I am not pleased, and the reason that I am not pleased is that I do not have anyone with whom to play.' So a girl came out. They played together. (When you see a girl, you do not laugh but you are pleased in your heart: the satisfaction remains there and there is no need of more.) Then they started to play like children in the way that, as you know, they love each other. And they bore a child. And they saw that that was sweet and they went on loving each other and they loved each other a lot.

God came and said: 'Now I shall go and I shall give you good, but you will not taste of that tree.' A wise creature (mugambi) that crawls on the earth as a snake came and asked them: 'Don't you want to eat of those fruits?' 'No, our chief (munene) told us not to eat of that tree.' He rejoined: 'If you eat of those fruits you will have intelligence as he has. So the woman climbed on the tree, picked a fruit and ate it. She picked a second one and gave it to her husband. The man refused. But the woman said: 'If you refuse, I will leave you alone.' The man on hearing that he would be left alone, took the fruit and ate it. Having eaten it, his throat-apple [Adam's Apple] came out. It is since then that man has got a throat-apple.

And now, God came and said: 'You knew that you should not have eaten of those fruits. Tell me, why did you eat of them?' The man said: 'It is the snake that deceived me and I ate the fruit. God said to the snake: 'I know that you are full of falsehood, therefore your head shall be crushed.' As for the man he sent for the mole to tell [him] that all men will die and then arise. While the mole was on his way he met the hyena. The hyena asked him: 'Where are you going?' 'It is God that sent me. He told me to go and tell man that they will die and arise.' 'No,' said the hyena, 'if you go and say so, what shall I eat?' The mole said: 'No, I will tell them.' The hyena said: 'Do you want me to eat and swallow you as you are?' So the mole became afraid on hearing that. He went and said: 'You will die and not arise.' And the mole returned to God and told him: 'I went, but the hyena deceived me and forced me to say: you will die and not arise.' On hearing that, God answered: 'You will now live under the earth, far away from me in heaven.' From that day the mole made a hole in the earth and he never comes out except during the night when he is not seen by man.[25]

Early missionaries recorded many Creation stories based on popular mythology, and it is possible that some of these stories have been reformulated under the influence of Christian teaching. Even before the arrival of Europeans, however, African traditional religions were constantly incorporating new ideas, modifying old ones, and adapting their rituals to accommodate immigrants. Ngwabi Bhebe, a distinguished Zimbabwean historian, relates how the primordial ancestors of the Zansi people, after completing their work of creation, returned to the earth as snakes. The Zansi were the original followers of Mzilikazi who emigrated from Zululand to what is now Zimbabwe, where, in the caves of the Matopos hills, they came into contact with the cult of the high-god, Mwari, whom they then began to worship.

Ancestral Snakes

The Zansi believed in a creator called Nkulunkulu. *They thought of him as the first human being, who with his wife* Mvelengangi *emerged out of a marshy place where there were reeds, and found cattle and corn awaiting them in abundance. They lived together and children were born to them, and having brought them up, given them various laws, customs, habits and property, the old people went underground again, became snakes, and have remained there in snake-like forms ever afterwards. . . .*

The Zansi conceived of man as consisting of three aspects: the material and two spiritual beings. Right from birth to death a person lived with a spirit — almost the equivalent of his shadow (isithunzi) *— which looked after him, and could bring good things or misfortune. This integral part of the person, but having extraordinary power, was also called an* idlozi *(spirit). Indeed, they spoke in terms of* idlozi lami *(my spirit) and* idlozi lake *(his spirit). . . .*

When a person died his spirit, as in the Christian idea of the soul, lived after him. The exact dwellings of the spirit are somewhat difficult to establish. The myth of Nkulunkulu described above points out that his spirit and that of his wife went underground with them but later emerged and went into the bodies of snakes. The spirits of their descendants behaved in a similar manner. Although the Zansi believed in the transmigration and reincarnation of the spirits and actually showed a great deal of deference to the animals supposed to embody them, they also thought of them as having at once fixed and unfixed places of abode. The fixed abode was the graveyard, while their spiritual nature made them air-like enabling them at the same time to live with their descendants and guard them wherever they went.[26]

Such ideas allow the ancestral spirits to accompany migrants on their travels, without being tied to the land in which their bodies are buried. The belief that human or other spirits may inhabit the bodies of certain animals is fairly widespread across Africa as in other parts of the world, although it is expressed in many different ways.

According to Peter Garlake, the San people (known as Bushmen) do not see the distinction between animals and people as something absolute or eternal, but as 'part of a historical process within time'. Their cave paintings portray animals and people inhabiting a single world in relations of equality, respect, interdependence and co-operation:

Animals are People

All San seem to have shared a fundamental belief in a unity of creation. In an ancient mythic time, the supreme god created a single living form, 'the people of the early race'. In this first world the differences between all living creatures were obscure: 'animals were people', they behaved in a fully human way and shared all human virtues and vices, emotion and reason, lusts and ambitions, plots and plans. Later, God named and distinguished the different species, and assigned to each a characteristic pattern of behaviour and determined their roles in the world. This amounted to a second creation. Thus, the distinction between animals and people and between different species of animals is neither absolute [n]or eternal but part of a historical process within time.

This process was also conceived in another way: animals evolved from humans. Humanity is overlaid or cloaked in a higher animality. The unity of the two is only superficially disrupted by external appearances. Animals retain elements of their human past and nature; they conceive of themselves as human, are interested and involved in human affairs, will interfere in, help and hinder them. Animal behaviour is no different from human behaviour: it is rational, purposive, directed by values and customs and institutions. Animals have language. Some practise sorcery. Their knowledge transcends that of humans in some areas, for instance, in their ability to fortell rain. A consequence of the interpenetration of the worlds of people and animals is that 'animals know all things', 'they know things that we don't', they know what is going to happen: 'an animal is a thing which knows of our death'.[27]

According to Credo Mutwa, Zulu people respect the Bushmen's remarkable ability to communicate with animals, particularly with dolphins. Moreover he maintains that in 'old Africa we did not regard ourselves as superior to the animals, the trees, and the fishes and the birds'.[28]

Dolphin the Redeemer

The Zulus call a dolphin an ihlengethwa, *which come from the verb* hlenga *which means 'to redeem', 'to ransom' or 'to save'. Thus the translation of the Zulu word* hlengeto *is 'the fish of salvation' or 'the redeemer fish'.*

The Zulu people believed, as did other nations in other parts of the world, that if a human being fell into the ocean, or was stolen from the seashore by waves and swept far out to sea, he could be saved from drowning, or from being mauled by sharks, by schools of dolphins which nudged the victim towards the shore.

The people also believed that, like the whale, the dolphin is gifted with speech and great telepathic power. When you are undergoing training as a high sanusi *, you are taught to communicate with dolphins. You are taught the clicks and the grunts which we are told are the language of the dolphin. . . . Our people believe that on the day we start communicating with dolphins and whales, great doors of knowledge and wisdom will be opened to us because these marine animals, the* umkhoma *and the* ihlengethwa, *are custodians of knowledge that we wretched human beings have not even dreamt about.*[29]

All this is not as fantastic as some Western theologians would like to believe. Zoologists are beginning to record the language of many different species and to decode it. In the case of dolphins and whales, Charlotte Uhlenbroek reports:

> Dolphins produce loud clicks and listen for echoes in order to sense their environment. Bottlenose dolphins (*Tursiops truncatus*), for example, can detect the presence of a steel sphere only about three centimetres in diameter as far away as the length of a football pitch. Sound is also the primary means by which dolphins communicate with each other. . . . there are strong bonds between particular individuals that can last a lifetime.
>
> Most surprisingly, the songs of humpback whales contain repeating refrains that form rhymes. This suggests that whales use rhyme in the same way as we do: as a mnemonic device to

help them remember complex material. The fact that whale song has so much in common with our own music, even though our evolutionary paths have not crossed for 60 million years, raises the possibility that rather than humans being the inventors of music, music may far predate humans. Every human culture has music and apparently when the Bushmen of the Kalahari were asked about the origins of music by the writer Laurens van der Post, they looked puzzled and replied, 'Can't you hear the stars singing?'[30]

In this Section we have sampled some of Africa's traditional wisdom about animals and Creation that has been collected by ethnographers and other scholars. It provides a rich resource, which is increasingly being made use of to develop new ways of studying theology in contemporary Africa, as we shall see in Section Six. In other Sections, the extent to which African traditional concepts of Creation may have influenced the development of Egyptian civilization and the religions of the Book will be considered.

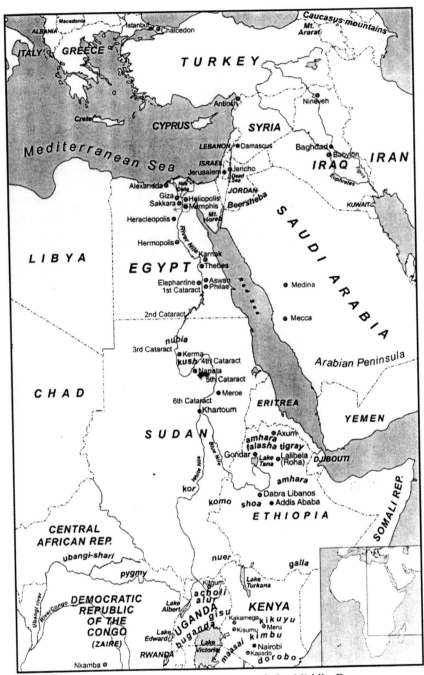

Map of North Eastern Africa and the Middle East

Early Civilizations of Egypt and the Nile Valley

List of Excerpts

Early Civilizations of Egypt
and the Nile Valley

Like other early African peoples, Egyptians saw spirits in trees, springs, stones, hill-tops, in birds and beasts, and in creatures thought to be possessed of a wisdom unknown to mankind, but, as James Henry Breasted observed nearly a hundred years ago: 'the earliest gods are the controlling forces of the material world.' The civilizations of Egypt and the Nile valley were dependent on both the sun and the waters of the Nile, which therefore came to be venerated as gods. Religious developments along the banks of the Nile, in what is now Egypt and Sudan, are the earliest for which records survive. Fifth and Sixth dynasty Pyramid Texts at Sakkara can be dated between 2625 and 2475 BCE, but contain much older material.[1]

Because Egypt is believed to have been colonized by 'Ethiopians' from further south at an early date, it is possible that many of the Egyptian gods originated in Ethiopia (or 'the land of the blacks').[2] According to Apuleius, Isis, mother of all the gods, was worshipped there, as she herself declared.

Queen Isis

I am nature, the parent of all the gods, mistress of all the elements, the beginning of all the ages, sovereign of the gods, queen of the manes [spirits of the dead], and the first of the heavenly beings. . . . My divinity, uniform in itself, is honored under numerous forms, various rites, and different names . . . but the sun-illumined Aethiopians, and the Egyptians renowned for ancient lore, worship me with due ceremonies, and call me by my real name, 'Queen Isis.'[3]

Plutarch considered Isis to be the earth, the feminine part of nature, while the Egyptians, considering the earth to be the parent of all things born, called her Mother, just as the Greeks called earth Demeter.[4] The cult of the Mother goddess was later adopted, or adapted, by the early Christian church in Egypt who passed it on along with other African traditions, to the rest of Christendom. Not only is the Christian title

Mother of God one of the titles of Isis, but her blue robe is one of her attributes that have passed into the Christian tradition concerning the Blessed Virgin Mary.[5]

Evidence of the merging of these traditions is found in Ethiopia too, where O'Hanlon claims the Bandlet of Righteousness, *Lefafa Sedek*, is similar to the Egyptian *Book of the Dead*. Although of Abyssinian origin, he thinks many of the beliefs expressed in the Bandlets are Egyptian. While containing much native Abyssian magic, some of the stories are Jewish, and the Virgin Mary plays the part which Isis plays in the *Book of the Dead*: 'Isis was regarded as a friend of the dead employing her powers for their benefit. According to Abyssinian tradition magical powers were bestowed on the Virgin by Christ Himself.' The Bandlets were originally inscribed strips of parchment the same length as the body with which they were buried"[6]

The *Book of the Dead* praises Osiris, god of the Nile, whose death and resurrection in late spring brought healing to the land.

Lord of Cattle
The Nile appeareth at thy utterance, making men live through the effluxes that come forth from thy members, making all cultivated lands to be green by thy coming, great source of things which bloom, sap of crops and herbs, lord of millions of years, sustainer of wild animals, lord of cattle; the support of whatsoever is in the heavens is thine, what is in the waters is thine.[7]

The annual resurrection of Osiris became a popular myth in Greek and Western European culture. The Stoic Seneca, in the first century CE, believed that the fecundity of the Nile could cure barren women, and that its source was not to be found in Ethiopian snows but in the 'veins and passages of underground caves and channels deep in the heart of Africa'':

> Only on the Nile was it possible, thought Seneca, that fluvial gladiators — crocodiles from the south and dolphins from the north — could have engaged in massed mortal combat. Only on the meandering Nile could the canny dolphins, the animals of peace and wisdom, have prevailed by tearing the reptile underbellies with their dorsal fins, salt water and fresh; mud and blood; life and death, tinting the sacred stream.

After quoting Seneca, Simon Schama explains that the annual rise of the Nile was originally celebrated on the island of Philae, just below Aswan, at the boundary of Nubia and Lower Egypt, where it could first be seen. Much later it came to be celebrated in every square of the French Republic after the Revolution, where officials planted

'Liberty Trees' which were 'politicized Maypoles' or emblems of 'the spring-like renewal of life', derived from the Osiris myth.[8]

The child-god Horus, was born of the union of Osiris, the god of the Nile, and Isis, the earth-mother, but death and sacrifice were seen as the precondition of rebirth. So, Osiris was incarnated as Apis, the Sacred Bull. According to Alexander Murray, this animal was allowed to live for no more than twenty-five years, at the end of which he was taken to the Nile and drowned. His death was followed by national mourning, giving place to national thanksgivings as soon as a new sacred bull, or Avatar, was discovered, by its identifying marks: a black coat, a white triangular spot on the forehead, a spot like a half-moon on its right side and under its tongue a knob like a beetle. The tradition was recorded by *Aelian*:

Apis, the Sacred Bull

As soon as a report is circulated that the Egyptian god has manifested himself, certain of the sacred scribes, well versed in the mythical marks, known to them by tradition, approach the spot where the divine cow has deposited her calf, and there, following the ancient ordinance of Hermes, feed it with milk during four months, in a house facing the rising sun. When this period has passed the sacred scribes and prophets resort to the dwelling of Apis, at the time of the new moon, and placing him in a boat prepared for the purpose, convey him to Memphis, where he has a convenient and agreeable abode, with pleasure grounds and ample space for wholesome exercise. Female companions of his own species are provided for him, the most beautiful that can be found, kept in apartments to which he has access when he wishes. He drinks out of a well, or fountain of clear water: for it is not thought right to give him the water of the Nile, which is considered too fattening. . . . The man from whose herd the divine beast has sprung is the happiest of mortals, and is looked upon with admiration by all people.[9]

The death and resurrection of this civilized creature could later be seen by Coptic Christians to prefigure that of the Saviour Jesus Christ.

Animals played an important part in Egyptian civilization, as evidenced by the fact that out of over seven hundred hieroglyphic signs, nearly one-fifth represent mammals and birds or parts of them.[10] The sun god was represented by a scarab beetle, *Khepra*, which deposited its seed in round pellets and rolled them with its back legs. This was a perfect analogy to the slow movement of the sun across the sky. Another form of the sun god was as *Ra*, flying perhaps more quickly with a human body and a falcon head, according to Molefi Kete Asante:

> Crowned with a solar disc and a cobra, Ra gained preeminence by the Fifth Dynasty and was considered the head of the pantheon. . . . In a mythopeical manner at dawn the sun was a child represented by the scarab beetle Khepra; at midday he was an adult male represented by Ra; and at sunset he was Atum, an old man who disappeared into the horizon. The most mysterious part of all was the night voyage. By night he sailed through the underworld and made it just in time for the dawn trip across the sky.[11]

The ancient Egyptians believed that human beings and other animals were equally children of the Creator, as a hymn dedicated to the sun god Re (or *Ra*) testifies: 'Thou art the begetter who causes thy children to come into being: men, gods, flocks, herds, and all creeping animals'.[12] In *The Book of Two Ways*, the All-Lord Re is identified as the Creator, who loves mankind. Leonard H. Lesko thinks the instruction of a king in Heracleopolis prior to the fall of the tenth dynasty (2040 BCE) provides 'in capsulized form the complete philosophy and theology of the Re religion'. Such documents reveal that two thousand years before Christ, and even before Abraham set out on his journey to the Promised Land, there was in Africa a concept of the Creator being 'hidden, omniscient, provident, responsive and just'. Long before Moses, Africans knew that 'men, who are created in the likeness of God, and for whom Heaven and Earth were created, must worship God, and provide for their fellow men'.

When They Weep He Hears

Serve God, that He may do the like for you, with offerings for replenishing the altars and with carving, it is that which will show forth your name, and God is aware of whoever served Him. Provide for men, the cattle of God, for He made Heaven and Earth at their desire. He suppressed the greed of the waters, he gave the breath of life to their noses, for they are likenesses of Him which issued from His flesh. He shines in the sky for the benefit of their hearts; he has made herbs, cattle, and fish to nourish them. He has killed His enemies and destroyed His own children, because they had planned to make rebellion; He makes daylight for the benefit of their hearts, and He sails around in order to see them, . . . and when they weep, He hears.[13]

The pharaohs protected the world from disorder while protecting settled farmers along the banks of the Nile from predators. In Egypt hunting particular animals, such as the hippopotamus and the lion, was a pharaonic prerogative, permitted only to the king's retainers by privilege. In Nubia, traces of a wildlife park have been found. Some wild animals were held in captivity to supply temple offerings, while others were domesticated. The striped hyena was used for offerings but also trained for hunting. Monkeys and baboons were trained and highly regarded for their understanding. It was this inate intelligence that led to their being associated with Thoth, the god of writing and wisdom.[14]

The pharaoh Akhnaton (*ca.* 1350-1334 BCE) introduced monotheism based on the worship of the sun. He wrote a hymn, praising the Creator's concern for 'strangers' and animals in other lands, for whom rain is provided, while the Egyptians have to rely upon the Nile's annual flooding to cover their fields with fertile black silt. Akhnaton (sometime spelt Ikhnaton) decreed that only the sun god, *Aton*, was to be venerated, and he built a sanctuary at Karnak where the anthropomorphic form of the sun god was replaced by a disk with radiating rays ending in hands holding the symbols of life.[15]

A Nile in the Sky

The lands of Khor and Kush and the land of Egypt: you have set every man in his place, you have allotted their needs, every one of them according to his diet, and his lifetime is counted out. Tongues are separate in speech, and their characters as well; their skins are different, for you have differentiated the foreigners. In the underworld you have made a Nile that you may bring it forth as you wish to feed the populace, since you made them for yourself, their utter master, growing weary on their account, lord of every land. For them the Aton of the daytime arises, great in awesomeness.

All distant lands, you have made them live, for you have set a Nile in the sky that it may descend for them and make waves upon the mountains like the sea to irrigate the fields in their towns. How efficient are your designs, Lord of eternity: a Nile in the sky for foreigners and all creatures that go upon their feet, a Nile coming back from the underworld for Egypt.[16]

This universal God of Egypt had a very different attitude towards neighbouring states from that of the God of Israel who emerged eight hundred years later. Akhnaton's vision of the Creator's embracing love for people of other lands is in stark contrast to the vengeful attitude expressed by Ezekiel, a priest and prophet who is called 'the father of Judaism':

> *The Lord Yahweh says this:*
> *Now I set myself against you, Pharaoh king of Egypt,*
> *you great crocodile wallowing in your Niles.*
> *You have said: My Niles are mine, I made them.*
> *I am going to put hooks through your jaws,*
> *make your Nile fish stick to your scales,*
> *and pull you out of your Niles*
> *with all your Nile fish sticking to your scales.*
> *I shall drop you in the desert, with all your Nile fish.*
> *You will fall on open ground and not be taken up or buried.*
> *I shall give you as food to the beasts of the earth and the birds*
> *   of heaven,*
> *so that all the inhabitants of Egypt may learn that I am Yahweh,*
> *since they have given no more support than a reed to the House*
> *   of Israel.* [17]

Although Akhnaton's monotheistic reform did not survive after his rule, it is thought to have influenced Hebrew religion as well as some African religions further south, so that ideas of universal justice and moral values were developed in Africa earlier than anywhere else. Fred Gladstone Bratton regards Akhnaton as a prophet centuries ahead of his time. He says: 'Ikhnaton's religion of cosmic theism is more challenging and more imperative in the shrunken world of the space age than it was in the fourteenth century B.C., because the present demands such a world outlook for survival'. [18]

The Psalms attributed to King Akhnaton may have inspired the Psalms of King David. [19] They include many references to animals and the worship daily offered by all the natural world to the Creator.

Dawn
Your dawn is beautiful on the horizon of the sky,
O living Aton who is the Beginning of life!
When you arose in the eastern horizon,
You filled every land with your beauty.
You are beautiful, great, glittering, high over every land,
Your rays encompass the lands, even to the end of all you have
*   made.*
You are Re, who penetrates to the very end of them;
You bind them for your beloved son.

Though you are far away, your rays are upon earth;
Though you are in the faces of men, your foot steps are unseen.

Night and Animals

Every lion emerges from his den,
All serpents, they sting.
Darkness broods,
The world is in silence,
He that made them rests in his horizon.

Animals and Plants

All cattle rest upon their pasturage,
The trees and the plants flourish,
The birds flutter in their marshes,
Their wings uplifted in adoration to thee.
All creatures that fly or alight.
They live when you shine upon them.

Day and the Waters

The barques sail upstream and downstream.
Every highway is open at your dawning.
The fish in the river leap up before you.
Your rays are in the midst of the great green sea.

Creator of Man and of Animals

Creator of the germ in woman,
Who makes seed into men,
Making alive the son in the body of his mother,
Soothing him that he may not weep,
You nurse him even in the womb,
Giver of breath to sustain alive every one created!
When he descends from the womb on the day of his birth,
You open his mouth, You supply his needs.
When the fledgling in the egg chirps in the shell,
You give him breath in it to preserve his life.
You ordered his term in the egg, and the time for breaking it.
He comes forth from the egg to chirp with all his might;
He goes about upon his two feet
When he comes forth.

Mother and Father of all

How beautifully you arise, O living Aton, Lord of Eternity;
You are glittering, beautiful, strong;
Your love is great and mighty,
Your rays furnish vision to every one of your creatures,

Your radiance brings life to the hearts of men,
When you have filled the Two Lands with love.
O God, . . . Creator of . . . men, all herds of cattle and the
*   antelopes,*
All trees that grow in the soil,
They live when you dawn for them,
You are the mother and the father of all that you have made. . . .
They see by means of thee.
Your rays illuminate the whole earth,
And every heart rejoices because of seeing you. . . .
They are drunken before you.
All cattle skip upon their feet;
The birds in the marsh fly with joy,
Their wings that were folded are spread,
Uplifted in adoration to the living Aton. . . .[20]

Akhnaton was succeeded by the nine-year old Tutankhamun, who
reigned from about 1334 to 1325 BCE, during one of the most glorious
periods of Egypt's long and distinguished history. Gradually, however,
the old gods reappeared and the priesthood was restored.

The Aton was still worshiped as a divinity, but no longer as the
sole god. According to Edward F. Wente, 'the counter-reformation
under Tutankhamun was more charitable and broad-minded' than
the iconoclastic reformation of Akhenaton had been. Indeed, he
says:

> An account of Tutankhamun's reforms, known as the restoration
> stele, is quite explicit about the disruption of the relationship between
> god and man that had occurred as a result of Akhenaton's innovation
> that made the king an intermediary in man's approach to god. With
> the counter-reformation under Tutankhamun it was once again
> possible for men to encounter the gods directly.[21]

The rule of law was not to be upheld by the Pharaoh alone, but by
all the gods. According to Gerald A. Larue, the Egyptian ethic was
based on *ma'at*, a concept of justice which includes order, truth, what
is correct and right action, established in the beginning by the gods
and guaranteed by the pharaoh. Officials appointed by the king to deal
with legal matters were called 'priests of *ma'at*'. Chapter 125 of 'The
Book of the Dead' contains a negative confession in which the deceased
recited before a panel of 42 divine judges a list of 42 sins not committed.
The crimes mentioned include mistreatment of animals, and Larue
explains why:

> The prohibition of cruelty to animals, which represents an

unusual ethical stance in the ancient world, rests in part on the Egyptian belief that when Ptah, the creator god of Memphis, brought life into being by his spoken word, creatures were manifestations of the divine. All that was, including the other gods, were projections of Ptah. Thus, Egyptians could imagine the creatures of the world welcoming and praising the rising sun as it was reborn each day, just as each Egyptian would do. Moreover, some gods assumed animal form. For example, Thoth could be either a baboon or an ibis, the sacred animal of the goddess Bast was the cat, Tauret was a hippo goddess, Sebek a crocodile and so on.[22]

Egyptian civilization was based on what has been called a 'culture of death'. Pyramid tombs provided the pharaohs with all they would need to carry them into their heavenly home. According to Mazrui, the pyramid builders 'recognised no fundamental break between living and dying. . . . To die was like changing your address'.[23]

Animals, who accompanied human beings on this heavenly journey, played an important part in Egyptian religion. Their bodies were sometimes mummified and carefully buried. At Abydos, a small Twelfth Dynasty pyramid tomb contained seventeen cat skeletons. Donkeys played an essential role as load carriers, and the word for donkey was simply *eeyore,* but the donkey was also associated with the god Seth.[24] *The Book of the Dead* suggests that words spoken by these familiar animals could open the way to eternal life for the righteous.

The Donkey and the Cat

I am one pure of mouth, pure of hands,
One to whom, 'Welcome' is said by those who see him;
For I have heard the words spoken by the Donkey and the Cat,
In the house of Eternity.[25]

The cat was associated with the moon, because of her nocturnal habits, and with fertility, because of her reproductive powers. Both the goddess Hathor, and later Bastet, were portrayed as cats playing a sistrum, a bronze musical instrument with a rounded open frame, suggesting a crescent moon, something like a fiddle. There is a sculpture (*ca.* 664-30 BCE) of Bastet playing a sistrum with kittens at her feet, which may be the source of popular European representations of 'the Cat and the Fiddle'. While Bastet protected the family, particularly women and children, the lion-headed female deity, Sekhmet, protected the whole nation.[26]

The lion god, Apedemak, was a god of war and one of the most powerful gods of Nubia and Meroe, although not worshipped further north in Egypt. His temples, with their square-chambered architectural style, differed from the characteristically rectangular Egyptian temples.[27] There were other Nubian gods who never became Egyptianized. However, Apedemak, who is often referred to as 'the Lion of the south, the foremost of Nubis', was in certain temple depictions placed alongside Isis and Horus as a trinity and was sometimes presented in a processional that included Thoth, the god of wisdom and learning.[28]

Lion of the South

Thou are greeted, Apedemek, lord of Naqa; great god, lord of Musawwarat es-Sofra; splendid god, at the head of Nubia. Lion of the south, strong of arm. Great god, the one who comes to those who call him. The one who carries the secret, concealed in his being, who was not seen by any eye. Who is a companion for men and women, who will not be hindered in heaven and earth. Who procures nourishment for all men in his name 'Perfect Awakener.' The one who hurls his hot breath against his enemy, in this his name 'Great of Power.' . . . The one who punishes all who commit crimes against him. Who prepares the place for those who give themselves to him. Who gives to those who call to him. Lord of life, great in his sight.[29]

There are many folk-tales of the lion's strength and wisdom, often contrasted with the wickedness of mankind. One of the earliest recorded is from a Demotic Papyrus of the Twenty-first Egyptian dynasty (*ca.*1070-945 BCE). A version of this story later appears in Aesop's fables.

The Lion in Search of Man

A mighty lion on the mountain met a panther whose fur was stripped and whose skin was torn, with horrible wounds. The lion said: 'How did you get into this condition? Who scraped your fur and stripped your skin?' The panther answered: 'It was man.' The lion said to him: 'Man, what is that?' The panther replied: 'There is no one more cunning than man. May you not fall into his hands!' The lion became enraged and ran off to search for man.

The lion encountered a team yoked so that one bit was in the mouth of the horse, the other bit in the mouth of the donkey. The lion said to them: 'Who is he who has done this to you?' They said: 'Our lord, there is not one more cunning than man. May you not fall into the hand of man!' The lion was outraged by the wickedness of man.

The lion met a bear whose claws had been removed and whose teeth had been pulled. He asked him, saying: 'Is man stronger than you?' He said: 'That is the truth. He removed my claws and my teeth. I have no food and no strength without them! He threw sand in my eyes and ran away from me.' The lion became even more enraged against man.

The lion boasted: 'Man, if you should fall into my hand, I shall give you the pain that you inflicted on my companions on the mountain!' Then, as the lion was walking in search of man, there strayed into his paw a little mouse, small in size, tiny in shape. The mouse said: 'Do not crush me, my lord the lion! If you eat me you will not be sated. If you release me you will not hunger for me either. If you give me my breath of life as a gift, I shall give you your own breath of life as a gift. If you spare me from your destruction, I shall make you escape from your misfortune.' The lion laughed at the mouse and said: 'What is it that you could do? Is there anyone on earth who would attack me?' But the mouse swore an oath: 'I shall help you escape from man one day!' Although the lion considered the words of the mouse as a joke, he reflected that she would not make much of a meal and so released her.

Now there was a hunter with a net who set traps and dug a pit which the lion fell into. The lion found himself caught in the net and bound with dry leather straps. As he lay suffering on the mountain, God made his joke come true, because of his boastful words. The little mouse appeared and said to him: 'Do you recognize me? I am the little mouse to whom you gave his breath of life as a gift. I have come in order to repay you for it today, and to rescue you from your misfortune, since you are suffering. It is beautiful to do good to him who does it in turn.' Then the mouse set his mouth to the fetters of the lion. He gnawed through all the dry straps with which he had been bound, and released the lion. The mouse hid himself in the lion's mane and went off with him to the mountain.[30]

Folktales and oral traditions were often recited in poetic form. According to Northrop Frye, the first phase of language is poetic, and the primary social function of the poet is connected with something very ancient in society's use of words:

The Elizabethan critics, for example, tell us that in pre-Homeric times, the days of the legendary Orpheus and Hermes Trismegistus, the poet was the repository of all wisdom and knowledge, the teacher, or, in Shelley's phrase about a later era of history, the 'unacknowledged legislator,' of his society. There were technical reasons for this: verse, with its formulaic sound-schemes, is the easiest vehicle for an oral culture in which memory, of the keeping alive of tradition, is of primary importance. As the critics of the god Thoth, the inventor of writing, remark in Plato's *Phaedrus*, the ability to record has a lot more to do with forgetting than with remembering: with keeping the past in the past, instead of continuously recreating it in the present.[31]

Thoth was the Egyptian god of the moon, messages and writing, whose sacred ibis, a lunar bird of the night, guided the souls of the dead. He was known to the Greeks as Hermes. Ibises were bred in sanctuaries and mummified for burial in Egyptian tombs in enormous numbers. One and a half million have been excavated from the Saqqara catacombs alone.[32] According to Brian Copenhaver, Thoth was given a title, the Demotic equivalent of *megistou kai megistou theou megalou Hermou* – two superlative forms of 'great' followed by a positive form of the same word, foreshadowing the Greek title, *Trismegistos,* which was later given to Hermes as author of the *Poimander*. It was 'the name that would signify a new way of sanctifying the heathen past for Christian scholars of the Renaissance'.[33]

The Word of the Lord

I am Light your god Mind
who gave myself to sight
before Dark Water's birth
the glowing Word Mindvoiced
is God's Son.

Know what hears in you and sees
is the Word of the Lord
your mind the Father God

Father and Son are One
this makes life
now turn towards the Light and understand.

. . . all this was in my mind
while I looked inside at the world
through Poimander's Word. . . .[34]

This divine *Word* prefigures later Christian definitions of the Trinity, just as Egyptian and other early writings can be seen to prefigure the Jewish wisdom tradition. The biblical book of *Proverbs* 'very faithfully follows the Egyptian maxims of Amenemophis' and 'the author of Tobit knew the *Wisdom of Ahikar*'.[35]

Ahikar was a high official at the Assyrian court under Sennacherib (704-681 BCE) and Esarhaddon III (681-669BCE). The earliest extant manuscript of his *Wisdom* is in Aramaic and was discovered in 1906 on the island of Elephantine in southern Egypt, the site of a Jewish military colony dating back to at least the fifth century BCE. This manuscript does not mention the God of Israel, but refers to at least three gods, El, Shamash, and Shamayn. As Porter points out, 'the Bible itself provides evidence that, before the Babylonian exile, the popular religion of Israel included the worship of the sun, the "Queen of Heaven", and other deities',[36] Ahikar extols not only the wisdom of gods but also that of animals.

Eternal Wisdom

From heaven the peoples are favored;
Wisdom is of the gods.
Indeed, she is precious to the gods;
her kingdom is eternal.
She has been established by Shamayn;
yea, the Holy Lord has exalted her.

Wisdom of Animals

The ass abandons his load and will not carry it. He will be shamed by his fellow and will have to carry a burden which is not his own; he will be laden with a camel's load. . . .

A leopard came upon a she-goat who was cold. The leopard said to the goat, 'Won't you let me cover you with my pelt?' The goat replied to the leopard, 'Why should I do that, my lord? Don't take my own hide away from me! For, 'A leopard does not greet a gazelle except to suck its blood."

A man said one day to the wild ass, 'Let me ride on you, and I will provide for you!' The wild ass replied, 'Keep your care and fodder; as for me, I want nothing to do with your riding!'[37]

Proverbs and folk-tales from Africa must have been well known to later Greek philosophers, who seriously debated whether or not species other than mankind had souls, and the extent to which their feelings should be respected. Some time after 530 BCE Pythagoras opposed animal sacrifice and meat eating. Unfortunately, the widespread acceptance of Aristotle's view that other creatures lack reason (*logos*) and belief (*doxa*), led to the subsequent justification of cruelty and abuse.[38] Apart from constant ritual slaughter in temples, the Roman occupation of North Africa led to the capture of many lions and other wild animals purely for entertainment in the games, where they were required to fight each other or to devour Christian martyrs.

As we have noted, Egyptians and inland Africans further south saw the sun and the waters of the Nile providing for all creatures equally, and the Creator God appeared to them in the form not only of a human being, but perhaps more often in the form of an animal. Therefore animals were given a respect in early civilizations of the Nile valley that was later denied them in the Roman Empire and in subsequent European Christendom.

African Judaism

List of Excerpts

African Judaism

In this Section we begin with the early roots of Judaism in Egypt, in the Nile Valley and in Ethiopia. The Hebrew Bible records many contacts between the Chosen People in the land we now call Palestine and the people of Africa. Most of those who survived the Babylonian conquest of Judah were deported by Nebuchadnezzar between 598 and 582 BCE, but other Hebrew communities settled on the banks of the Nile. There were in fact more Jews in the Diaspora than in their 'homeland'. Only after Cyrus permitted exiled Jews to return to Jerusalem in 539 BCE and to begin the rebuilding of the Temple, was there a slow growth in the number of Jews in Palestine.[1]

Hebrew communities in the Diaspora developed their own traditions, some of which are recorded in surviving ancient scriptures in Africa and nowhere else. They also preserved oral traditions forgotten or neglected in other parts of the world. Many of these myths and legends concern the creation of animals, as well as angels and human beings, and record the way in which each species was given its own kind of wisdom. African traditions, both oral and written, reveal more about life in the Garden of Eden and events leading up to Noah's Flood than can be found in the Hebrew Bible.

There are Judaic communities in Africa which developed with little or no contact with Palestine. The Falasha people of Ethiopia, known as *Beta Israel,* date back at least to the Babylonian Captivity if not before, while a totally different community in Uganda, known as the Abuyudaya, was founded less than a hundred years ago by people possessing only the (Christian) Old Testament, without having met Jews from any other part of the world.[2] These communities have almost no knowledge of the Hebrew language or of the Talmud.

Popular Jewish stories, known as Midrashim, were transmitted orally in the Diaspora long before some of them were codified in the Talmud. In these stories King Solomon is portrayed not only as understanding the language of animals, but as gaining some of his renowned wisdom from them. In the Book of Proverbs the lazy person is advised, 'Go to the ant; ponder her ways and grow wise'. One Midrash recorded by an English Rabbi, Schlomo Pesach Toperoff, concludes: 'It was a sufficient humiliation for man that he had to learn from the ant; had he learnt and acted accordingly he would have been sufficiently humbled but he did not learn from the wise ant.'[3] Toperoff maintains that animal welfare finds its roots in Jewish tradition.

The Ant is Wiser than Solomon

In the course of his wanderings Solomon heard an ant issuing orders to others to withdraw and so avoid being crushed by the armies of the king. Thereupon Solomon summoned the ant who informed him that she was the queen of the ants and offered reasons for her orders. Solomon wished to question her but she defiantly refused to answer unless the king took her and placed her on the palm of his hand. He acquiesced and repeated his question, 'Is there anyone greater than I am in the world?' asked Solomon. The ant promptly retorted, 'Yes, I am.' Solomon was taken aback, saying, 'How is that possible?' The ant, unperturbed, replied. 'Were I not greater than you, God would not have led you here to place me in your hand.' Exasperated, Solomon threw her to the ground and exclaimed, 'I am Solomon, the son of David.' Not to be intimidated, the ant reminded the king of his earthly origin and admonished him to be humble. The king went his way, feeling abashed. In this manner, the wise Solomon was outwitted by the unpretentious ant.[4]

King Solomon was able to communicate not only with insects, but also with birds. There is a popular legend that the lapwing or hoopoe delivered a letter from Solomon to the Queen of Sheba.[5] Solomon also called on these birds for help in his travels.

King Solomon flies South and rewards the Birds

Solomon thought he would make for himself a magic carpet that was invisible and yet would be able to move in any direction at word of command. One day he told Genu, who attended him, that he would fly southward. He commanded: 'Carpet, become small enough to hold me in comfort and fly with me southward. Do that I may see manifold variations of life that God has made.'

Immediately Genu took up the carpet and the king was wafted southward. As he travelled, the sun became hotter and hotter. When the sun was directly overhead, the king tried to shelter himself from its rays. He saw some vultures flying near him.

He called, 'Come spread your wings, fly over my head and shelter me from the sun.' But the vultures refused – the sun helps us to find decaying food on which we live; we will not offend the sun. The sun grew hotter and hotter and a small cloud appeared and the king could see presently a flock of birds flying toward him. He called out to them to shelter him from the sun's rays and they answered, 'Willingly, O king – we are very small but we are numerous, if we spread our wings, they may be a protection to your head.' In gratitude King Solomon promised them a reward.

He said, 'Come and tell me in three days' time what you would like.' For three days the birds set up a council but could not come to an agreement until the king of hoopoes suggested that their queen should choose a suitable reward, and they flew to King Solomon and asked for the golden crown. Solomon was shocked and exclaimed, 'Vanity of vanities – I warn you that admiration often creates jealousy, but if that is your wish, you shall have it.'

Trouble first came with the fowler and his gun, as he killed many of them for their beauty. Then the hunters set traps of cages with looking glasses inside. The foolish hoopoes came to see how beautiful they had become, but they found they had been made prisoners. Then they were sold for their plumage. In great alarm the king of the hoopoes went to Solomon: 'What have you done to us; you have returned evil for good. Before we helped you, none sought our lives, now we are in danger of being utterly destroyed.' King Solomon replied: 'I now see that some creatures are incapable of choosing best for themselves and it is necessary for the wiser men rulers to help them choose. I warned you that vanity would be your downfall. Now let me choose. I suggest that all golden crowns be changed to feathers.' And turning the magic ring the king pronounced the necessary words and it was done. The hoopoes said, 'Wise and great is Solomon the king – he has given us warmth and security.'[6]

This Midrash illustrates not only Solomon's legendary relationship with animals, but also his interest in African lands to the South, particularly Ethiopia, where gold was to be found. A mutual exchange of goods and ideas developed between the two countries, and by the fourth century CE Hebrew scriptures were translated into *Ge'ez* (Ethiopic).

The Ethiopian epic, *Kebra Nagast*, refers to the Ark of the Covenant as the first of all things in creation, which came to earth containing the

Mosaic Law. It relates how, after visiting Jerusalem, Queen Makeda returned to Ethiopia bearing King Solomon's son, Menelik. This young prince later visited his father and was educated in Jerusalem. When he returned home to his mother some 'first-born of the leaders of Israel' accompanied him, carrying the Ark of the Covenant with them.

The Falasha Jews claim to be the descendants of the bodyguard provided by King Solomon for his son on this journey.[7]

When Islam became dominant in North Africa and Arabs controlled the trade route along the Red Sea, Ethiopian Jews became isolated from their co-religionists. As a result the Falasha are unfamiliar with the Talmud, which was only codified around 500 CE. The Torah they use is written not in Hebrew but in *Ge'ez*, and although they retain only a few Hebrew words in their prayers, they strictly observe the Sabbath, adhere to the dietary commandments in the Book of Leviticus, and celebrate the new moons and festivals as prescribed in the Pentateuch. Ethiopia's Jews regard the weekly Sabbath not simply as a day of rest, but more importantly, as a *holy person*. This metaphysical being is female and is seen as the manifestation on earth of the heavenly world – to which end she is given names: 'Luminous', 'Vivifying', 'Rejoicing' and 'Beloved'. She constantly intercedes with God on behalf of both the righteous and sinners, reminding the Almighty that she is a 'sign' and a witness to the people.[8]

According to Edward Ullendorff, 'A dispassionate appraisal of the ethnic and religious position of the Falashas places them squarely into the mainstream of Ethiopian life, yet outside the doctrinal tradition of monophysitism'. He regards them as descendents of those elements of the Axumite kingdom who resisted conversion to Christianity, but 'Ethiopians in general are the heirs of a civilization in which the veneration and imitation of the Old Testament occupy a central and enduring position'.[9]

The Falasha Jews have much in common with their Christian neighbours: the language of their prayers is the same, both groups carry out circumcision on boys and excism on girls, and, surprisingly, monasticism plays an important part in both religions. J.M. Flad, a missionary of the London Jews' Society stationed in a Falasha village not far from Gondar, in the middle of the nineteenth century, wrote about the Hoharewa cave, a place of pilgrimage, guarded by a community of about two hundred *Jewish* monks:

> The founder of their order of monks, Aba Zebra, lived in the fourth century after Christ, in the province Armatshoho, in a cavern called Hoharewa. There he spent his whole time in the study of the law, and it is related that he healed the sick through prayer, and the laying-on of hands. Great crowds followed him,

to whom he preached the word of God, exhorting them to fear God and to lead a holy life. The gifts brought to him by those who sought his aid he distributed among the poor and needy. He himself lived on herbs and roots. His self-denying life, and the respect paid him by the Falashas, excited in other minds a desire to follow his example.[10]

According to Flad, the Falasha not only observe the feasts and sacrifices laid down in the Pentateuch in a way no longer practised by Rabbinical Judaism, they add some practices which probably derive more from African traditional religion than from Christianity.

Blood Sacrifice

One peculiar custom common to Falashas and Christians is that they never reside in a newly-built house until, as they say, blood has flowed in it. This is a special sacrifice, usually of a sheep, or amongst the poorer classes, of a hen. . . . If this sacrifice is not observed, which is often the case with Europeans, and a death occurs in the house shortly after, the natives consider it a clear proof that the house, or rather the spirits presiding in it, have required their offering. Also in the granary a white hen is sacrificed.[11]

Besides their Old Testament, which includes the Apocrypha, Flad found that the Falasha possessed other sacred books written in Ge'ez on parchment, including the *Gedala Adam* (History of Adam), and *Siena Aihud* (History of the Jews, a translation of Josephus). Since 1856 the Falasha have also been in possession of the Christian Amharic Bible.[12]

The Bible of the Ethiopian Church has always included various scriptures not found in either the Hebrew Bible or the Septuagint, notably the *First Book of Enoch* (known as *Ethiopian Enoch* because it has been preserved in its entirety only in Ethiopia) and *The Book of Jubilees*. These pseudepigrapha describe the creation of the universe in greater detail than the Book of Genesis does, explaining how first angels, then human beings and other animals fell into sin, and why the Creator had to send the Flood to cleanse the earth. Clement of Alexandria, Irenaeus and Tertullian all regarded the *Book of Enoch* as 'canonical' and, although it was later rejected by Jerome and Augustine, in the Eastern church it continued to be treated with great respect.[13] The epistle of St Jude in the New Testament quotes *Enoch,*[14] but for centuries non-Ethiopian biblical scholars were unable to identify the source of Jude's quotation, because the *Book of Enoch* was not in their Bible of sixty-six books. For Ethiopian scholars, whose Bible contains eighty-one books, locating the passage in *Enoch* 1:9 was not a problem. It is only since fragments of *Enoch* were found in Aramaic at Qumran among the Dead Sea Scrolls that Western scholars have begun to appreciate the value of the Ethiopian manuscripts and to make translations from the *Ge'ez*.[15]

The Book of *Jubilees* (also known as *The Little Genesis*)[16] is thought to have been originally composed in Hebrew or Aramaic some time between *ca.*175 and 140 BCE. In this book the weekly Sabbath is viewed as especially sacred, and time is measured in weeks, jubilees (forty-nine years) and weeks of jubilees (seven times forty-nine).[17] According to the Book of *Jubilees,* the Mosaic Law requires even the angels to observe the Sabbath according to a solar calendar of 364 days. Both *Jubilees* and *Enoch* claim that the Jews went astray during the Babylonian exile in adopting a lunar calendar, which gave a 354-day year plus an intercalated month every three years. According to *Enoch,* the sun alone dictates the proper days for Sabbaths and feasts, and *Jubilees* states that at Creation, 'God appointed the sun to be a great sign on the earth for days and for Sabbaths and for months and for feasts and for years'. The angel Uriel foretells the dire consequences of confounding holidays with 'unclean' days, thereby disturbing the divinely appointed order of the cosmos.[18]

From *Jubilees* we learn that Adam spent six days naming the animals 'and everything that moves on the earth' before God decided to create a 'helper' for him. The woman (created from Adam's rib) did not enter the Garden of Eden until the eighth day. Adam and Eve then lived naked in the garden for seven years before the serpent approached Eve, and during that time angels taught Adam 'all the details of the gardener's craft'. As will be seen from this excerpt, prior to their expulsion from the Garden, animals were able to communicate with one another in a common language. Adam made a daily offering at sunrise, which did not involve animal sacrifice, although garments were made of their skins.

The Garden of Eden

And He [the Creator] made for them garments of skin and he dressed them and sent them from the Garden of Eden. And on that day when Adam went out from the garden of Eden, he offered a sweet-smelling sacrifice – frankincense, galbanum, stacte, and spices, in the morning with the rise of the sun from the day he covered his shame. On that day the mouth of all the beasts and cattle and birds and whatever walked or moved was stopped from speaking because all of them used to speak with

*one another with one speech and one language. And he sent
from the garden of Eden all of the flesh which was in the garden
of Eden and all of the flesh was scattered, each one according
to its kind and each one according to its family, into the place
which was created for them. But from all the beasts and all the
cattle he granted to Adam alone that he might cover his shame.
Therefore it is commanded in the heavenly tablets to all who
will know the judgment of the Law that they should cover their
shame and they should not be uncovered as the gentiles are
uncovered.*

    *And on the first of the fourth month Adam and his wife went
out from the garden of Eden and dwelt in the land of 'Elda, in
the land of their creation. And Adam named his wife Eve. They
had no son until the first jubilee but after this he knew her.
And he tilled the land as he had been taught in the garden of
Eden.*

    *And in the third week in the second jubilee, she bore Cain.
And in the fourth she bore Abel. And in the fifth she bore 'Awan,
his daughter. . . . And Cain took his sister, 'Awan, as his wife,
and she bore for him Enoch at the end of the fourth jubilee.*[19]

The Book of *Jubilees* adds a good deal to the story of Creation,
found in the canonical Book of *Genesis*. Moreover, Norman Cohn
regards it as a true apocalypse, in that the story is presented as a
secret revelation originally transmitted by angels to Moses on Mount
Sinai. The narrative is interspersed with prophecies of the great
consummation and foreshadowings of the final cataclysm.[20] In
Jubilees angels are referred to as *Watchers,* because they came down
to earth to teach men and women what to do. It relates how some of
the Watchers fell into sin themselves, fornicating with 'the daughters
of men', and 'sinning against beasts, and birds and everything which
moves or walks upon the earth.' They caused such havoc that the
Creator had to send a Flood to destroy their tyranny. Although the
book of Genesis mentions wicked angels, the Nephilim, corrupting
womankind and begetting giants, it says nothing about the corruption
of animals which, according to *Jubilees,* produced terrifying monsters.
It simply records that among mankind, only Noah was found worthy
to be saved along with his immediate family, and that he was
commanded to build an ark to rescue the innocent animals. Thereafter
God established a Covenant with every living creature that came out
of the ark, and the rainbow became a sign of this Covenant.[21]

    To what is recorded in *Genesis*, *Jubilees* adds that Noah was given seven commandments, which had originally been delivered to Adam for all mankind. These prohibit the worship of other gods, blasphemy, murder, incest, adultery, and theft. In addition, Noah was commanded to eat only permitted foods and to establish courts of law.[22] These Noachide laws were important for the later development of Judaism in Africa, because Hellenized Jews, preaching to gentiles who were not descended from Abraham or Moses, could thereby claim Noah's more universal and prior authority. Noah was the saviour not only of all mankind but of all God's Creation. His universal message, as recorded in *Jubilees*, focuses on the serious consequences of the shedding of blood, and on the virtue of honest husbandry.

Cover the Shed Blood

For whoever sheds man's blood, and whoever eats the blood of any living creature shall be destroyed altogether from the earth. And no man that eats blood shall be left on earth, or that sheds the blood of man, nor shall there be left to him any offspring or descendants under heaven; for to Sheol shall they go, and into the place of punishment shall they go down, and to the darkness of the deep shall they all be removed by a violent death. There shall be no blood seen on you of any of the blood shed when you kill any animals or cattle or birds on the earth; and do then what is right and cover what has been shed on the earth. And you shall not be like the man that eats meat with the blood still in it, and take care that no one eats blood in your company: cover the blood, for so I have been commanded to instruct you and your children and all mankind.[23]

The First Fruits

And now, my children, listen: act justly and do what is right, so that you may be planted in righteousness over the whole earth and your glory exalted before my God, who saved me from the waters of the flood. And behold, you will go and build yourselves cities and you will plant in them all the plants that there are upon the earth, and also all trees that bear fruit. For three years the fruit of everything that can be eaten must not be gathered; and in the fourth year its fruit shall be reckoned holy, and they shall offer the first fruits, acceptable before the Most High God, who created heaven and earth and all things. Let them offer it sprinkled with the first of the wine and the oil as first-fruits on the altar of the Lord, who receives it; and what is left let the servants of the Lord's house eat before the altar which receives it. And in the fifth year let the land lie fallow, so that you let it lie fallow in righteousness and honestly; and you will be righteous, and all your orchards will be ritually pure. For so your great-grandfather, Enoch, commanded his son Methuselah, and Methuselah his son Lamech, and Lamech commanded me to observe everything his fathers had commanded him.[24]

Muslims believe that Adam was the first of the prophets. From a manuscript recently discovered at Nag Hammadi in Upper Egypt, the *Book of the Apocalypse of Adam*, we learn that Adam had foretold the Flood and prophesied to Seth that Noah and his sons would rule the earth 'in kingly fashion', but that subsequently a wicked generation not descended from Noah would arise. This indicates that Noah's family were not to be the only ones to survive the flood.[25]

Another scripture, known as *The Penitence of Adam*, like the Book of *Jubilees*, describes how God sent an angel to teach Adam and Eve to make clothing out of animal skins, using 'spines from the thorn-bush.' It also records how wicked angels appeared as mermaids to tempt them with sins of the flesh, but after much prayer and fasting, God allowed Adam and Eve to enter chastely into the sacrament of matrimony, which suggests that their 'original sin' had been forgiven. This lends little support to the Christian doctrine of Original Sin but reflects a view found in the Talmud. Although the Rabbis agreed that the sin in the Garden of Eden had repercussions on all subsequent generations, that did not mean that sin is inherited. According to Cohen: 'He may be burdened by the consequences of the wrongdoings of his forefathers; but no Rabbi of the Talmudic age would admit that any human being committed a wrong for which he or she was not personally responsible'.[26]

Mermaids tempt Adam and Eve

Satan was filled with envy against them, and he and ten of his company took the form of maidens of incomparable beauty, and coming out of the waters of the river they came before Adam and Eve. And they said: 'We desire to look upon the faces of Adam and Eve who are on the earth, and to see whether they are beautiful and whether they are different from our own.' And they came upon the bank near to Adam and Eve; they saluted them and stood before them amazed, and Adam and Eve looked upon them and were astonished by their beauty, and said to them: 'Is there then another world where there

*exist such beautiful creatures?' And the maidens answered and
said to Adam and Eve: 'There is, and we are but a part of a
great number.' And Adam said to them: 'And what is it that has
caused you thus to multiply?' And they answered: 'We have
men who marry us and we conceive and bear children, and our
children grow and so our race is multiplied. And if you do not
believe us, we can bring it about that you shall see our husbands
and our children.' And they called their husbands and their
children, and men and children came up out of the water, and
began each to go to his wife and to take his own children. And
when Adam and Eve saw these things they were filled with
amazement. And the maidens said to Adam and Eve: 'You have
seen our husbands and our children; and now Adam, you must
do as we shall tell you so that you also shall have children and
shall perpetuate your race.' For Satan thought in his heart:
'God forbade Adam to eat of the tree and Adam disobeyed his
command and has suffered great punishment; and now I shall
bring him to go in unto Eve without the command of God, and
God will be wrath with him and will destroy him.'*

*But Adam thought he should offend God, and he fell to praying,
as did Eve also, and Satan and his company plunged again
into the waters, and Adam and Eve returned to their cave as
was their wont, and the hour of evening was come. And in the
night they rose to pray, and Adam said: 'Lord, thou knowest
that we disobeyed thee, and through our fault our bodies have
become as those of the brutes. Show us what is thy will, O
Lord, and let not Satan come to trouble us with deceiving
visions, lest we are led again to do that which will offend thee,
so that thou art wrath with us and destroy us utterly.' And God
heard the words of Adam, and saw that they were true and that
he was not able to resist the attacks of Satan; and the word of
God came to Adam and said: 'The pains thou now sufferest
would never have come upon thee hadst thou not provoked my
wrath, so that I drave thee from the garden.'*

*And to Adam he sent the angel who had brought to him gold,
and the angel who had brought to him incense, and him who
had brought to him myrrh; and the angels said to Adam: 'Take
the gold and give it to Eve as a marriage gift, and make a
covenant with her, and give her the incense as a pledge that
thou and she shall be one flesh.' And Adam heard the voice of
the angel and took the gold and put it in the skirt of Eve's
garment, and they made a covenant together, joining their*

hands. And the angels commanded Adam and Eve to pass forty days and forty nights in prayer, and then Adam might go in unto his wife, for then it would be in purity and not in impurity; and she should bear him children and they would fill and people the earth. And Adam and Eve heard the voice of the two angels, and the angels left them. And Adam and Eve fasted and prayed until the forty days were accomplished, and then they lay together as the angels had told them. And from the expulsion of Adam to the day when he wed Eve there were 223 days, that is, seven months and three days.[27]

The Penitence of Adam indicates that angels were very busy in the Garden of Eden. Whereas in the Hebrew Bible, angels are primarily seen as messengers, in the Pseudepigrapha they have more varied and extensive roles. They control natural phenomena; there is an angel of peace and an angel of death; and, as we have already noted, there were the Watchers. There is, as Porter observes, 'a whole range of celestial beings whose primary function is to guard God's heavenly throne; these are not really distinguishable from angels except that they have distinctive names, such as seraphim, cherubim, and ophannim'.[28]

The Ethiopian *Book of the Conflict of Adam* describes the various orders of angels and the tasks that God assigns to each of them. From this it is worth noting that, while mankind is watched over by the lowest order, other species are entrusted to a higher order of Archangels, perhaps because they are more precious to God or more in need of care and attention.

Angelic hierarchy

The lowest order is that of the Angels, and the task which has been entrusted to them by God is to watch over each man. To every man living in this world is allotted as his guardian an angel of this lowest order, and this is his office.

The second order is that of the Archangels, and their task is to make all things to live according to the order of God's ordering. All that exists in creation, animals of the earth, or winged animals, or reptiles, or fishes of the sea, all creatures that are in the world save man alone are entrusted to their care and government.

The third order is that of the Principalities, and their task is to hie themselves to the places where the clouds rise from the ends of the earth, according to the word of David, and to cause the rain to descend from thence upon the earth. All the changes in the air, rain and hail and snow and dust-storms and showers of blood are all produced by them, and to them also belong the storm-clouds and the lightening.

The fourth order is that of the Powers, and their task is the government of all light-giving bodies, such as the sun and the moon and the stars.

The fifth order is that of the Virtues, and their task is to prevent the demons from destroying the creation of God for envy of man. For if it were allowed to the accursed race of demons to do their own will for one hour, then on an instant they would overturn the whole of creation. . . .

The sixth order is that of the Dominations, and their task is to have the oversight of all kingdoms. In their hands are victory and defeat. . . . All victories and all defeats, these are they who decide them according to the sign of God who has entrusted to them the overseeing of war.

The other orders are those of the Thrones, the Seraphim and the Cherubim. These are they who stand before the greatness of the Lord and serve his throne and continually at all times make him offerings and worship him. The Cherubim with all reverence hold up the throne and the seal of God is in their hands. The Seraphim wait upon our Lord. The Thrones stand at the door of the Holy of Holies. Such are in truth the divisions of the tasks entrusted to the angels who have the government of this world.[29]

The continuing importance of angels in Ethiopian culture today may be due to the sacred status the Ethiopian Church accords to the *Book of Enoch*. Enoch is believed to have been 'the first among men born on earth to learn to write',[30] and *Ethiopian Enoch* has been described as the 'richest of the surviving apocrypha of the Old Testament'.[31] It is made up of five originally independent texts: the *Book of the Watchers*, the *Parables*, the *Astronomical Treatise*, the *Dream Visions*, and the *Letter* to his children. In addition *Ethiopian Enoch* includes fragments of an earlier *Book of Noah*, enlarging, like *Jubilees* and other pseudepigraphica, upon the brief passage in Genesis concerning sons of God (angels) who literally fell for daughters of man (womankind) and, after seducing them, begot giants who terrorized and corrupted not only mankind but other animals and all creation.[32]

Angels Fall for Daughters of Man

In those days, when the children of man had multiplied, it happened that there were born unto them handsome and beautiful daughters.

And the angels, the children of heaven, saw them and desired them; and they said to one another, 'Come, let us choose wives for ourselves from among the daughters of man and beget us children. And Semyaz, being their leader, said unto them, 'I fear that perhaps you will not consent that this deed should be done, and I alone will become responsible for this great sin.' But they all responded to him, 'Let us all swear an oath and bind everyone among us by a curse not to abandon this suggestion but to do the deed. . . .' And they were altogether two hundred. . . .

And they took wives unto themselves, and everyone (respectively) chose one woman for himself, and they began to go unto them. And they taught them magical medicine, incantations, the cutting of roots, and taught them about plants. And the women became pregnant and gave birth to great giants whose heights were three hundred cubits. These (giants) consumed the produce of all the people until the people detested feeding them. So the giants turned against (the people) in order to eat them. And they began to sin against birds, wild beasts, reptiles, and fish. And their flesh was devoured the one by the other, and they drank blood. And the earth brought an accusation against the oppressors.[33]

Ethiopian Enoch records that Noah, the son of Lamech, was an unusual baby – his hair was 'white as wool' and his body white as snow and red as a rose – causing his parents some apprehension. When he opened his eyes, he lit up the whole house like the sun. His parents feared he might be a giant begotten 'from the angels', so Lamech consults first his father, Methuselah, and then his grandfather, Enoch, who by this time was living somewhere at the ends of the earth 'with the angels'. Lamech is reassured to learn from him that Noah is destined to 'comfort the earth after all the destruction'.[34]

From these scriptures we see that the original sin of the angels proved to be much more serious in its consequences than the temptation of Adam and Eve. While our human ancestors repented, the wicked angels did not. Angels, who later came to be identified with gods of the ancient world, taught mankind innumerable skills, which could be used for evil or benign purposes. These skills included astronomy, botany, biology, medicine, metallurgy, mathematics, physics and engineering, in which the Egyptians and the Greeks later became proficient. Greek philosophy encompassed all these disciplines and was able to provide a view of the world more complex than that found in the Hebrew Bible.[35] Under the influence of Hellenism, Jewish communities in Africa gradually adapted their Judaism to Greek philosophy.[36] The Jewish philosopher, Philo of Alexandria (20BCE – 50CE) taught that when the first man, *Adam*, named the animals, he both defined their natures and established his authority over them.

Wisdom of the first Man

Moses does well to ascribe the giving of names to the first man, for that is the function of wisdom and royalty, and the first man was wise with a wisdom taught by Wisdom's own lips; he was also a king, and it belongs to a king to bestow titles on each of his subjects. It was a most high sovereignty that invested that first man, since God had formed him with such care to be worthy of the second place, making him his own viceroy and governor of all others.[37]

Philo thus brings Greek philosophy and Hebrew theology together. Taking the Greek legend of Mnemosyne, mother of the Muses, Philo offers a midrashic reinterpretation, in which he sees Virgin Memory giving birth to the Muses who sing the praises of the Creator God.[38]

Virgin Memory

There is an old story on men's lips. . . . When they say, the Creator had finished the whole cosmos, He inquired of one of His subordinates whether he missed anything that had failed to be created, aught of created things beneath the earth or beneath the water, aught found in air's high realm of heaven's, furthest of all realms that are. He, it is said, made answer that all were perfect and complete in all their parts, and that he was looking for one thing only, namely the word to sound their praises. . . . The story runs that the Author of the universe on hearing this commended what had been said, and that it was not long before there appeared the new birth, family of the Muses and hymnody, sprung from the womb of one of His powers, even virgin Memory, whose name most people slightly change and call 'Mnemosyne.'[39]

When asked whether the Serpent in the Garden of Eden spoke 'in the manner of men', Philo reflects on the understanding and speech of animals at the time of Creation. He believes that being without sin, they were endowed with 'philosophical sight and hearing'.[40]

Animals share in Speech

First, it is likely that not even in the beginning of the world's creation were the other animals without a share in speech, but that man excelled in voice (or utterance), being more clear and distinct. Second, when some miraculous deed is prepared, God changes the inner nature. Third, because our souls are filled with many sins and deaf to all utterances except one or another tongue to which they are accustomed; but the souls of the first creatures, as being pure of evil and unmixed, were particularly keen in becoming familiar with every sound. And since they were not provided only with defective senses, such as belong to a miserable bodily frame, but were provided with a very great body and the magnitude of a giant, it was necessary that they should also have more accurate sense, and what is more, philosophical sight and hearing. For not inaptly do some conjecture that they were provided with eyes with which they could see those natures and beings and actions which were in heaven, and with ears to perceive sounds of every kind.[41]

Philo was wrestling with questions about the language of animals that have baffled generations of zoologists since Darwin. Only recently have scientists been able to appreciate the extent to which other species communicate with each other, as has been beautifully illustrated by Charlotte Uhlenbroek.[42] Philo was succeeded by other distinguished African scholars in what became known as the Alexandrian School, to which further reference will be made in Section Four.

One of the greatest of the African-Jewish scholars, Moses Maimonides, lived long after Egypt had come under both Christian and Muslim influence. He is revered by Jews all over the world in the saying: 'From Moses to Moses there was none like Moses'. Born at Cordoba (*ca.*1135), but driven into exile, he spent most of his life in Africa. His family settled at Fostat, where Moses practiced medicine and became a leader of the Jewish community in Old Cairo. His Commentary on the Mishnah was written in Arabic and subsequently translated into Hebrew and other languages. Maimonides death in 1204 'was the cause of great mourning to all Jews'.[43] Excerpts from his *Guide for the Perplexed*, concerning the imagination of animals and the prohibition of cruelty, exemplify the contribution of African Judaism to Animal Theology.

The Imagination of Animals
Mark, O reader, that if you know the nature of the soul and its properties, and if you have a correct notion of everything which

concerns the soul, you will observe that most animals possess imagination. As to the higher class of animals, that is, those which have a heart, it is obvious that they have imagination. Man's distinction does not consist in the possession of imagination, and the action of imagination is not the same as the action of the intellect, but the reverse of it. For the intellect analyses and divides the component parts of things, it forms abstract ideas of them, represents them in their true form as well as in their causal relations, derives from one object a great many facts, which – for the intellect – totally differ from each other, just as two human individuals appear different to the imagination it distinguishes that which is the property of the genus *from that which is peculiar to the individual, – and no proof is correct, unless founded on the former; the intellect further determines whether certain qualities of a thing are essential or non-essential. Imagination has none of these functions. It only perceives the individual, the compound in that aggregate condition in which it presents itself to the senses; or it combines things which exist separately, joins some of them together, and represents them all as one body or as a force of the body. Hence it is that some imagine a man with a horse's head, with wings, etc. This is called a fiction, a phantasm; it is a thing to which nothing in the actual world corresponds. Nor can imagination in any way obtain a purely immaterial image of an object, however abstract the form of the image may be. Imagination yields therefore no test for the reality of a thing.*

Cruelty to Animals

The commandment concerning the killing of animals is necessary, because the natural food of man consists of vegetables and of the flesh of animals; the best meat is that of animals permitted to be used as food. No doctor has any doubts about this. Since, therefore, the desire of procuring good food necessitates the slaying of animals, the Law enjoins that the death of the animal should be the easiest. It is not allowed to torment the animal by cutting the throat in a clumsy manner, by poleaxing, or by cutting off a limb whilst the animal is alive.

It is also prohibited to kill an animal with its young on the same day (Lev. xxii. 28), in order that people should be restrained and prevented from killing the two together in such a manner that the young is slain in the sight of the mother; for the pain of the animals under such circumstances is very great. There is no difference in this case between the pain of a man and the pain of other living beings, since the love and tenderness of the mother for her young ones is not produced by reasoning, but by imagination, and this faculty exists not only in man but in most living beings. This law applies only to ox and lamb, because of the domestic animals used as food these alone are permitted to us, and in these cases the mother recognizes her young.

The same reason applies to the law which enjoins that we should let the mother fly away when we take the young. The eggs over which the bird sits, and the young that are in need of their mother, are generally unfit for food, and the mother is sent away she does not see the taking of her young ones, and does not feel any pain. In most cases, however, this commandment will cause man to leave the whole nest untouched, because [the young or the eggs], which he is allowed to take, are, as a rule, unfit for food. If the Law provides that such grief should not be caused to cattle or birds, how much more careful must we be that we should not cause grief to our fellow-men.[44]

Since the time of Maimonides, Judaism has no doubt continued to develop in different parts of Africa, drawing on ancient traditions and adapting them to modern conditions. Further study is required to discover in what ways such developments may be able to contribute to current ecological concerns.

Early African Christianity

List of Excerpts

Early African Christianity

Before the end of the third century, nearly all the books of the Bible had been translated into Coptic, and by the fifth century into Ethiopic (Ge'ez)[1] In addition, early African Christians were nourished by numerous other writings. As was seen in Section Three, there are many Old Testament manuscripts extant in Africa that were not included in the Hebrew Bible. Similarly, many Christian gospels, acts and epistles, written or translated in Africa, were not included in the New Testament canon and later came to be regarded as apocryphal or pseudepigraphical by the Church of Rome. Not only has the Ethiopian Orthodox Church preserved Ge'ez translations of scriptures not included in the canon, but since the end of the nineteenth century, writings have been discovered in Egypt which 'may yet substantially alter our concepts of ancient Christian history'. Although some of these are known as 'gnostic gospels', they often preserve older traditions and reveal the different ways in which the words of Jesus were remembered and interpreted.[2]

We begin this Section with an excerpt from the *Odes of Solomon*, which like similar works found among the Dead Sea Scrolls, belong to a poetic genre that was influenced by the images and concepts of the Bible.[3] Although the *Odes*, unlike the *Psalms of Solomon*, are of Christian origin, some of them exemplify a theology of creation that has survived in African Judaism and is being rediscovered today by feminist theologians.

The Two Breasts of the Father
A cup of milk was offered to me,
and I drank it in the sweetness of the Lord's kindness.
The Son is the cup,
and the Father is he who was milked;
and the Holy Spirit is she who milked him;
Because his breasts were full,
and it was undesirable that his milk should be released without
*   purpose.*
The Holy Spirit opened her bosom,
and mixed the milk of the two breasts of the Father.
Then she gave the mixture to the world without their knowing,

and those who have received it are in the perfection of the
   right hand.
The womb of the Virgin took it,
and she conceived and gave birth.
So the Virgin became a mother with great mercies.[4]

Apart from revealing the motherhood of God, some stories show
'how often early Christians exercised their imagination about Jesus
and the world of animals', as Andrew Linzey points out. For
instance, a Coptic manuscript describes how Jesus healed a pack-
mule. This is consistent with a variety of Jewish themes which
would have been common at the time of Christ: the religious duty
of compassionate treatment—especially to beasts of burden; the
acknowledgement of the suffering of animals; the association of
righteousness with righteous acts towards animals and, not least
of all, the explicit acceptance of the view that since the Creator's
mercy extends to all things so should humans be likewise merciful.[5]

Jesus heals the Pack-Mule

*It happened that the Lord left the city and walked with his
disciples over the mountains. And they came to a mountain,
and the road which led up it was steep. There they found a
man with a pack-mule. But the animal had fallen, because
the man had loaded it too heavily, and now he beat it, so
that it was bleeding. And Jesus came to him and said, 'Man,
why do you beat your animal? Do you not see that it is too
weak for its burden, and do you not know that it suffers
pains? But the man answered and said, 'What is that to
you? I may beat it as much as I please, since it is my
property, and I bought it for a good sum of money. Ask
those who are with you, for they know me and know about
this.' And some of the disciples said, 'Yes, Lord, it is as he
says. We have seen how he bought it.' But the Lord said, 'Do
you then not see how it bleeds, and do you not hear how it
groans and cries out?' But they answered and said, 'No, Lord,
that it groans and cries out, we do not hear.' But Jesus was sad
and exclaimed, 'Woe to you, that you do not hear how it
complains to the Creator in heaven and cries out for mercy.
But threefold woes to him about whom it cries out and
complains in its pain.' And he came up and touched the animal.
And it stood up and its wounds were healed. But Jesus said to
the man, 'Now carry on and from now on do not beat it any
more, so that you too may find mercy.'*[6]

A lively awareness of God's love for other creatures is expressed by the mother of the Virgin Mary, who saw the birds and the beasts and even fish being blessed by the Creator, while she waits for her heartfelt prayer to be answered, as recorded in *The History of James*.

Anna's Lamentation

Anna sighed towards heaven, and saw a nest of sparrows in the laurel tree and immediately she made lamentation within herself:

'Woe to me, who begot me,

What womb brought me forth?

For I was born as a curse before them all and before the children of Israel,

And I was reproached, and they mocked me and thrust me out of the temple of the Lord.

Woe is me, to what am I likened?

I am not likened to the birds of the heaven;

for even the birds of the heaven are fruitful before thee, O Lord.

Woe is to me, to what am I likened? ...

I am not likened to the beasts of the earth;

for even the beasts of the earth are fruitful before thee, O Lord.

Woe is me, to what am I likened?

I am not likened to these waters;

for even these waters gush forth merrily, and their fish praise thee, O Lord.

Woe is me, to what am I likened?

I am not likened to this earth;

for even this earth brings forth its fruit in its season and praises thee, O Lord.'

And behold an angel of the Lord came to her and said: 'Anna, Anna, the Lord has heard your prayer. You shall conceive and bear, and your offspring shall be spoken of in the whole world.'[7]

Many of the stories recounted in the *Infancy Gospel of Thomas* and the *Protevangelium of James* also appear in the *Gospel of Pseudo-Matthew*, which was translated into Latin by Jerome and was very influential in Europe in the Middle ages. It is from this 'apocryphal' gospel that the popular image of an ox and an ass round the manger at the Nativity is derived: the presence of these creatures is not explicitly mentioned in the canonical gospels. As Elliot says, 'Much medieval art is indecipherable without reference to books such as *Pseudo-Matthew*'.[8]

There are Greek, Latin, Slavonic, and Ethiopic versions of *The Infancy Gospel of Thomas*. The popular story of Jesus and the sparrows is found in the majority of Ethiopic manuscripts of the Miracles of Jesus, but J. K. Elliott suggests that the 'different forms in which infancy stories about Jesus have been preserved suggest that there was a continuing oral development of such episodes even after the first written accounts were circulating'.[9]

Jesus and the Sparrows

When this boy Jesus was five years old he was playing at the ford of a brook, and he gathered together into pools the water that flowed by, and made it at once clean, and commanded it by his word alone. He made soft clay and fashioned from it twelve sparrows. And it was the sabbath when he did this. And there were also many other children playing with him. Now when a certain Jew saw what Jesus was doing in his play on the sabbath, he at once went and told his father Joseph, 'See, your child is at the brook, and he has taken clay and fashioned twelve birds and has profaned the sabbath.' And when Joseph came to the place and saw it, he cried out to him, saying, 'Why do you do on the sabbath what ought not to be done?' But Jesus clapped his hands and cried to the sparrows, 'Off with you!' And the sparrows took flight and went away chirping. The Jews were amazed when they saw this, and went away and told their elders what they had seen Jesus do.[10]

Neighbours and friends who knew the Holy Family in Egypt, either in Jerusalem, or Nazareth, will have remembered many stories concerning this remarkable child. Apart from the one incident recorded in the canonical New Testament when his parents found him in the Temple sitting among the doctors, 'listening to them, and asking them questions' (*Luke* 2: 41-50), the Infancy gospels record other memorable events.

The *Arabic Infancy Gospel* contains stories about the birth of Jesus and his miracles in Egypt, most of which are taken from the infancy Gospel of Thomas. Thanks to this translation into Arabic, these legends became known to Mohammed, who included some of them in the Koran.[11] One story in the *Arabic Infancy Gospel* portrays Jesus as a precocious child wanting to play with other children who somewhat mysteriously appear to be goats.

Children and Goats

One day the Lord Jesus went out into the street and saw children who had come together to play. He followed them, but the children hid themselves from him. Now when the Lord Jesus came to the door of a house and saw women standing there, he asked them where those children had gone. They replied that no one was there; and the Lord Jesus said: 'Who are those whom you see in the furnace?' 'They are three-year-old goats', they answered. And the Lord Jesus said: 'Come out to your shepherd, you goats.' Then the children in the form of goats came out and began to skip round him. When those women saw this, they were seized with wonder and fear, and speedily fell down before the Lord Jesus and implored him, saying: 'O our Lord Jesus, son of Mary, truly you are the good shepherd of Israel, have mercy on your handmaids who stand before you and have never doubted: for you have come, our Lord, to heal and not to destroy.' The Lord Jesus answered and said: 'The children of Israel are like the Ethiopians among the peoples.' And the women said: 'You, Lord, know everything, and nothing is hidden from you; but now we beg and implore you of your mercy to restore to their former state these children, your servants.' So the Lord Jesus said: 'Come, children, let us go and play.' And immediately in the presence of these women the goats were changed into children. [12]

However the reference to Ethiopians in the above passage may be interpreted, the author obviously knew that while in Egypt the child Jesus would have encountered many black people from the South. Indeed, there are legends that the Holy Family actually travelled as far as Ethiopia, and that the Apostle Matthew later preached there and baptized the king. [13]

Apart from stories of Jesus' concern for animals, there are numerous legends of the apostles being recognized by animals who converse with them, or provide assistance when required. M.R. James describes *The Acts of Philip* as 'grotesque' but 'yet a catholic novel'. Although translated into Coptic and Ethiopic, the complete work is no longer extant. [14] In it a great leopard relates to Philip and Bartholomew how it seized a kid, who wept like a child and cried out,

> O leopard, put off your fierce heart and the beastlike part of your nature, and put on mildness, for the apostles of the divine greatness are about to pass through this desert to accomplish perfectly the promise of the glory of the only-begotten Son of God. So the leopard was led to repentance.

The Kid and the Leopard
And in that hour the leopard and kid rose up and lifted up their fore-feet and said, 'We glorify and bless you who have visited and remembered us in this desert, and changed our beastlike and wild nature into tameness, and granted us the divine word,

*and put in us a tongue and sense to speak and praise your
name, for great is your glory.' And they fell and worshipped
Philip and Bartholomew and Mariamne; and all set out together,
praising God.*[15]

According to *The Acts of the Holy Apostle Thomas,* some time after
the Ascension, the apostles gathered in Jerusalem and 'divided the
regions of the world, that each one of us might go to the region which
fell to his lot, and to the nation to which the Lord sent him'. Thomas,
a carpenter, was not at all happy when India fell to his lot. 'How can I,
who am a Hebrew, go and preach the truth among the Indians?' he
asked. Even after the Saviour had appeared to him in a dream, he was
not convinced until he was sold as a slave to an Indian merchant.[16] A
tame colt and even wild asses recognized his calling however, and
came forward to assist him on his journey.

Concerning the Colt

*While the apostle was still standing in the highway and
speaking with the crowd, an ass's colt came and stood before
him, opened its mouth and said: 'Twin brother of Christ,
apostle of the Most High and fellow-initiate into the hidden
word of Christ, who dost receive his secret sayings, fellow-
worker of the Son of God, who being free didst become a slave
and being sold didst lead many to freedom; thou kinsman of
the great race which condemned the enemy and redeemed his
own, who has become a cause of life for many in the land of
the Indians – for thou didst come to the men who erred, and
through thine appearance and thy divine words they are now
turning to the God of truth who sent them – mount and sit upon
me and rest until thou enter the city.' . . .*

*'I am of that race that served Balaam, and thy Lord and
teacher also sat upon one that belonged to me by race. . . .'
But the apostle said to it: 'He who has bestowed on thee this
gift (of speech) is able to cause it to be fulfilled to the end in
thee and in those who belong to thee by race; for as to this
mystery I am weak and feeble.'*[17]

Concerning the Wild Asses

*So the apostle went out to depart on his way. . . . But when they
went off along the road, it befell that the beasts became weary
with the great heat, and could not move at all. The captain was
vexed and altogether in despair, and thought of going on his
own feet and bringing other animals for the wagon. But the*

apostle said: 'Let not thy heart be troubled or afraid, but believe in Jesus Christ whom I declared to thee, and thou shalt see great wonders.' And looking about he saw a herd of wild asses grazing beside the road. And he said to the captain: 'If thou dost believe in Jesus Christ, go to that herd of wild asses and say: Judas Thomas, the apostle of Christ the new God, says to you, Let four of you come, of whom we have need.' And the captain went, although he was afraid; for they were many. And as he went, they came to meet him. And when they drew near he said to them: 'Judas Thomas, the apostle of the new God, commands you: Let four of you come, of whom I have need.' When the wild asses heard this, they came to him with one accord at a run, and having come they did him reverence. But the apostle said to them: 'Peace be with you! Yoke four of you in place of these beasts that have come to a stand.' And every one of them came and pressed to be yoked. Now there were four there, stronger than the rest, and these were yoked. As to the others, some went before and some followed. But when they had travelled a short distance he dismissed them, saying: 'To you dwellers in the wilderness I say, Go to your pastures! For if I needed all, you would all come with me. But now go to your place. . . .'[18]

Thus in many early writings, not only the Saviour, but also his apostles are portrayed as being able to communicate with animals and as having concern for their well-being and salvation.

The *Acts of Paul* was translated into many languages (Coptic, Ethiopic, Syriac, Arabic, Armenian, Slavonic, as well as Latin and Greek). It was well known and respected by many of the early church fathers, including Origen, and yet it was eventually rejected by Jerome and not included in the Canon. According to Tertullian, the author was a presbyter in Asia Minor, who ' "out of love for Paul" gathered up whatever legends were in circulation, set them in order, and also surely elaborated and expanded them'. The *Acts of Paul* is thought to have been written between 185 and 195 CE and to be indebted to an original Greek version of the *Acts of Peter*.[19] It relates not only the various ordeals suffered by Paul, but also the sufferings of his devoted follower, St Thecla.

Thecla's Ordeal
Thecla was taken out of Tryphaena's hands and stripped, and was given a girdle and flung into the stadium. And lions and bears were set upon her, and a fierce lioness ran to her and lay down at her feet. And the crowd of the women raised a great

shout. And a bear ran upon her, but the lioness ran and met it, and tore the bear asunder. And again a lion trained against men, which belonged to Alexander, ran upon her; and the lioness grappled with the lion, and perished with it. And the women mourned the more, since the lioness which helped her was dead. Then they sent in many beasts, while she stood and stretched out her hands and prayed. . . .

And the governor summoned Thecla from among the beasts, and said to her: 'Who art thou? And what hast thou about thee, that not one of the beasts touched thee?' She answered: 'I am a handmaid of the living God. As to what I have about me, I have believed in him in whom God is well pleased, His Son. For his sake not one of the beasts touched me. For alone is the goal of salvation and the foundation of immortal life. To the storm-tossed he is a refuge, to the oppressed relief, to the despairing shelter; in a word, whoever does not believe in him shall not live, but die for ever.'[20]

Paul baptizes a Lion

There came a great and terrible lion out of the valley of the burying-ground. But we were praying . . . when I finished praying, the beast had cast himself at my feet. I was filled with the Spirit and looked upon him, and said to him: 'Lion, what wilt thou?' But he said: 'I wish to be baptized.' I glorified God, who had given speech to the beast and salvation to his servant. Now there was a great river in that place, and I went down into it. . . . I cried out, saying: 'Thou who dost dwell in the heights, who didst look upon the humble, who didst give rest to the afflicted, who with Daniel didst shut the mouths of the lions . . . accomplish thy plan. . . .' When I had prayed thus, I took the lion by his mane and in the name of Jesus Christ immersed him three times. But when he came up out of the water he shook out his mane and said to me: 'Grace be with thee!' And I said to him: 'And likewise with thee.' The lion ran off to the country rejoicing.[21]

A Coptic fragment of *The Acts of Paul* relates that when the Apostle was thrown to the beasts at Ephesus, he recognizes one of them as the lion that he had baptized in Judea:

And borne along by faith Paul said, 'Lion, was it you whom I baptized?' And the lion in answer said to Paul, 'Yes.' Paul spoke to it again and said, 'And how were you captured?' The lion said with its own voice, 'Just as you were, Paul.'[22]

Maureen Tilley maintains there is a 'role reversal' in which the persecutors of the saints behave like animals, while animals assume saintly qualities. For example, in stories about Thecla, Perpetua and Felicitas, a bear brought in to torture the martyrs refuses to come out of its cage, and a boar even turns against the Romans instead.[23]

All this is very different from the gnostic heresy which later divided the Church. 'Gnosticism' is a modern name given by scholars to a religious movement which was widespread in the second century CE, but largely disappeared after the fourth century. Only since 1945 with the discovery of a large collection of writings in Coptic at Nag Hammadi in Upper Egypt, dating from the fourth century, has the complexity of Gnostic ideas begun to be seriously studied. According to J.R. Porter:

> For the Gnostics, Christ comes to earth to reveal to human beings the truth about themselves: his teaching, rather than his miracles, death, and resurrection, is the means of salvation. The Gnostic Christ appears in spiritual form as a heavenly Redeemer, and Gnostic writings do not concern themselves with what could be described as 'the historical Jesus.'[24]

Clement of Alexandria (ca. 150-215 CE), who combined Hellenic culture with a profound knowledge of the Scriptures, taught at a school under ecclesiastical authority, preparing young Christians from the most cultivated families for baptism. According to Baur, Christian theology, in the proper sense of the word, first started in Alexandria. Confronted with Gnostic speculations, mixed with Egyptian pagan rituals, 'the Alexandrian theology school was able to quench the thirst for knowledge of the young Christians of Egypt, and avoid the pitfalls of the Gnostics without condemning outright any speculations, as the bishops usually did'. Clement warned his students against the errors of the philosophers, but insisted on accepting from the Hellenes 'whatever is good, whatever is beautiful'.[25] His *Paedogogus* ends with a hymn, inspired by both the Bible and Plato, which was perhaps the Alexandrian 'School Song'.

Hymn to Christ the Saviour

Bridle of untamed colts,
Wing of the birds in steady flight,
strong Rudder of the ships,
Shepherd of the royal sheep,
gather together the flock of your pure children,
that they may praise with holiness and sing with sincerity,
with lips without guile, the Christ who leads his children.
Sovereign of the saints, invincible Word of the Father all-high,

Prince of wisdom, Support of our labours, eternal Joy:
O Jesus, Saviour of our mortal race,
Shepherd, Worker, Bridle and Rudder,
Wing towards heaven of the company of the saints:
Fisher of men whom thou willest to save,
on the sea of sin thou dost catch pure fishes;
from the menacing wave thou leadest them to the life of bliss.
Guide thy flock of the sheep of wisdom;
lead, O King, thy children without blame.
The footsteps of Christ are the way to heaven.
O God eternal, Age without end, Light immortal,
Fountain of mercy, Worker of virtue, Life to be revered of those
*   who sing to God!*
O Christ Jesus, thou art the heavenly milk of the sweet breasts
*   of a young bride, of the graces of thy wisdom.*
We, little children, whose tender mouths quench their thirst
*   from thee, are refreshed in all chastity by the spring of the*
*   Spirit.*
Let us sing together pure songs, loyal hymns, to Christ our
*   sovereign, sacred prize of the life given by his voice.*
Let us praise with sincere hearts the Son almighty.
Let us who are born of Christ form the choir of peace;
people of wisdom, sing all together to the God of peace.[26]

With its poetic reference to the 'heavenly milk' of Jesus we are reminded of *The Two Breasts of the Father*, our first excerpt above.

The work of combining faith and philosophy into a theological system was later undertaken by Origen (*ca.* 185-254 CE), and in the Alexandrian school they were followed by an even more famous theologian, St Athanasius (*ca.*296-373), the great defender of the Council of Nicaea. His treatise on the Incarnation expounds his teaching that the Creator, in his mercy, has given the human race a share in the divine life of the Logos. Nevertheless, Athanasius has 'a very strong sense that creation includes both the material and the spiritual', and the spiritual is not to be pursued at the expense of the material. In writing *The Life of Antony*, Athanasius did not regard the monk's retreat to the desert a flight from the material to the spiritual. The flight is not a 'washing one's hands' of the State or the Church, but a critique of it.[27]

Antony of Egypt, who is regarded as the originator of monasticism, had a precursor in one Paul of Thebes in Upper Egypt. A book very popular in the early church was St Jerome's *Life of Paul the First*

Hermit, which introduced an entirely new genre into Latin literature and was soon translated into Greek, Coptic, Syriac, and Ethiopic. According to Jerome, when Antony discovered Paul in his secluded cave he was already 113 years old, and in the end Antony buries the old hermit with the help of two grief-stricken lions.

Paul the First Hermit

This Saint was born in the lower Thebais, a province of Egypt, in the third century, of Christian parents, who being wealthy in worldly riches took care to give him a liberal education, and to train him up both in the Greek and Egyptian literature; yet without any prejudice to his innocence, or Christian piety; for which he was remarkable from his childhood; being always of a meek and humble disposition, and greatly fearing and loving his God. His parents dying when he was about fifteen years of age, left him their estate which he had not long enjoyed, when that bloody persecution, set on foot by the Emperor Decius (who employed all manner of torments to oblige the Christians to renounce Jesus Christ, and offer sacrifice to idols,) had reached Egypt and Thebais; where it made many martyrs; and drove many others into the deserts and mountains; where great numbers of them perished with hunger or sickness, or fell a prey to robbers and wild beasts; as we learn from St. Denys, who was at that very time bishop of Alexandria, in his epistle to Fabius, bishop of Antioch.

Paul also withdrew . . . into the wilderness, where he purposed to pass his time till the danger was over. Here, as he advanced still further and further into the remoter parts of the desert, he came at last to a rocky mountain, at the foot of which he found a large den or cave; and going in, he there discovered a kind of a spacious porch, open at the top to the heavens, but protected by an old palm-tree, which covered it with its spreading branches: near which there was a spring of clear water: and in a hollow part of the mountain, several cells or rooms, which, by the instruments he found there, appeared to have been formerly occupied by coiners. This place the Saint judged to be very proper for his abode; and embraced it as a dwelling assigned him by divine providence for the remainder of his life.

And thus he who thought only at first to hide himself for a while in the wilderness from the fury of the persecutors, was by the design of God conducted thither, to be an inhabitant for life, and the first that should dedicate, and as it were, consecrate, those deserts to divine love; by living there for so many years a perfect model of an entire separation and disengagement from all ties and affections of this world; for the instruction and encouragement of many thousands, who should, by his example, in following ages, embrace a recluse or eremitical life. . . .

Our saint had now lived in his solitude to the age of one hundred and thirteen years when St. Antony, who was then about ninety years old, was one day thinking with himself that no one amongst the religious of Egypt had penetrated further into those wildernesses than he had done. Whereupon he was one night admonished in a dream, that there was one still further on in the desert much better than himself; and that he should make haste to visit him. In compliance with this divine admonition, Antony set out at break of day in quest of this servant of God, with great confidence that he who had sent him forth, would conduct him to the place where he should find him. Thus he spent two whole days, fatigued with the labor of the journey, and broiled by the heat of the sun, which is violent in those sandy deserts, meeting with no creature the whole way, except two in monstrous shape; the one representing a centaur, *half man and half a horse, and the other a* satyr, *made up of a man and a goat: which whether they were phantoms and illusions of the enemy, or monsters bred in those vast wildernesses, is uncertain. The saint, when he opposed to these frightful figures his usual arms, the shield of faith and sign of the cross, neither of them offered him any harm; but on the contrary the former, on being asked where the servant of God dwelt, pointing towards the place, ran swiftly away, and disappeared; and the latter brought him some dates for his food; and being asked, who or what he was? Delivered an intelligible answer, (by some supernatural power) with an acknowledgment of God, and of Jesus Christ, his Son; which gave the Saint occasion to glorify our Lord, and to reproach the unbelieving city of Alexandria, which refused to acknowledge the true and living God, whom even beasts adored, and worshipped these very beasts instead of him. At which words of the Saint the monster fled away with incredible speed, and was seen no more.*

Antony having spent two nights watching in prayer, at break of day on the third morning, he perceived a wolf at a distance panting for thirst, going into a cavern at the foot of the mountain. Whereupon coming up to the place after the beast was gone, he ventured into the cave, advancing cautiously and silently in the dark, till at length he perceived at some distance a glimmering of light (from the opening from above over the porch of the cell of the Saint) upon which in hastening forward he stumbled upon a stone, when the noise gave occasion to St. Paul to shut his door and fasten it within. Antony was now convinced that he found the person whom he sought: and coming up to the door earnestly begged for admittance, with many tears, lying prostrate on the ground from morning till noon (to teach us the necessity of fervor and perseverance in prayer, if we would obtain what we ask), till at length the holy old man opened the door to him. Then after falling upon each other's neck, embracing each other, and calling one another by their proper names, as if they had been of long acquaintance, they joined in giving thanks to God.

When they had sat down together, Paul said to Antony, behold here the man whom thou hast taken so much pains to seek, and who very speedily must return to dust: tell me, then, if thou pleasest, how mankind goes on; what is the present state of the empire; are there any still remaining that worship devils, &c.? — Whilst they were discoursing on these matters, they perceived a raven alighting upon one of the branches of the palm-tree, which descending gently dropped a loaf of bread before them, and then flew away. Behold, said Paul, how our loving and merciful Lord has sent us a dinner? There are now sixty years elapsed since I have daily received from him half a loaf, but upon thy coming, Christ hath been pleased to send his soldier a double portion. Then after praying and thanksgiving, they sat down by the edge of the spring to take the meal which God hath sent them: but not without an humble contention who should break the loaf; which they at last decided by breaking it conjointly. After taking a moderate refreshment, they laid themselves down to sip at the fountain: and then returned to prayer and the praises of God, in which they spent the evening, and the whole of the following night.

The next morning Paul thus accosted Antony: 'it is a long time, brother, since I have known of your dwelling in these regions: and the Lord long ago promised me your company. But as my time is now come to go to rest, (as I have always desired to be dissolved and to be with Christ), and my race being finished, the crown of justice waits for me, thou art now sent by the Lord to cover this body with ground, or rather to commit earth to earth.' Which when Antony heard, breaking out into sighs and tears, he began to entreat him not to leave him, but to take him along with him for his companion in so happy a journey.

'Thou oughtest not,' said Paul, 'to seek in this thy own interest, but what may be for the good of others. It would be expedient indeed to thee to lay down this load of flesh, and to follow the Lamb: but it is necessary to the rest of the brethren, that thou shouldest continue here, to instruct them by thy example. Wherefore go, I beseech thee, if it be not too much trouble, and bring hither the cloak which was given thee by bishop Athanasius, to wrap up my body for its burial:' ...

Antony being astonished to hear him speak of Athanasius, and of the cloak (of which he could not otherwise have been informed but by revelation) as if he saw Christ himself in Paul, without making any further reply, kissed his hands with tears, and departing from him, made the best of his way home to his own monastery. Here his two disciples (Amathas and Macarias) asked him where he had been so long? To whom he made no answer, but, 'woe to me a sinner, who deserve not to bear the name of a religious man! I have seen Elias: I have seen John in the wilderness: I have seen with truth, Paul in paradise.' And thus without explaining himself any further, he went into his cell, striking his breast, and taking up the cloak, instantly hastened away without staying to take any refreshment; having Paul continually in his mind, and fearing, that which indeed happened, lest Paul should die before he reached his cave.

On the second morning, when he had travelled for about three hours, he saw the soul of Paul encompassed in great glory ascending to heaven, attended with an innumerable multitude of angels and saints. At this sight, falling down on the ground, he cried out lamenting and mourning: 'O Paul, why does thou leave me? Why dost thou go without letting me salute thee? Too late have I come to know thee, and dost thou depart from me so soon?' Then rising up he went on the remaining part of the way, notwithstanding his great age, and his having been before greatly fatigued, with such unaccustomed speed, that, as he himself afterwards relates, he seemed rather to fly than to walk.

When he arrived and had entered into the cave, he found the body of the Saint in the posture of one at prayer, kneeling with uplifted hands; so that thinking he might be yet alive, he knelt down to pray with him. But not perceiving him to sigh, as he was accustomed at his prayers, he was convinced he was dead. Wherefore weeping and embracing the dead body, he wrapt it up in the cloak, and carried it out singing hymns and psalms according to the Christian tradition. But here no small difficulty occurred, how he should bury the body, having no spade or other instrument to dig a grave: so that what to do he knew not: to go back to the monastery, was three days' journey; to stay where he was, was doing nothing.

Whilst he remained in this perplexity, behold two lions, from the remoter part of the wilderness, came running with all speed toward him. At the sight of them Antony was at first surprised; but presently recollecting himself in God, he shook off all fear, and stood his ground till the beasts coming up to the place, went and laid themselves down at the feet of the deceased saint, and seemed, in their way, to lament his death. Then going a little distance off, they began to scratch up the sandy ground with their claws, and did not cease till they had made a hole big enough to answer the purpose of a grave; which when they had done, coming to Antony as it were for their wages, wagging their ears and hanging down their heads, they licked his hands and feet. The Saint conceiving that in their mute way they craved his blessing, took occasion to praise and glorify God, whom all his creatures serve; and then prayed in this manner: 'O Lord, without whose disposition not a leaf falls from the tree, nor a sparrow to the ground, give to them as thou knowest best' and so making them a sign with his hand he sent them away.

Then taking the dead body of St Paul, he laid it down in the grave which they had made, and covered it with the earth; and so returned home, carrying with him the garment made of the leaves of the palm-tree, which Paul had worn (which for the remaining years of his life he always put on upon the solemn festivals of Easter and Pentecost,) and related all that he had seen and done to his disciples, from whom St. Jerome had his account.[28]

Apart from this *Life* by St. Jerome, no evidence Paul of Thebes survives, although much has been recorded about Antony and other desert fathers. For more than a hundred years after Antony's death in

356 CE, men and women flocked to the desert in their thousands.[29]
Today, the women may not be as well known as the men, but St
Sophronius, Patriarch of Jerusalem, wrote the *Life of St Mary of Egypt*,
describing her as a black-skinned harlot who had accompanied pilgrims
to Jerusalem. After a conversion experience in the Holy Sepulchre,
she spent the next forty-seven years alone in the desert without food
or clothing. Although she never learnt to read the gospels or to write
her name, her sanctity was recognized by St Zosimus, who spoke to
her, and by the lion, who helped him bury her.

The Devoted Lion

*The next year Zosimus going out in Lent, according to the
custom of the monastery, into the desert, made the best of his
way towards the place where he had first seen the Saint, in
hopes of being still more edified by her sight and heavenly
conversation, and of learning also her name, which he regretted
not have inquired after when he last saw her. After a long and
painful journey, when he arrived at the dry torrent, he found in
the higher part of that concavity the dead body of the Saint
extended decently on the ground, with her hands crossed, and
her face turned towards the east. Hereupon he fell down at the
feet of the holy corpse, which he washed with his tears, and
then began to sing the psalms and recite the prayers for the
burial of the dead, when behold he perceived on the ground
these words written in the sand: 'Father Zosimus, bury the
body of poor Mary; render to the earth what belongs to the
earth; and in the name of God pray for me on the ninth day of
April, the day of the passion of our Lord, after the communion
of the divine supper.' The old man, reading these words, could
not conceive by whom they were wrote, as the Saint had assured
him she could neither read nor write. He was however not only
pleased to have found out her name, but also astonished to
think how quickly she had been brought back in the space of
one night after receiving the holy communion, over as large a
tract of ground as had taken him twenty days travelling without
ceasing. Hence it appears that after her return her blessed
soul had left her body, and taken its flight to heaven.*

*But now his greatest solicitude was how he should contrive
to bury her body, as he had no proper instrument to open the
earth, or dig a grave. But he was not long under this perplexity
before he perceived a great lion standing by the body of the
Saint, and licking her feet. To recover himself from the terror*

excited by the sight of so tremendous an animal, he made the sign of the cross, trusting that God and her holy body would protect him from all dangers, when behold he found the lion began to fawn upon him, as if he proffered him his service! So that being convinced that God had sent the beast to make a grave for his servant, he commanded him in the name of God to set about that work with his claws. The lion obeyed, and presently made a sufficient grave, in which Zosimus interred the body of the Saint, covering it only with the mantle she had received of him, and with many tears, having recommended both himself and the whole world to her prayers, he departed praising God, whilst the lion, like a tame lamb, went his way into the remoter parts of the desert.[30]

African Christians treasured not only the lives of the desert mothers and fathers, but also their homilies and writings. St Pachomius was born in Thebais, upper Egypt, in about 292 CE. Many versions of his *Life* are extant, in Arabic, Syrian and Latin, but the Coptic versions are the earliest.[31] His monastic order, established in Egypt in 323 CE, appeared in Ethiopia at the end of the fifth or the beginning of the sixth century, when Abba Aragawi and his eight companions, popularly venerated as 'The Nine Saints', built a monastery in Tigray.[32]

Another desert father venerated in the Coptic Church to this day is St Macarius. He is listed in the Roman Martyrology, although his exact identity is debated. Palladius (ca. 363-431 CE) wrote of an ascetic, Macarius the Alexandrian (ca. 295-394 CE) who headed a monastic colony in the Nitrian desert, but also of a more important figure known as Macarius the Egyptian, in the desert of Scetis, who lived as a hermit for sixty years before being exiled in his old age by the Arians to an island in the Nile. Of the *Fifty Spiritual Homilies* attributed to him, the one on Ezekiel's vision is an important reminder that the angelic world includes non-human species.[33] These same 'four non-incarnated animals' are still invoked today in the Coptic Orthodox Liturgy of St Mark.

Four Spiritual Animals

When Ezekiel the prophet beheld the divinely, glorious vision, he described it in human terms but in a way full of mysteries that completely surpass the powers of the human mind. He saw in a plain a chariot of Cherubim, four spiritual animals. Each one had four faces. On one side each had the face of a lion; on another side that of an eagle while on the third side each had the face of a bull. On the fourth side each had the face of a human being. To each of the faces were attached wings so that one could not discern any front or posterior parts. Their backs were full of eyes and likewise their breasts were covered with eyes so that there was no place that was not completely covered with eyes. . . .

The four animals that bore the chariot were a type of the leading characteristics of the soul. For as the eagle rules over all the other birds and the lion is king of the wild beasts and the bull over the tamed animals and man rules over all creatures, so the soul has certain dominant powers that are superior to others. I am speaking of the faculties of the will, conscience, the mind and the power of loving. For it is through such that the chariot of the soul is directed and it is in these that God resides. In some other fashion also such a symbolism can be applied to the Heavenly Church of the Saints.

In this text of Ezekiel's vision it is said that the animals were exceedingly tall, full of eyes, it was impossible for anyone to comprehend the number of eyes or grasp their height since the knowledge of such was not given. And in a like manner the stars in the sky are given for man to gaze upon and be filled with awe but to know their number is given to no man. So in regard to the Saints in the Heavenly Church it is permitted to all who only enter into it and enjoy it as they but strive to live in it, but to know and comprehend the number of the Saints is given only to God.[34]

In another homily, Macarius reveals not only the close relationship between Adam and the creative Word, who was with him 'in the beginning', but also affirms that Adam was taught and guided by the Holy Spirit.

Adam and the Word of God

Question: *Since Adam lost his own image and also that heavenly image, therefore, if he shared in the heavenly image, did he have the Holy Spirit?*

Answer: *As long as the Word of God was with him, he possessed everything. For the Word Himself was his inheritance, his covering and a glory that was his defense (Is. 4:5). He was his teaching. For He taught him how to give names to all things: 'Give this the name of heaven, that the sun; this the moon; that earth; this a bird; that a beast; that a tree.' As he was instructed, so he named them. . . .*

We know, therefore, that every creature of God is under His dominion. For He Himself has made heaven and earth, the animals, reptiles, the beasts that we see but whose number we cannot know. Who among men knows? Only God Himself knows who is in all things, even in the not yet perfectly formed embryos of animals. Does He Himself not know all things under the earth and above the heavens?[35]

Maloney regards Macarius as an 'outstanding spiritual spokesmen for the charismatic Christians of the desert in the fourth century', who had enormous influence in the early Church, and was 'one of the first witnesses of what modern Christians would call the Baptism in the Holy Spirit'.[36]

A later desert father, St Isaac the Syrian, expresses an awareness of the unity of creation, which was shared by all the hermits of the desert who had encountered other creatures capable of worshipping their one Creator God. He was born in Nineveh and became bishop of that city, but soon retired to 'his beloved Skete in the wilderness' and died towards the end of the sixth century. His writings were translated into Coptic and became influential in Ethiopia. Today they are also preserved in Syriac, Arabic, Greek and Russian.[37]

The Humble Man

He who speaks contemptuously against the humble man and does not consider him an animate creature, is like one who has opened his mouth against God. And though the humble man is contemptible in his eyes, his honour is esteemed by all creation. The humble man approaches ravening beasts, and when their gaze rests upon him their wildness is tamed. They come up to him as to their Master, wag their heads and tails and lick his hands and feet, for they smell coming from him that same scent that exhaled from Adam before the fall, when they were gathered together before him and he gave them names in Paradise. This was taken away from us but Jesus has renewed it, and given it back to us through His Coming. This it is which has sweetened the fragrance of the race of men.[38]

The idea that different animal species have some wisdom to impart to mankind became very popular in medieval Christendom. The oldest philosophical text in Ethiopia, known as *The Physiologue* was widely translated. It inspired popular medieval art in European cathedrals, in illuminated manuscripts and bestiaries. In translating a Latin *Bestiary*, T.H. White points out that:

> There is no particular author of a bestiary. It is a compilation, a kind of naturalist's scrapbook, which has grown with the additions of several hands. Its sources go back to the most

distant past, to the Fathers of the Church, to Rome, to Greece, to Egypt, to mythology, ultimately to oral tradition which must have been contemporary with the caves of Cromagnon. . . an anonymous person who is nicknamed 'the Physiologus' appeared between the second and fifth centuries A.D., probably in Egypt, and wrote a book about beasts, possibly in Greek. The book was a success and was translated north and south into Syriac, Armenian and Ethiopian. The earliest Latin translation of him which we have is of the eighth century.[39]

The *Physiologue* is a description of animals, plants and stones, which stand as symbols for moral values. Ethiopian culture is highly symbolic, according to Sumner: 'Each animal, plant or mineral is symbolic of moral values. In all the "philosophical" Ethiopian works which follow *The Physiologue*, the prevalence of moral concerns is strongly underlined. Here, however, we are dealing with a text which gives us the complete set of values which characterizes Ethiopia.' The *Physiologue* provides many Christian symbols, including the phoenix as the symbol of Christ's resurrection and the pelican as the symbol of His self-offering on the cross: 'in *The Physiologue* the naturalistic and symbolic elements are fused with true artistry and each chapter is something of a creative masterpiece'. Sumner sees it as an essential source of Ethiopian philosophy: 'Without the later developments of Ethiopian philosophy, *The Physiologue* is deprived of its significance; without *The Physiologue*, Ethiopian philosophy is deprived of its roots'.[40]

The Phoenix

The bird penetrates into the city of the sun, and the perfume ascends above the altar while the bird of its own self is consumed, becoming ashes. When later the priest examines the ashes, he finds a worm which on the third day is changed into a small chick; on the fourth day this fledgling becomes a big bird, it shows itself to the server, greets the priest and returns to its place.

Since the bird has the power to kill itself and to rise again, how then is it possible for the Jews to murmur against our Redeemer for having said: 'It is in my power to lay down my soul and to take it up again?' The phoenix is an image of our Redeemer: He has filled his two wings with sweet scent, with beauty and strength, and He has come down to us. Let us in our turn spread out to Him our hands in prayer in order to fill ourselves with the fragrance of His grace in our beautiful homeland.

The Serpent

Our Lord says: 'Be cunning as serpents and yet as harmless as doves.' The serpent has four characteristics. The first is that when it grows old its eyes become dim, and if it wants to be young again, it stays awake, fasts for forty days and forty nights, till its skin splits and cools; then it searches for a narrow cleft in the rock, thrusts its head into it and sloughs its skin; then it becomes young again.

You indeed, O man, if you want to cast off the man of old, adjust your body to the narrow door that leads to Life, and you will become a new man.

The second characteristic. When the serpent drinks water, it loses its poison.

Let all evil leave us and let it stay far away from our heart, as we desire to sate ourselves with the water of life, which is the new doctrine from the books of the Godhead, and as going to church, we also desire to receive the mysteries of the Son of the Lord, the Word from heaven.

The third characteristic. The serpent is frightened by someone without clothes; but should it see someone who is clothed, it strikes at him. If he is pursued, anyone who knows this will cast off his clothes and escaping naked will be saved.

We know that when our father Adam was naked in Eden having need of nothing, the serpent could not hurl itself upon him. And so, O man, is it with you, if you have abandoned the possessions of this world, the clothing of the man of old, that you may acquire all good, the serpent cannot thrown itself upon you.

The fourth characteristic. When a man tries to kill the serpent, it leaves its whole body uncovered, but protects its head.

Likewise our flesh is exposed to suffering, but our head is protected, and after the manner of the holy martyrs we do not deny our head and leader, Christ; for it has been said: 'Christ is the head of all men, and the head of Christ is the Lord of all things.'

The Ant

And the Physiologue *says: 'The ant has three characteristic sorts of wisdom. The first is that when the ants hurry along in single file, each one carries a grain of corn in its mouth. Any that has none does not say to the others: 'Give me your grain of corn' and does not turn upon them although itself is without; it simply goes and rests.'*

This surely is akin to those who are foolish and those who are prudent.

Moreover when the ant stores grain in the earth, it separates the grain into two parts, so that when the rainy season comes, it will not become damp and germinate, and the ant die of hunger.

But you, O man, reject the Law of old from your heart, so that the written letter will not kill you! For Paul says: 'The Law is the spirit of life.' By bringing it to an end, the Jews will die of hunger and will become their own murderers.

Moreover, at the time of harvesting, the ant goes far away into the country and climbs up the ear of corn in order to bring down a grain. It sniffs the stem and from its smell it knows whether it is barley or wheat; it leaves aside the barley and climbs the wheat stem, because barley is the food of domestic animals.

Job says: 'Where once was wheat, there let brambles grow.' But you, O man, shun that which is comparable to the food of animals for the satisfaction of the stomach, and gather wheat for storing. Moreover he has compared food of four-legged beasts with the science of hypocrites and wheat with the true faith of Christ.

The Siren and the Onocentaur

From the navel to the feet the sirens look like a bird, while from the face to the navel they are like a horse.

Isaiah said: 'Evil spirits and rustic demons and devils will dance in Babylonia.' These sirens are murderous and there is nothing more enticing than their voice. The onocentaurs, on the other hand, are human from the face to the loins, their back is that of a donkey, their feet are solid, and furthermore their behaviour is perturbing.

Likewise there are men who resemble these animals. They assemble in the churches, outwardly behave in a correct manner, while in point of fact they deny the strength of the Church. They call themselves Christians, but in reality they have left the Church and they will perish. Those who are like them resemble the sirens and the onocentaurs. While appearing to be faithful, they oppose themselves to the mysterious strength of the Church, and with the softness of their voice they seduce simple people into error, as it is written: 'A virtuous habit may be ruined by an unvirtuous conversation.' Rightly did the Physiologue *speak.*

The Panther

The panther is a small animal. The prophet says: 'I mean to be like a panther to Ephraim.' The Physiologue *says: 'The nature of the panther is such that it is the friend of all beasts, but it is enemy to the snake. It seems to be of many colours, like Joseph's coat, and it is very beautiful. It is a quiet and peaceful animal. When it has eaten a little and is satiated, it will fall asleep in its cave. On the third day, however, it will rise from its sleep and roar with a formidable voice; both those who are nearby and those who are further off will hear its voice. Its mouth exhales an odour of sweetness which draws all the other animals towards it one after another.'*

Likewise the perfume of our Lord Jesus Christ, who rose from His slumber, attracts to Himself both those who are distant and those who are nearby, as the Apostle says: 'We have Christ's sweet smell and great is the wisdom of our Redeemer.' The psalmist says: 'On your right stands the queen arrayed in gold.' The many-coloured apparel of Christ our Redeemer is woven with virginity, with strength and with purity, with clemency and with grace, with peace and with perseverance. Moreover the slayer of the serpent dwells in heaven. And no groundless statement is found in what is written about the birds and the beasts.

The beast called Unicorn

It is said in the psalm: 'You raise my horn as if I were a unicorn.' This is its natural characteristic: it is a small, wild animal, similar to the goat. The hunter cannot touch it on account of its strength. It has one horn in the middle of the head. How is it captured? The hunters adorn with splendid ornaments a beautiful virgin, and place her in front of it: the animal goes near her, leaps forward and takes shelter in her bosom; the virgin is heaped with gifts from the king and having found favour in his sight she receives great riches.

This is in the image of our Redeemer, who has raised up for us the horn of our salvation in the House of His servant David; the forces that are on high cannot come close to Him and touch Him, but he reclines in the shadow of the Virgin Mary's womb. The Word made flesh has lived among us.

The animal called Elephant

It lives in uninhabited country. It is an intelligent animal devoid of passion. If it wishes to have an offspring, it goes to the East towards Eden: there is in the land of Sirones a certain tree; the

*female and the male go there together. If the female reaches
this place first, she snatches a bit from the tree, gives it to her
mate and plays with him, until he also takes it, eats it and is
found with her. Then she conceives. When the time for laying
down has arrived, she goes into a great river, she enters the
water until it comes to her breasts, and lays down her offspring,
staying there until the young one takes her nipple and sucks.
But the father elephant carries his young one protecting it
against the snake, because the snake is the enemy of the
elephant's offspring. And if it finds a snake, the elephant
tramples upon it with its foot and kills it.*

*Such are the natural characteristics; if it falls, it cannot rise
again, because it cannot bend its knee. If it wants to sleep, it
leans upon a tree and thus supported falls asleep. The hunters
who know its habits and its abode, go and cut the tree till only
a small part remains of it; when the animal comes to lean upon
the tree it falls and begins to howl and to lament. Its partner,
upon hearing it, comes to help it, but does not succeed and
howls. Many others come, but cannot raise it. After them all,
comes a small elephant, a young one, that places its foot under
the side of the fallen elephant, upholds it and raises it. This
small elephant strikes fear in the evil spirits, and the serpent
does not come near it.*

*Likewise when Adam and Eve were in the garden of delights,
they did not know evil, and hence no one could win over them.
But when she had eaten and had made him eat from the tree of
knowledge of good and evil, then she acted in an evil way; she
knew her husband and she gave birth to Cain. And the Lord
said to them: 'Be cold like water', as David said: 'Save me,
God! The water is already up to my soul.' When the big elephant
came, it was unable to raise the fallen elephants, and after it
came many elephants, and they could do no better: these are
the great prophets and the twelve minor prophets, who could
not raise Adam; the new elephant, our Redeemer, came, He
assumed the appearance of Adam, and having taken the
condition of a slave He raised us and lifted us high into heaven
with Him. And this elephant is in His image.*[41]

The baby elephant here is a type of Christ. A version of this story
found its way into a medieval European Bestiary, which also draws
a parallel with Eve, who 'brought forth Cain above the waters of
shame'. It is worth quoting the version from this Bestiary, which

demonstrates the influence of early African literature on later European thought:

> Now if the elephant wishes to beget children it goes to the East to paradise; and there is a tree there which is called Mandragora, and it goes with its female, who first takes of the fruit of the tree and gives it to her male. And she beguiles him until he eats, and immediately she conceives. . . when the time for bringing forth has come, she goes into a pool so deep that the water comes up to the udders of the mother. But the male elephant guards her while giving birth because of the dragon which is the enemy of the elephant.[42]

Ethiopian philosophers of this early period, like their Greek counterparts, taught their disciples not only by holding discourse but by answering questions put to them. *The Maxims of Skendes* were derived from the *Book of Secundus*, which exists in Greek and Latin versions as well as in Syriac, Arabic and Ethiopic. According to Sumner:

> A careful comparison between the Ethiopic and the Arabic texts shows that the Ethiopian translator is clearly distinguishable as a deeply thinking person with a very sensitive power of perception. The Secundus story as it is conveyed in Ethiopic is the most perfect, the most morally chastened of all the preserved Secundus accounts.[43]

Creation

They questioned the wise man and said to him: which is the first of all creation, the heaven, the earth or the waters? He answered:

'The heaven where God lives is the first of the whole creation and his throne, where he first dwelt, is there. It is invisible. God cannot live absolutely without a place. After this heaven, comes the waters. He created this world out of the waters. The sky that we see is the dwelling of all the angels.'

Clothing

They questioned the wise man and said to him: what did the skin Adam dressed himself with look like? He answered:

'All the animals and beasts are covered with hair, for any place that has no hair is cold. Adam put on a kind of cover as is seen on iron [namely: rust]. Adam's body grew hair. It is the weak parts of the body that grow hair abundantly till they are covered with it. For these parts took away the light that formerly covered the body, [the parts] of the bestial sexual intercourse. The place of lust is much more covered with hair than any

other place. That is why young children are not ashamed when naked – until they reach adulthood. Then they become aware of nakedness. For the shameful parts of the body are from the knee to the navel.'

Language

They questioned the wise man and said to him: when the serpent spoke to Eve, did it do so in human language, or in the language of serpents? He answered:

'Adam and Eve were under the influence of the Holy Spirit, and nothing on earth could be secret to them: whether it was the language of serpents, of animals, of all that crawls on earth, not only of [those] that are on earth, but also of [those of] the sky – they knew all. Hence Eve knew the power the righteous have over the serpent: to this day they know all things by the virtue of grace. If the language of the serpent was like that of human beings, there was no need for her to fear and to run away.'*

Enemies

They questioned the wise man and said to him: do animals, beasts and birds have enemies other than human beings? He answered:

'Each living being has its own enemy. There are the enemies of sheep, [for instance:] the lion. The enemy of the lion is the snake. The enemy of the snake is the porcupine. And the enemy of the porcupine is the dog. And the enemy of the dog is the wolf. And the enemy of the wolf is the swine. And the enemy of the swine is the elephant. And the enemy of the elephant is the camel. And all that these fear is man. . . .'[44]*

A very different document, the *Kebra Negast* (Glory of Kings), is not merely a literary work but, according to Edward Ullendorff, 'it is the repository of Ethiopian national and religious feelings.'[45] Written in Ge'ez in the fourteenth century by an Ethiopian cleric named Yeshaq (Isaac), this epic elaborates on the biblical story of King Solomon and Makeda, the Queen of Sheba, perhaps to legitimate the Solomonic dynasty which in 1270 CE had wrested the throne from previous Aksumite rulers of Ethiopia. Ethiopians believe that Solomon could not persuade Menelek, the son Makeda bore him, to remain in Jerusalem. He quite naturally wanted to return to the beautiful land of his African mother, carrying the Ark of the Covenant with him.[46] The *Kebra Nagast* compares Ethiopia with Judah, a land flowing with milk and honey; when the headmen of Tamrin the merchant were asked to stay on and settle in Judah, they replied:

Our Country is Good

Our country is the better. The climate of our country is good, for it is without burning heat and fire, and the water of our country is good, and sweet, and floweth in rivers; moreover the tops of our mountains run with water. And we do not do as ye do in your country, that is to say, dig very deep wells in search of water, and we do not die through the heat of the sun; but even at noonday we hunt wild animals, namely, the wild buffaloes, and gazelles, and birds, and small animals. And in the winter God taketh heed unto us from year to the beginning of the course of the next. And in the springtime the people eat what they have trodden with the foot as in the land of Egypt, and as for our trees they produce good crops of fruit, and the wheat, and the barley, and all our fruits, and cattle are good and wonderful.[47]

Ethiopia's favourite Bible quotation, 'Ethiopia will extend her hands to God and He will turn to her with honour' is used as a motto in heraldic devices, and is quoted twice in the *Kebra Nagast*.[48] The Queen of Sheba is portrayed as having wisdom before she met Solomon and converted to the God of Israel. It records that she was delighted by Solomon's humility, and that not only human beings, but also animals and birds, were attracted by his wisdom.

Love of Wisdom

And the Queen said unto them, 'Hearken, O ye who are my people, and give ye ear to my words. For I desire wisdom and my heart seeketh to find understanding. I am smitten with the love of wisdom, and I am constrained by the cords of understanding; for wisdom is far better than treasure of gold and silver, and wisdom is the best of everything that hath been created on the earth. . . .

And the King answered and said unto her, 'Verily, it is right that they (i.e. men) should worship God, Who created the universe, the heavens and the earth, the sea and the dry land, the sun and the moon, the stars and the brilliant bodies of the heavens, the trees and the stones, the beasts and the feathered fowl, the wild beasts and the crocodiles, the fish and the whales, the hippopotamuses and the water lizards, the lightnings and the crashes of thunder, the clouds and the thunders, and the good and the evil. It is meet that Him alone we should worship, in fear and trembling, with joy and with gladness. For He is the Lord of the Universe, the Creator of Angels and men. And it is He Who killeth and maketh to live, it is He Who inflicteth punishment and showeth compassion, Who raiseth up from the ground him that is in misery, Who exalteth the poor from the dust, Who maketh to be sorrowful and Who maketh to rejoice, Who raiseth up and Who bringeth down. No one can chide Him, for He is the Lord of the Universe, and there is no one who can say unto Him, 'What hast Thou done? And unto Him it is meet that there should be praise and thanksgiving from angels and men. And as concerning what thou sayest, that 'He hath given unto you the Tabernacle of the Law', verily there hath been given unto us the Tabernacle of the God of Israel, which was created before all creation by His glorious counsel. And He hath made to come down to us His commandments, done into writing, so that we may know His decree and the judgement that He hath ordained in the mountain of His holiness.'

And the Queen said, 'From this moment I will not worship the sun, but will worship the Creator of the sun, the God of Israel. And that Tabernacle of the God of Israel shall be unto me my Lady, and unto my see after me, and unto all my kingdoms that are under my dominion. And because of this I have found favour before thee, and before the God of Israel, my Creator, who hath brought me unto thee, and hath made me to hear thy voice, and hath shown me thy face, and hath made me to understand thy commandment.' Then she returned to her house. . . .

Now it was not only the Queen who came [to hear the wisdom of Solomon], but very many used to come from cities and countries, both from near and from far; for in those days there was no man found to be like unto him for wisdom - and it was not only human beings who came to him, but the wild animals and the birds used to come to him and hearken unto his voice, and hold converse with him - and then they returned to their own countries, and every one of them was astonished at his wisdom, and marvelled at what he had seen and heard.[49]

In the above passage it is very clearly stated that the Tabernacle of the God of Israel 'was created before all creation', a belief that is prevalent among both Jews and Christians in Ethiopia, but perhaps not elsewhere. The Queen gives the *Tabot* a provocative title, 'my Lady', suggesting the connection that is made by Christians between the Ark of the Covenant and the Blessed Virgin Mary.[50]

In the seventeenth century there was something of a cultural renaissance in Ethiopia.[51] A philosopher by the name of Zera Yacob wrote a *Treatise* (in the year 1667 by the Gregorian Calendar) recording both his life and his thoughts. Sumner thinks this is the earliest known autobiography in Ethiopic literature. Yacob, who lived about a century and a half after the emperor of the same name, was the son of a poor farmer near Aksum. In the traditonal schools of Ethiopia he studied the *Psalms* of David, sacred music, the *qene* ('poetry' or 'hymns') and Ethiopian 'belles-lettres'. According to Sumner:

> The language of Zera Yacob is pure *qene* Geez: it reveals no foreign influence. Indeed it is the jewel, the masterpiece of Ethiopian literature. But the import of the *qene* school on Zera Yacob went further than mastery of the Ethiopian language. In such a school questions and discussion are encouraged. Students are trained to reflect and criticize, and hence they have been dissenters more often than not. Indeed it can be said that Ethiopian philosophy in the sense of philosophy based on primacy of thought originated in the *qene* school.[52]

Zera Yacob confesses that he began by questioning the inerrancy of scripture and the variety of interpretations given to it by people of different faiths:

Truth is One

I thought, saying to myself: 'Is everything that is written in the Holy Scriptures true?' Although I thought much about these things, I understood nothing, so I said to myself: 'I shall go and consult scholars and thinkers; they will tell me the truth.' But afterwards I thought, saying to myself: 'What will men tell me other than what is in their heart?' Indeed each one says: 'My faith is right, and those who believe in another faith believe in falsehood, and are the enemies of God.' These days the foreigners tell us: 'Our faith is right, yours is false.' We on the other hand tell them: 'It is not so; your faith is wrong, ours is right.' If we also ask of the Mohammedans and of the Jews, they will claim the same thing, and who would be the judge for such a kind of argument? No single human being can judge: for all men are plaintiffs and defendants between themselves ... then, where could I obtain a judge that tells the truth? As my faith appears true to me, so does another one find his own faith true; but truth is one. While thinking over this matter, I said: 'O my creator, wise among the wise and just among the just, who created me with an intelligence, help me to understand, for men lack wisdom and truthfulness; as David said, no man can be relied upon.'[53]

When King Susenyos professed the Christian faith, Zera Yacob was forced to flee and took refuge in a cave for two years before settling at

Enfraz, south of Gondar, where he married, raised a family and eventually wrote his *Hatata* (Treatise). He lived to be ninety-three.

The Beauty of God's Creatures

I know that our heart is always in the hand of God; it is possible for God to make us happy and content if we are in difficulties, poverty and sickness; again it is possible for him to make us miserable even if we live in wealth and all the luxuries of this world. Hence we see every day poor wretched people enjoying the bliss of their heart; but the rich and the kings are sad and depressed in their riches, because of their limited desire. Sadness springs in our heart, without our willing it and without our knowledge of the cause of its beginning. We need to pray to God that he grant us joy and felicity and keep us happy on earth. God makes his light to dawn for the just and his joy dawn for upright hearts; he knows and governs all the ways of our heart. . . .

With these words was I praying day and night: I was admiring the beauty of God's creatures according to their orders, the domestic animals and the wild beasts. They are drawn by the nature of their creation towards the preservation of their life and the propagation of their species. Moreover trees in the fields and plants which are created with great wisdom grow, bloom, flourish, produce the fruit of their respective seed according to their orders and without error; they seem to be animated. 'Mountains, valleys, rivers, springs, all your works praise your name, O lord: highly praised is your name on earth and in heaven. Great are the works of your hands! Behold the sun, source of light and source of the light of the world, and the moon and the stars which you made and which do not deviate from the paths you prescribed for them.' Who can know the number, the distance and the size of the stars which, because of their remoteness, appear so small? Clouds give out showers of rain to make plants green. All things are great and admirable, and all are created with great wisdom.

Thus did I remain for two years admiring and praising the creator. I thought within myself: 'The work of God is splendid and the thought of him whose wisdom is ineffable is deep indeed. How then can man who is small and poor lie by saying: 'I am sent by God to reveal to men his wisdom and his justice?' But man reveals to us nothing but vain and contemptible things, or things whose nature is by far inferior to the reason that the creator gave us that we may understand greatness.' And I said: 'I am little and poor in your sight, O Lord; make me understand what I should know about you, that I may admire your greatness and praise you every day with a new praise.'[54]

Zera Yacob's devoted disciple, Walda Heywat, made the works of his master more widely known by writing his own *Treatise,* in which he expresses his joy in the pleasures of life.

The Wonders of Our Creator

What tongue can utter or what hand can write the wonders of our creator? As he drew from the earth corn with a pleasant taste and a life-giving power, so that our life be strengthened as we seek the pleasantness of the food, likewise he implanted in the dust of our body an admirable instrument for procuring delights which are greater than all pleasures and for increasing mankind, which surpasses all works of creation. . . .

We who live today, who were not yesterday and tomorrow will disappear, we were created *and likewise all that we see in this world is transitory and* created: *how can it be* created *without a* creator? *For each* creature *is finite and weak; it has no power to* create *from nothing. Therefore there needs to be* one essence, that existed before all creatures, without beginning or end, *that* created *from nothing all that is dense, and thin, visible and invisible. . . .*

We should admire and praise the creator *in all his work, even if we do not understand, and thank him, because* he created us *and placed us among these beautiful and admirable* creatures, *and made us superior to them all; he gave us the reason and the science of which he has not endowed the other* creatures *besides us, and made us lord and reign over all* creatures ; *if God had* not created *other things inferior to us, we would not have known our superiority. As therefore we are superior to animals and trees of the fields, we should thank our* creator *who has exalted us, crowned [us] with glory and splendour, made us lord over the work of his hands, set all things under our feet; for man is the king of this world, commands all, reigns over all; the other* creatures *obey him and serve him, or fear and flee from is face; there is no king for man except God alone. Therefore man should adore the one who placed him and exalted him over all his works, and should serve him with all his heart and fulfil the will that he showed him through the light of his reason, by which the good and the evil become apparent.*

Therefore, without prayer the soul of man falls from its elevated order, and is numbered among the orders of animals which have no reason and is reduced to their share; it is not worthy of the blessing of its creator because it has repudiated him, ignored him, refused to come near him; it stayed away from the source of all blessing, preferred malediction, an enemy to the giver of life so that, expelled into darkness, it fell where the sun of justice does not shine; it did not want to remain in its creator as a branch in the trunk of a tree; and just as branches cut off from the stem have no life, so our spirit cannot live unless it is close to its creator, and dwells in him, in prayer, thanksgiving and constant adoration.[55]

Walda Heywat goes on to express an amazingly egalitarian philosophy, in which all creatures deserve equal respect whatever their religion may be, and hermits are to be regarded as no more holy than anyone else.

The Creator is Father of All

If a person approaches his creator and remains as if he were elevated with him in his prayer and his thanksgiving, he should not remain aloof from his fellow men, because God ordered men to unite and cooperate with their neighbours. God did not create man that he be busy only with himself, but he created him with the need for the society of other men. For man cannot live by himself; one is in need of the other. All men should help one another; whoever breaks away from the company of men, abrogates the law of his creator. Therefore do not praise those who isolate themselves from men that they may live as hermits in country caves. They have ignored the will of the creator who ordered that each and every man help one another; now a solitary man is useless to human society as if he were already dead; God does not accept the service of such a man who refuses to walk through the path he would have led him by and does not want to serve in the well-determined service that he had imposed on him.

Moreover God created all men equal just like brothers, sons of the one father; our creator himself is the father of all . . . for all men are our fellow men whether they are good or evil, Christians, Mohammedans, Jews, pagans: all are equal to us and our brothers, because we are all the sons of one father and the creatures of one creator. Therefore we ought to love one another. . . .

Let us not love one another like those who love their relatives, their friends, those who share their faith, but hate the aliens and those who do not belong to their faith; their love is not perfect, we ought to know that all men are equal by creation and all are sons of God; we err if we hate them on account of their faith because each man should believe what seems true to him. Faith cannot be strengthened or made to appear right in the heart of men by force and excommunication but by science and doctrine; as we should not hate men because of their science, so should we not hate them because of their faith.[56]

Theologians and ecclesiastical historians may do well to reflect on the radical pacifism and ecumenism of these African teachers at a time when Europe was being torn apart by the Reformation. This Section has shown that African Christians retain an active faith in the power of angels and spirits who were created by God not only to rule the cosmos, but to share the life of humans and other animals on earth. A contemporary Ethiopian scholar, Tsehai Berhane-Selassie, observes that Orthodox Christians today see no contradiction between the biblical creation stories and the world of spirits, some of whom are believed to be children of Eve. Such beliefs are shared by Muslims and Jews, and she reflects on the way Ethiopian Orthodox Christians use creation myths to incorporate 'other belief systems, including the basic African polytheism'. She also highlights some valuable ecological side-effects of their sense of sacred space, particularly in the preservation of endangered species.

Animal Sanctuaries

The grounds around churches are considered holy. Within a certain radius, depending on the size of the grounds, the wood and even the leaves are not to be cut and the land is not to be farmed or 'bled'. Monasteries have huge grounds which are kept holy; small churches often have only a small fenced-in compound immediately around them.

As a result, the surroundings of many churches are home to wild animals which have almost disappeared elsewhere. Around monasteries in the highlands one may see rare animals such as the colobus monkey, much hunted for its beautiful skin, baboons, leopards, huge snakes and birds of all sorts. The forests are still more or less intact. Many indigenous trees, which in some places have been destroyed completely over the last forty years, are still found standing on their own in the grounds of remote rural churches. Bees make honey inside the roofs of some churches without being disturbed, and doves and other birds make nests even on the ground.[57]

This Section shows the tremendous variety of scriptures and other resources to be found in Africa. Many African Christians retain, perhaps more than Western missionary churches, a lively appreciation of this material, which they use in a variety of ways, as is shown in Section Six.

African Islam

List of Excerpts

African Islam

In this Section, attention will be drawn to the ways in which African Islam has modified or adapted Koranic teaching about Creation, particularly as it affects human relations with the animal kingdom. Perhaps because the Koran's explanation of events is sometimes at variance with the biblical record, Africans have attempted to reconcile these different accounts with both their own traditions and with the Bible, by expanding on them. For example, the Queen of Sheba's visit to Jerusalem is portrayed rather differently in the Koran from the brief account in the Hebrew Bible, which makes no mention of Solomon's summons nor of a letter being delivered by a bird (although this remarkable means of communication was recorded in the Talmud).[1]

In the Name of God, the Compassionate, the Merciful
[When] Solomon succeeded David he said: 'Know, my people, we have been taught the tongue of birds and endowed with all good things. Surely this is the signal favour.'

His forces of jinn and men and birds were called to Solomon's presence, and ranged in battle array. When they came to the Valley of the Ants, an ant said: 'Go into your dwellings, ants, lest Solomon and his warriors should unwittingly crush you.'

He smiled at her words, and said: 'Inspire me, Lord, to render thanks for the favours You have bestowed on me and on my parents, and to do good works that will please You. Admit me, through Your mercy, among Your righteous servants.'

He inspected the birds and said: 'Where is the lapwing? I cannot see him here. If he does not offer me a good excuse, I shall sternly punish him or even slay him.'

The bird, who was not long in coming, said: 'I have just seen what you know nothing of. With truthful news I come to you from Sheba, where I found a woman reigning over the people. She is possessed of every virtue and has a splendid throne. But she and her subjects worship the sun instead of God. Satan has seduced them and debarred them from the right path, so that they might not be guided to the worship of God, who brings to light all that is concealed in the heavens and the earth and knows what you hide and what you reveal. God; there is no god but Him, the Lord of the Glorious Throne.'

He replied: 'We shall soon realize if what you say is true or false. Go and deliver to them this message of mine. Then turn aside and wait their answer.'[2]

In East Africa this story figures in Swahili *tenzi* (long religious poems recalling deeds of Muslim heroes) which take up such Koranic texts and make them more dramatic by incorporating traditional myths and legends from a pre-Islamic past. While the Arabic Koran states that *Nabii Sulemani* (King Solomon) had been taught the tongue of birds and that he could understand what the queen of the ants was telling her subjects, one Swahili version recorded by Jan Knappert refers to a much wider knowledge of the languages of Creation:

A Secret Language

Sulemani bin Daudi, King Solomon, ruled many peoples, human, animal and invisible. Allah gave him wisdom and knowledge, so that he understood the secrets of the stars as well as the languages of the animals. He could hear what the cocks crowed, what the horses neighed, what the snakes hissed. He also knew the languages of the fishes in the sea and of the demons in the fire; yes, he could even understand the intentions of the trees rustling with their leaves, or the moods of the winds, whispering and roaring. But he had to keep all this secret – for otherwise he would die.[3]

Whereas the Koran depicts Solomon deploying his forces of jinn and men and birds in battle array, in the Swahili legend he also commands animals to assist in his building operations and other more peaceful activities. Moreover, the king overhears some lazy animals plotting to avoid recruitment by outwitting each other in an amusing way reminiscent of Aesop's fables.[4]

Again, the Koran makes a curious reference to Solomon's control of the wind and the sea not found in the Hebrew Bible:

To Solomon We subjected the raging wind: it sped at his bidding to the land We had blessed. We had knowledge of all things. We assigned him devils who dived for him into the sea and who performed other tasks besides. Over them we kept a watchful eye.[5]

The idea of devils diving into the sea for King Solomon may have inspired the following Swahili story about Allah's reason for creating the dolphin.

The Dolphin dives for the Ring

In the days of King Sulemani there were no dolphins. Sulemani ruled the animals and the birds, the fishes and the insects, the demons and the human mortals. All the king's regal power lay in his ring. Allah had given him the ring: on this ring there was a seal, and in this seal there was engraved Allah's one hundredth name. Only the prophet Sulemani and the prophet Mohammed have ever known this holy name of God.

One ominous day, when the king was asleep, the devil came and stole the ring. Now the devil, ugly Satan, took the shape of King Sulemani and sat down on his throne, ready to rule men and animals. Soon, however, he was bored with sitting there and decided to go on a voyage. He ordered a ship to be made ready and sailed out. In the middle of the Ocean he lost the ring, which sank and sank and sank in the water, until Allah sent a fish along to look for it. This fish was the dolphin, which Allah created for the purpose. If you go out sailing on the Ocean you are likely to see the dolphins still diving for the magical ring.[6]

Solomon's ring and seal, with its secret name, is well known for its magical power in Ethiopia, where it is depicted in talismanic scrolls.[7]

According to the Swahili *Maulidi* ('nativity') cycle, Mohammad, although entirely human, was conceived in a miraculous manner that affected all the animal kingdom.

Animals announce the Birth

The night of the conception of the Prophet was indeed a night of wonders. When his mother Amina lay between sleeping and waking that night, an angel came down to her and said: 'Amina, this night it has pleased Allah to fill your womb with the light of Paradise. You will become the mother of the Lord of all the Arabs, of the last Prophet God will send to earth before Judgement. When he is born, call him 'Mohammed', the praised one, for that is his earthly name.'

That night the Lord God ordered His angel Ridhuani to open the gates of Paradise, so that the pleasant fragrance of the Perfumed Garden would spread over the valleys of the earth. And with this life-giving breath of heaven, all the female animals of the Kureshi clan became pregnant, so that in

*due course they dropped many lambs and kids. . . . Not only
did angels speak to people in the night of Mohammed's
conception, the spirits of the mountains, too, called to each
other that the prophet was conceived, and that the time of
Islam would soon come. The animals of the East brought
the message to the animals of the West, and many people
heard the animals speak in human language, announcing
the imminent birth of the Best of men.*

*Amina's pregnancy was light and easy, but alas, her husband
died during those months. The angels of heaven wept when
Abdullah died, and asked God why He had made his prophet
an orphan. The answer was: 'Allah suffices as a guardian.'*

*Every month the angels announced to the inhabitants of
the earth that Mohammed, the seal of the prophets, would
soon be born; and the animals again began to speak.*[8]

The Maulidi cycle relates that at Mohammed's birth, his mother was
attended by 'four heavenly women' including Mariamu (Mary), the mother
of the Prophet Îsâ (Jesus), while a beautiful bird sat on her breast and
showed her the horizons of the earth, on which 'were planted the flags of
Mohammed'.[9] According to Grierson and Munro-Hay, Islamic
tradition affirms that even before the angel Gabriel informed the prophet of his
unique calling, animals and birds had recognized it. Even the stones and trees
would cry out to him, 'Peace unto you, Apostle of God!' Jewish rabbis, Christian
monks and Arab magicians had all been predicting the arrival of a prophet in
Arabia, and while Mohammed was travelling with one of the Meccan caravans 'a
monk recognized that his body bore the signs that marked him out as a prophet'.[10]

The Koran records how, after the angel Gabriel had called
Muhammad to be a prophet, he was then commanded to tell the story
of the Virgin Mary, who had also been visited by Gabriel. According
to this account in the Koran, she gave birth to *Îsâ* (Jesus) not in a
stable with animals but alone, under a palm tree near a brook.

Mary in a Solitary Place

*And you shall recount in the Book the story of Mary: how she left her
people and betook herself to a solitary place to the east. We
sent to her Our spirit in the semblance of a full-grown man.
And when she saw him she said: 'May the Merciful defend me
from you! If you fear the Lord, leave me and go your way.'*

*'I am the messenger of your Lord,' he replied, 'and have
come to give you a holy son.'*

*'How shall I bear a child,' she answered, 'when I am a virgin,
untouched by man?'*

'Such is the will of your Lord,' he replied. 'That is no difficult thing for Him. 'He shall be a sign to mankind,' says the Lord, 'and a blessing from Ourself. That is Our decree."

Thereupon she conceived, and retired to a far-off place. And when she felt the throes of childbirth she lay down by the trunk of a palm-tree, crying: 'Oh, would that I had died and passed into oblivion!'

But a voice from below cried out to her: 'Do not despair. Your Lord has provided a brook that runs at your feet, and if you shake the trunk of this palm-tree it will drop fresh ripe dates in your lap. Therefore rejoice. . . .'

On returning home as a single parent, Mary was challenged by 'her people', but the new-born child himself spoke up for her, saying: 'I am the servant of Allah. He has given me the Gospel and ordained me a prophet.'[11]

Before Mecca became the centre of pilgrimage for Muslims, it had been a holy place for Jews, Christians and pagan Arabs; so that when Muhammad entered Mecca in triumph (*ca.* 630 CE) 'paintings of Jesus and the Virgin Mary, among others, were still visible on the inner walls of the Ka'ba.'[12] The chapter in the Koran called *The Elephant* is believed to relate to an attempt made by the Christian kingdom of Ethiopia to capture Mecca in the year of Muhammad's birth (*ca.* 570 CE), when flocks of birds came to the rescue.

Flocks of Birds

Have you not considered how God dealt with the Army of the Elephant? Did He not confound their stratagem and send against them flocks of birds which pelted them with clay-stones, so that they became like the withered stalks of plants which cattle have devoured?[13]

According to Alfred Guillaume 'The point of the legend is that Mecca, the sanctuary founded by Abraham, is God's house, and that He miraculously saved it from violation'.[14]

When Muhammad's followers had to flee from Mecca, some of them took refuge amongst the Christians of Abyssinia, whom the Prophet commends: 'You will find the most affectionate friends will be those who say, "We are Christians" '.[15] Arab traders later brought their new faith to the coastal people of East Africa and Zanzibar, but in fact Islam already had a foothold in Christian Africa before it was established at Mecca or anywhere on the Arabian peninsula.

The first *muezzin* to call people to prayer from the top of the *Ka'bah* at Mecca was Bilal, a black slave from Abyssinia who, because his master severely mistreated him for his religious beliefs, was ransomed

and freed by his fellow-convert, Abu Bakr. When the call to prayer –
rather than a summons by bells – was instituted at Mecca, Bilal was
chosen for his fine voice.'[16] The rulers of Mali claimed to be descended
from Bilal, and other West African kings also traced their ancestry to
heroic Muslim migrants.

Berber and Tuareg migrants who crossed the Sahara and settled
peacefully in Hausaland, assimilated some of their ancient traditions
with local ones. The oldest Hausa state of Daura traces its kings to an
exiled prince from Baghdad, called Bayajida (Abu Yazid). Before his
advent, Daura had been terrorized by a snake which occupied the
town's only well, so Bayajida slew the snake and married the Queen.
He became the grandfather of Muslim princes of other Hausa city-
states: Kano, Gobir, Katsina, Rano Daura, Garun Gabas, and Zazzau,
which date back to the eleventh century. Although Hausa kingdoms
trace their origins back to legendary queens who were overthrown by
patriarchal Muslim leaders, at least one female ruler was still powerful
in the fifteenth century. Known as *Gumsu*, Queen Amina the Great of
Zazzau was renowned for her conquest of other Hausa states and is
remembered in a Muslim prayer, bestowing her with the qualities of
various animal relations.[17]

Queen Amina the Great

Queen Gumsu, owner of Maradi town, never looks behind her:
Owner of the city of Yam and the land of Yemen,
And of N'gasargamu and Njimi town.
Your mortar is made of the scented Guinea-pepper wood,
You own a pestle of polished silver.
Gumsu Amina, daughter of Talba,
A descendant of the great, The great and the blessed,
Good morning, good morning!
You are like the moon at its full, Like the morning star,
Precious as gold, daughter of a bush-cow, you are a bush-cow
     among women:
Gumsu, daughter of a lion: She is a lion as precious as gold
     among all women,
Like silver, Amina, daughter of Talba:
May Allah give you the long life of a frog
And the dignity of an eagle.[18]

The mention of animals betrays an assimilation of traditional forms of
worship within African Islam, which is also exemplified by a prayer of
Dhu 'l-Nun, who became very influential in West Africa. This Egyptian,
who died in the Muslim year 246 (861 CE), and whose tombstone is

to be found at Giza, is remembered as 'an almost legendary figure, half-mystic half-alchemist'. He is said to have known the ancient Egyptian hieroglyphs and to have been familiar with the Hermetic wisdom.

Voices of the Beasts

O God, I never hearken to the voices of the beasts or the rustle of the trees, the splashing of waters or the song of birds, the whistling of the wind or the rumble of thunder, but I sense in them a testimony to Thy Unity (wahdn+ya), *and a proof of Thy Incomparableness; that Thou art the All-prevailing, the All-knowing, the All-wise, the All-just, the All-true, and that in Thee is neither overthrow nor ignorance nor folly nor injustice nor lying. O God, I acknowledge Thee in the proof of Thy handiwork and the evidence of Thy acts: grant me, O God, to seek Thy Satisfaction with my satisfaction, and the Delight of a Father in His child, remembering Thee in my love for Thee, with serene tranquility and firm resolve.*[19]

In addition to prayers, Muslims also assimilated traditional folk-tales about animals and the respect that should be given them. Some years ago H. A. S. Johnston made a collection of Hausa stories, and the one reproduced here was translated by Alhaji Abubakar Imam and published in 1960.

Auta and the Animals

There was once a farmer who had a son called Auta. He told the boy that he must go hunting every day and get something for the pot. So Auta was always out with his bow and he seldom returned home without a hare or an oribi or a duiker. If he failed, as now and again he did, his father swore at him and sometimes even beat him into the bargain.

Now after a time the animals grew tired of being killed and went and complained to their Chief, the lion. Well', said the lion 'what are we going to do about it? You all know that men are creatures to be feared.'

'God give you long life' said the hyena, 'there's only one thing for it and that is to bring this boy here and then you can do as you think best.'

'That's it', said the other animals, 'what Kura says is right.' With this they took leave of the lion and departed.

Now it happened that soon afterwards the boy Auta was out hunting and met the jackal. He bent his bow and was about to shoot when the jackal spoke. 'Stop', he said. 'If it's food you want I'll take you to where you'll find plenty of it with no trouble at all.'

Auta thought that the jackal was telling the truth and so he followed him to a great cave where the lion was wont to hold his court. At the entrance to the cave the jackal told the boy to put aside his bow so that the other animals should not know him for a hunter. So Auta laid his bow down and the jackal hid it. Then they went into the cave together and there they found the lion seated on his throne and all the other animals gathered round him like courtiers. The jackal immediately prostrated himself and did obeisance.

'Here, you!' said the hyena looking at Auta, 'aren't you going to pay your respects to the Chief?'

'What business is it of yours?' asked Auta. 'You didn't bring me here.' Nevertheless he turned to the lion and bowed respectfully.

When they were all seated the lion spoke. 'Is this the one', he asked the jackal, 'who has been troubling you?'

'God give you long life' said the jackal. 'It is he.'

'Well, young man', said the lion to Auta, 'why are you going about killing our people?'

Before Auta could answer the lion's question, the hyena interrupted again. 'He's trying to insult us' he cried. 'Just look at his body – tanned all over.'

At this Auta did obeisance to the lion. 'God give you long life', he said. 'There is one thing I must ask before I speak: are you the Chief here or is the hyena?'

This made the lion very cross with the hyena. 'I don't want to hear any more from you', he said. 'Now young man, let's have your answer.'

Auta did obeisance again. 'The elders of our town', he said, ' told me to come here and kill your people so that we could judge whether the things which the hyena told us about you were true.'

'What did the hyena tell you about me?' asked the lion.

'We wanted to drive out our own Chief,' Auta went on, 'because he had no patience or pity. We thought we would make you our Chief in his stead so that you could rule over both men and beasts. In this way we should have been united in following you and would have done or not done whatever you commanded. Well, we were debating this plan when one day the hyena came

into the town. He told us that you had sent him and that you had said that there could be no dealings between us except war. We asked him about you, and he said that among all the rulers of the world there was no tyrant as great as you. A man had only to give the slightest offence, he said, and you at once had him put to death. It was because of this that I was ordered to come and kill your people so that we could see whether you would put me to death. And so if you have me killed the hyena will be proved right, but if you let me go free he will be proved a liar.'

When he heard this the lion rounded furiously on the hyena. 'Who told you to go among men?' he asked.

'He's lying' said the hyena, who was now befouling himself with fright. 'I've never been into the town in my life.'

'Who are you calling a liar?' asked Auta. 'Have you forgotten how we put a chair out for you to honour the Chief who had sent you?'

The hyena was about to say something when the lion sprang at him and bowled him over. Then all the other animals went for him and bit and clawed him until he was dead.

After that the lion gave the boy gifts of merchandise (which had been taken from traders in the past) and dismissed him. Auta thanked him and promised to tell the people at home all that had happened.

Even now, if you meet a lion, he will do you no harm so long as you make obeisance and say: 'God give you long life.'[20]

In western Sudan, during the centuries when Islam was becoming Africanized, the bards or *griots* of the Soninke and Malinké assimilated elements of Islamic tradition in their oral records. For instance, the *Epic of Njaajan Njaay* begins by tracing the ancestry of the founder of the Waalo empire back to Noah and his son Ham, referring to the biblical story of a curse laid on Ham's descendants because he had seen his father naked,[21] with echoes from Islam, Judaism, and Christianity.[22]

The Creation of a Black Race

Noah woke up and said: 'From today on, you, Ham, you will be the precursor of the black race. You, Sham! You will beget all white people.' Thus Sham begot two persons called Yajojo and Majojo. Ham begot a son called Anfésédé. . . . Ham also begot two black children, one male and one female. Ham said to his wife: 'These two children are not mine.' The wife replied:

*'What? You are the father. Remember that it takes two people
to make a child: me and you.' Ham went into exile. He arrived
at the shores of the River Nile. That was the beginning of the
black race. Thus, Ham went into exile. Ham's children grew
up. They became very strong. They didn't know their father.
They asked their mother: 'Mother, where is our father?' The
mother replied: 'I don't know where your father is.' The two
children left in their turn. They journeyed for many months
until they arrived at the banks of the River Nile. There they
met Ham. The latter asked them: 'Where are you going?' They
answered: 'We are looking for our father.' Ham said: 'What is
your father's name?' They replied: 'Our father's name is Ham;
We were told that Noah is Ham's father; Noah is then our
grandfather. We were also told that our father went to exile just
after our birth. Now we are fully grown up; we want to find
him.' Ham replied: 'The man you have in front of you is your
father. I am Ham.' Ham created a settlement on the banks of
the Nile. The settlement was called Nobara.*[23]

According to the Hebrew Bible, when Noah and his family emerged
from the Ark they were permitted for the first time to sacrifice an
animal and eat its flesh.[24] However, according to the Koran, this right
was strictly limited, much as it has always been in most ATRs.

The Onus of Gratitude

*Though, for a due period you derived benefit from the animals
you sacrifice, their final destination is the ancient house. For
every community We have ordained a sacred rite in which to
name the Name of God over the animals of the flock He has
bestowed upon them. Your Lord is One God: to him be
surrendered and bring good news to the humble whose hearts
are filled with awe at the mention of the Name of God and who
bear patiently whatever befalls them, who fulfill the prayer-
rite and expend of their substance given at Our hand. As for
the beasts of sacrifice, We appointed them for you as God's
symbols for your good. Recite, then the Name of God over
them when they are lined up in sacrificial order and, after
ritual slaughter, eat of their flesh and feed the needy – the
quiet, contented ones as well as those who are clamorous. It is
thus that We have placed the beasts within your power, laying
on you the onus of gratitude.*[25]

The heritage of African Islam includes many stories concerning animal sacrifice. When Muslims make the *Hajj* to Mecca they are, of course, required to offer sacrifice. According to popular legend, when the ancestral hero of the Mande people, Fa-Jigi, undertook this arduous trans-Saharan pilgrimage, his travelling companions were various friendly animals.

In one amusing version of the story, Fa-Jigi makes the pilgrimage to atone for the sin of incest, which he committed with his mother, and he persuades some animals to join him when they confess that the sin of incest is common to all the animal kingdom. Because they too have sinned, they are perfectly prepared to sacrifice their lives in order to achieve salvation. At the market in Mecca, Fa-Jigi exchanges these repentant animals for amulets and magic powders which he takes back to Mande, so that the Komo secret society is able to claim that its skills of sorcery and its powerful *boliw* (fetishes) are of Muslim origin.[26]

Sorcery from Mecca
There was no sorcery in Mande,
There were no powerful sorcerers in Mande,
There was no Nama Komo in Mande,
The bird dance did not exist in Mande,
There were no stilt-dancers in Mande,
There was no Komo in Mande,
There were no magic powders in Mande.
All these things were brought from Mecca by Koroma-Jigi. . . .
The porcupine was traded for magic powder.
The ram was traded for magic powder.
Fa-Jigi returned from Mecca with nine horns of magic powder.
Nine birds' heads dangled from his bonnet when he came from
 Mecca.
Fa-Jigi had a bark-dyed sorcerer's bonnet,
And he had the sorcerer's shirt.
Fa-Jigi got all those things in Mecca.[27]

In such oral epics, traditions and practices from a pre-Islamic past are skillfully included and given legitimacy, while sins such as incest are underlined in a memorable way for didactic purposes. However, in Islamic accounts of Creation one is unlikely to find anything like the Christian concept of Original Sin. Muslim ethics derive from the concept of *taqwa* in the Koran, which is defined by Azim Nanji as the 'human quality that encompasses . . . on the one hand, the moral ground that underlies human action, while on the other, it signifies the ethical conscience which makes human beings aware of their responsibilities to God and society, making a truly moral community.'

Taqwa

O humankind! We have created you out of male and female and constituted you into different groups and societies, so that you may come to know each other – the noblest of you, in the sight of God, are the ones possessing taqwa.[28]

Other more philosophical and spiritual concepts that have been assimilated by African Muslims may derive from Christianity. The well-known Sufi mystic Muhyi-D-Din Ibn 'Arabī (1165-1240 CE) is considered a bridge between the Sufi traditions of Spain and Morocco and the eastern Sufism of Egypt and Syria. In his reflection on Koranic references to *Bilqis* (the Queen of Sheba), it is remarkable that Ibn 'Arabi sees her as Wisdom personified, like Jesus.

Bilqis on her Throne

On the day of parting they did not saddle the full-grown reddish-white camels, until they had mounted the peacocks upon them. Peacocks with murderous glances and sovereign power: thou wouldst fancy that each of them was a Bilqis on her throne of pearls. When she walks on the glass pavement thou seest a sun, a celestial sphere in the bosom of Idris. When she kills with her glances, her speech restores to life, as though she, in giving life thereby, were Jesus.

Commentary:

The full-grown camels, i.e. the actions inward and outward, for they exalt the good word to Him who is throned on high, as He has said: 'And the good deed exalts it' (Koran 25:11). The peacocks' mounted on them are his loved ones: he likens them to peacocks because of their beauty. The peacocks are the spirits of those actions, for no action is acceptable or good or fair until it hath a spirit consisting in the intention of desire of its doer.

'With murderous glances and sovereign power': he refers to the Divine Wisdom which accrues to a man in his hours of solitude, and which assaults him with such violence that he is unable to behold his personality.

'A Bilqis on her throne of pearls': he refers to that which was manifested to Gabriel and the Prophet during his night journey upon the bed of pearl and jacinth in the terrestrial heaven. The author calls the Divine wisdom 'Bilqis' on account of its being the child of theory, which is subtle, and practice, which is gross, just as Bilqis was both spirit and woman, since her father was of the Jinn and her mother was of mankind.

*The mention of Idris alludes to her lofty and exalted rank.
'In the bosom of Idris', i.e. under his control, in respect of his
turning her wheresoever he will, as the Prophet said: 'Do not
bestow wisdom on those who are unworthy of it, lest ye do it
wrong'.*[29]

Mystical experience confirmed for Ibn 'Arabī 'the unity of religious
forms despite their external divergences; he spoke of a *hāl*, or a spiritual
state, in which he was joined to the nature of Jesus'. His great Muslim
heart is ready to embrace all faiths and appears amazingly ecumenical
at a time when European Christendom was launching its crusade against
'the infidel'.

Religion of Love
*My heart is open to all forms;
it is a pasturage for gazelles and a monastery for Christian
monks
a temple for idols and the Ka'bah of the pilgrim
the tables of the Torah and the book of the Koran.
Mine is the religion of Love
Wherever His caravans turn,
the religion of Love shall be my religion and my faith.*[30]

In eighteenth-century North Africa, a new Sufi movement, known as
the Tijaniyya, sprang up named after its leader Abu al-Abbas Ahmad
Ibn Muhammad Ibn al-Mukhtar al-Tijani, who was born in 1737 CE
in southern Algeria. After spending some time in the desert, where he
received a divine revelation in 1798, al-Tijani began to preach in
Morocco. After his death, the movement continued to grow and spread
south of the Sahara. According to Hilliard,

> It gained a strong following among the Fulbe or Fulani ethnicity
> of the western Sudan and became the rallying cry for a series
> of holy wars launched in the eighteenth and nineteenth centuries
> to purify Islam in West Africa.[31]

A follower of the Tijaniyya Sufi order, Cerno Bokar Saalif Taal,
born about 1883 in Segu, West Africa, grew up under French colonial
power and the concurrent erosion of Tijani political and religious
authority. According to Louis Brenner, Cerno taught that 'God caused
a rain of passions to shower upon the original human principle which
He planted in our father Adam; these are estimated to comprise nine-
tenths of the states of the soul.' He likened the struggle to overcome
these passions, to Abraham's preparation to sacrifice his son Isaac,

but like Isaac, the soul is spared and becomes the vehicle for spiritual transformation.[32] This meditation in which Cerno learns from his faithful dog who, like Isaac, trustingly follows his master, ends with an exhortation which might inspire conservationists today to 'respect the present great garden' which God has given us.

The Dog and the Shade Tree

One day I was going to the fields, accompanied by my faithful dog, guardian of our farms and sworn enemy of those monkeys who devastate them. It was the time of the great heat of April. My dog and I were so hot that it was only with great pain that we were able to breathe properly. I had no doubt that in the end one of us, perhaps myself, would faint. Thanks to God, we came upon a thicket of clustered branches, with a thick covering of green leaves. My dog, whimpering slightly, raced toward the shadow. But when he reached it, he did not stay there, but returned to me, his tongue hanging out, his lips sagging, his pointed, white teeth bared. His sides throbbed rapidly making me realise how exhausted he was. I moved toward the shade, and the dog became happier. But I decided to continue on my way. He whined plaintively, but nonetheless followed me, his head more bowed, his tail curled between his legs. He was visibly in despair, but decided to follow me whatever the consequences.

This faithfulness touched me deeply. I did not know how to appreciate the act of this animal, ready to follow me to the death without any need of his own, and without being constrained to do it by anything whatever. He was loyal just because he considered me his master. He proved his attachment to me by risking his life with the sole aim of following me and being at my side.

'Lord,' I cried in an outburst of feeling, 'cure my troubled soul. Make my fidelity similar to that of this being whom I disparagingly call 'dog'. Give me, like him the strength to be able to scorn my life when it is a question of accomplishing Your will. And give me the strength to follow the road on which You place me without asking where I am going. I am not the creator of this dog, and yet he obeys me blindly and follows me docilely at the cost of a thousand pains which weigh heavily on his life. It is You, Lord, who has endowed him with this virtue. Give, Lord to all those who ask You, and to me in particular, the virtue of love and the courage of charity.'

I retraced my steps and sat down in the shade. My companion, now very happy, lay down in front of me so that his eyes were turned toward mine as if to have a serious conversation with me. He extended his two front paws, raised his head up, and while lying there, kept watch on me so as not to miss any of my movements. A few minutes we had no more trace of fatigue.

God has no need of reason nor of human intelligence; he gave them to us for use in this life. We are not therefore to bring them untouched to the grave, that is, to live and die without meditating on and drawing spiritual profit from the events which happen to us and from the things which we ascertain. I began to meditate. Where am I? I am under a tree with thick foliage. The words 'thick foliage' caused my mind to reflect on verses 13 and 16 of Sura *LXXVIII:*

And [We] have appointed a dazzling lamp,
And have sent down from the rainy clouds abundant water,
Thereby to produce grain and plant,
And gardens of thick foliage.

The two last words forcefully hold my attention. They constitute the subject of my meditation.

Since I have been under this thickly foliated tree I have begun to feel relaxed and restored. When I was in the sun, I was beginning to lose my sensibility and my capacity for movement and to lapse into a state of faintness, death's younger brother. I can say as much about it as about my companion.

Why these two states? They are the result of two phenomena. Far from the tree — that is, in the sun — there is an atmosphere which boils the head and compresses the chests of both humans and animals. Under the tree there is a temperate atmosphere which restores our physical organs to their normal functions. Additional data or reflection are not required to enable us to realise the existence of two elements. In the sun there is an element which can kill men or animals by acting against their organs or respiration. In the shade of the plant there is a vivifying element which destroys the unbreatheable element spread by the solar heat.

In Fulfulde the first element is called olowere *and the second* yarara. Olowere *derives from the overheating of breatheable air by the sun's rays. This phenomenon is identical to what occurs when food is over-heated and cannot be consumed without danger. Similarly, air which is overheated by the sun cannot normally be breathed without burning the passages of the respiratory organs. Yarara in this case is inherent in the green leaves of the foliage. Why green? Because (according to my experience) the tree covered with dead leaves does not provide the same wellbeing. From all this, I draw the conclusion that green plants contain a vivifying property with the power to transform an atmosphere that has been overheated by the sun into breatheable and comforting air. Therefore, in a green plant there is a principle necessary for the maintenance of the life of men and animals.*

This principle which emanates from green plants awoke in me another idea, this time on the immaterial place: paradise, as it is metaphysically described in the Qur'an. In my opinion, the green of paradise is a spiritualisation of the green plants of the material world. This comparison caused a brilliant flame of comprehension to spring up in my mind, which allows me to say that paradise, as it is described, is a symbolic garden of eternal verdure. This eternal verdure attenuates the rays of divine light which are too strong to be supported by our vision. In this garden, which is forever green, the elect can look on the Essential Light and assimilate the emanations of the source of eternal life while listening to the voice of their Lord with ears purified from all materialism. They thus enter into the state of beatitude described in verses 10 and 11 of Sura LXXXVIII: 'In a high Garden/ Where they hear no idle speech.'

Brother in God, while awaiting the opportunity to enter the celestial garden of tomorrow, respect the present great garden which constitutes the vegetable kingdom. Refrain from uselessly destroying the least plant, for it is an allegory which God causes to emerge from the earth for our instruction, our nourishment and our comfort.[33]

Louis Brenner began to explore the spiritual search of Cerno Bokar after reading a biography by Hampaté Bâ, which also inspired the Nobel Laureate Wole Soyinka. The biographer thought that

Tierno [Cerno] had taken full measure of the disequilibrium from which the entire African society suffers. . . . Understood in the most general sense of a cultural disintegration, the phenomenon from which the African society suffers seems infinitely tiresome to the Sage of Bandiagara, who knows only too well that the remedy is in the cultural foundations of the races themselves.[34]

Like Brenner, Wole Soyinka appreciates this simple narrative of 'the growth of wisdom in an individual whose largeness of vision enables him, even while lauding the superiority of Islam over Christianity, to preach the accommodation of the rival faith within the spirit of tolerance.' However, he regards the work of Cheikh Hamidou Kane, from which our next excerpt is taken, to be in a 'very different class of writing, far less didactic but pervaded more deeply by the mystical aura of Islam.' Its vision of a new African consciousness shaped by the wisdom of Islam only 'occasionally, very occasionally', suggests the animism of African traditional beliefs.[35]

Being Nature Herself

You have not only raised yourself above Nature. You have even turned the sword of your thought against her: You are fighting for her subjection — that is your combat, isn't it? I have not yet cut the umbilical cord which makes me one with her. The supreme dignity to which, still today, I aspire is to be the most sensitive and the most filial part of her. Being Nature herself, I do not dare to fight against her. I never open up the bosom of the earth, in search of my food, without demanding pardon, trembling, beforehand. I never strike a tree, coveting its body, without fraternal supplication to it. I am only that end of being where thought comes to flower.[36]

A further exploration of Muslim writings in the Francophone Africa would doubtless reveal an awareness of the natural world and of the animal kingdom comparable to what we have seen in the English translations presented here.

What can be seen is that in the past, if not in more recent times, African Islam often proved more ecumenically minded, more tolerant of traditional beliefs and more 'environmentally friendly' for indigenous populations than Christianity. It has been argued that even the climate and the ecology on the east coast of Ethiopia favour Islam. The low rainfall calls for an economy based on livestock rearing, and especially of the dromedary, whose meat is forbidden to Coptic Christians. Moreover, the 180 days of fasting prescribed by the Ethiopian Christian calendar are often beyond the capacity of people living in the arid zones of the east. Thus, many who were baptized under the policy of Amharisation of Haile Selassi eventually went over to Islam, seeing it as more congenial to their environment.[37] In other parts of Africa wild animals, as well as livestock, are generally respected by Muslim communities as much if not more than they are by post-colonial Christian and secular societies.

African Theology Today

List of Excerpts

The Divine Presence
The Invisible Forces of Nature
A Forest of Symbols
The Tale without a Head
Gotami's Strange Land
Theology of Nature
The Liberation of Creation
The Divinisaton of Humanity
The Company of Many Guardians
Forces of Nature
Cosmic Consciousness
God in Creation
Preaching to All Creation
Carving Animals of Stone
It is our Animal
Purification Ritual
Water Spirits
The Holy Spirit as Earthkeeper
The Ancestors are the Land
Healing Water
The Compost Makers
Blood Buys the Land
The Three Horses
Prophetic Choice of Animals
The Creative Word

African Theology Today

This Section presents the writings of African scholars, academic theologians, preachers, poets, and novelists, but also includes reports of theological and spiritual initiatives taken by traditional leaders and lay people who are concerned about the preservation of natural resources and wildlife in Africa.

Samson K. Gitau's book, *The Environmental Crisis*, challenges African Christianity to do something to ensure the preservation of the natural environment. He acknowledges that 'under the impact of modern "scientism", the African spiritual wisdom in regard to environment has suffered greatly' and needs to be recovered. He explains how traditional African communities are concerned to protect their environment by, for example, not allowing people to defecate near a watering place. There are also 'holy' trees which should not be cut, such as the *mugambo* (fig tree) among the Kikuyu, and traditionally, sacrifice to God is made through the spirits before new ground is broken for cultivation. In Africa the term 'environment" means simply 'life in its totality'.

The Divine Presence

Indeed, the African traditions of spiritual wisdom are striking for the sense of the numinous in the created world. African prayers for instance, are alive with the sense of divine presence in the water, the earth and the sky. Nature in the broadest sense of the word is not an empty impersonal object or phenomena. It is filled with religious significance. African religious heritage links Africans with creation of universe whether visible, invisible or below. The stars, moon, sun, clouds, mist, rain, wind, lightening, storms, animals, plants and rivers all manifest the presence of the creator.

Furthermore, in the traditional African conception of man's identity, the environment plays a fundamental role. Nature is viewed as part and parcel of man. Other than being 'master over' nature he is seen as partner with it. Man came from nature and shall go back to it.[1]

Ancestral spirits are believed to control the environment. Moreover, they are able to influence and interact with animal and nature spirits for good or ill, but since the advent of Western missionary education, they have not been adequately remembered or consulted.

One distinguished Roman Catholic theologian, the Rt Rev. Patrick Kalilombe, M.Afr., suggests that the present generation needs to re-establish links with the past and remember the wisdom of the ancestors for the sake of future generations.

The Invisible Forces of Nature

The world of the invisible is indeed quite wide. It includes, first of all, the heavens where God resides. It also includes divinities and nature spirits for those cultures whose world view reserves a place for them. And almost everywhere in Africa the spirits of the dead (especially the dead ancestors) are the central area of the invisible . . . . But other parts of the universe are also potential fields for the invisible: animals, vegetation and other objects. . . .

The family and the community are thus not limited to those presently alive: they include members of the past and also future members. This link is seen in real terms as a continuing flow of the same life. The life of the present generation is not a novel creation; it is a carry-over from those who preceded us. Even physically we owe it to them, and we cannot understand who we are or what our exact identity is except by remembering them.

In the same way, the present generation does not have to reinvent the rules or the art of successful and harmonious living or take the risk of making fatal mistakes in the process. Its best bet is to interrogate the past and receive the accumulated wisdom of those who have gone ahead. That is why there is much store laid by the traditions of the ancestors, their customs, taboos, instructions and directives.

But there is more. Having passed through death, they have become prominent members of the invisible world, whereby they share in mystical powers not ordinarily available to those presently alive. They are nearer to God, the invisible par excellence, with whom they are able to communicate and to whom they can present more effectively the needs of those still alive. They are also nearer to the other invisible forces, such as those in the 'bush' (animals, vegetation, the landscape, the elements and other forces of nature), and so are in a position

to mobilize them for good or for ill toward the living. . . .
Contact with God is maintained through the mediation of the
spirits. In a way, the spirits render the transcendent immanent,
but in such a way that the transcendent becomes 'tamed',
manageable and even negotiable. The remembrance of the spirits
assures the benefits of care, protection and involved interest
from the invisible. But there remains the possibility of rendering
the invisible humanly manageable, since the living have some
grip over the spirits. Thus, there is an intrinsic danger when
religion is centred too much on the remembrance of the spirits:
it tends to lower religious practice down to a humanly
manageable enterprise. But this should not make us forget the
positive advantages of such a spirit-centred religion. [2]

A Francophone theologian, Jean-Marc Elà, promotes the importance
of symbolism in African thought. He demands an epistemological break
with the chains of Western rationality, which ridicule symbolic thought:
'Catholicism has made the language of Aristotle its official theological
language. Yet Jesus of Nazareth, whose manner of speech echoed that
of peasants and shepherds, did not use it; neither do Blacks in Africa.'
Jesus told stories and used symbols in his teaching much as traditional
African story-tellers still do.

A Forest of Symbols

Technologically deprived black Africa is overwhelmingly richer in
signs and symbols than it is in physical tools. In a universe where
all things speak, signs play an important role in every socio-religious
practice. In one sense, the African civilization is a civilization of
symbols. In it, relationships between one human being and another,
and between human being and nature, pass through the invisible,
the symbolic place where all reality acquires meaning. Then the
truly real is invisible and visible is only appearance – all is symbol.
Africans move then in a 'forest of symbols', a unique way of
maintaining their relationship to the universe. . . .

In particular, the animal world of the black African story-
teller is an inexhaustible well of symbols pertaining to daily
life. The turtle incarnates wisdom, prudence, and skill in the
stories of the forest peoples. Among the Bambara, the elephant
represents the immensity of knowledge; the lion stands for the
'educative and noble aspects of training'; and the hyena for
'objective knowledge available to human beings.'

The story also has an initiatory function, as seen in the story
of the hare that always triumphs over the hyena. Here African

*pedagogy introduces the young to the basic symbolism of life
and death. The deep meaning of the characters in the story is
related to the drama of the creation of the world that has been
disrupted by a rebellious creature and put back in order by
ritual activity. These stories illustrate at the same time both
the order and disorder of the universe, and the triumph of life
over death. Furthermore, their cosmic aspect is augmented by
the cathartic function of laughter.*[3]

In pre-literate societies, stories were recited in poetic language, and today
African poets and novelists still use traditional idioms. An example is an
epic poem originally written in the Shona vernacular fifty years ago by
the first black African barrister in Southern Rhodesia. Later killed in the
Chimurenga war, Herbert Chitepo is now remembered as a national
hero. He called his epic *Soko Risina Musoro*, 'The Tale without a Head',
implying a nonsensical message; yet, as George Kahari explains, it is
'quite simply, the tale of a people afflicted by drought with no knowledge
of where to turn, since all of their sacrifices have failed'. The people
address their chief, Mutasa, who passes on their petitions to Nyatene,
their Creator God. In the midst of sorrow and nihilism the poem 'does
offer some hope for the drought of the mind' and the ultimate triumph
of the spirit 'is magnificently and beautifully expressed'.[4]

The Tale without a Head

A Councillor. *O King, lord of the land, the new seed of the tree
of the Lion, the stout tree that lies straight and still, we are the
family of Nyatene, but we are also your family. Today we have
come to you, but we have not come with gifts. Gifts come from
the earth and the heavens – the heavens are bare and the earth
is cracking. Your gifts, it is you who must give us them, you
are receiver and giver together. Sire, the bull of the veld, we
have come but we have come empty-handed.*

King: *You have spoken, Grandson of Zvimbi. The earth is
mine, but it is not mine. It is my father's, but it is not even his.
The earth is God's – God the creator, who dwells in the earth,
the wind and the rain. You healers, and all you wise princes,
where is your might in the land? Where is your wisdom? I,
Mutasa, rule, but I rule in the wisdom of my councillors. There
was a time, long ago, when I sat upon this throne, governing
all the land. I ruled, but with the power which comes from my
forefathers, the power without beginning, which I thought was
endless. We fought battles and were victorious, and returned
home with gold and riches.*

Be silent, my people, look into the sky and behold the love of God. Set your ears to the ground and hear the words of hope, the words of the mercy of God.

'There is no death, there is no life.' We created beings have kinship with the red earth which makes the crops to grow. Our kindred are the birds, our elder brothers the beasts, but our father and mother are the soil, the trees and the rain. God alone is the first ancestor. Where is death? The shade of a man is the spirit of the deceased, his body and his life, we have them both — where is death?

The people were silent and listened to the King's speech, and each one in his heart questioned and answered himself.

'Where has it gone, the courage I thought was mine? Yours? Where did you get it poor receiver?

Where has it gone, the strength which I thought I had? Yours? What is yours, you who are swept away by the wind?

Where is that wisdom I thought was strength? Yours? What is yours, O child still wanting care?

Where is my path which I thought I had beaten out? Have you no eyes, you self-deceiver?'

The Wanderer, who had followed them, sat among them and thought his own thoughts among the strangers.

'Listen, my child, friend of the blind. We are all limbs, we are branches of the same tree, the tree of the eyeless creatures. He who has eyes is Nyatene, He who has power is God, He who has wisdom is the Heavenly One, the judge of the heart is God. His power is within himself, since He dwells everywhere. Look not far, He is near to you, He waits only for you to give yourself to him.'

Let us sing and be mindful of our gifts. A fair land with mountains which shine and shimmer in the haze; rivers which run down dancing to the place whence they came; fields which lie bare and silent in the spring and are dark [green] with crops in the summer; and the plains filled with countless trees, many-coloured with flowers and leaves. Let us dance, we who are blessed, we have powerful bodies with mighty bones. Let us thank God, let us praise him, for He, He is the giver of life, and the receiver of gifts. . . .

'We blind wanderers, as blind men let us walk, let us walk and be humble in the darkness which is before us whether we go, the darkness which is behind whence we have come. God alone is the light.'[5]

Such an epic poem loses something in translation even when, as in this case, it is made by the author himself.

Chenjerai Hove, a popular Zimbabwean author writing in English, expresses hope for an earthly paradise restored in the land of Chief Gotami in his poetic novel, *Ancestors*. When a deaf-mute woman who died a century ago speaks prophetically through spirit mediums, she describes Gotami's land as a place where lions are tame, where men, women and children, live in harmony and where an old man communes with nature.

Gotami's Strange Land

Imagine, forests and animals sitting alongside men and women, talking about the destiny of the land. Lions which come to houses and sit, listening to the conversations of the night, telling their own stories to the children, men and women. Friends of the dogs and children. People singing the songs of lions and the lions roaring back, imitating the songs of human beings, thanking everyone for living together, sharing the forests, the water, the food. Children stand up to brush the manes of the lions, brushing their teeth, playing with their tails, as you have heard in the folktales.

The land is rich, father talks on into the night. The land with grass as tall as the tallest man in the village. Father talks for the whole night about the enchanting songs of the birds of the new lands, birds whose songs no one has ever heard, songs which change into stories for those who have ears to hear. The eagles too, and the vultures, they swarm the sky, circling, reading the map of the land, seeing each grain of sand in its place, telling the little mice in the bush to keep watch before they swoop down to capture them in their hot claws. Vulture, vulture, warn me if there is buffalo nearby, the songs of the children go, in the night.

It was a strange land, he says, panting for breath. The honey-bird can lead you to where the honey is if you obey all the laws of Gotami's lands. But if you despise Gotami and defile his people's soil because of their backwardness, if you insult their trees and hills, their animals, the honey-bird too gets angry and leads you to a cave where an angry black mamba waits for you with its sharp fangs. Fangs which jut out like sharp thorns. The honey-bird knows the laws of the shrines of the land, Gotami's land, far away near the land of the Tonga people, near the waters of the Zambezi, where they say fish the size of human beings have been caught by Tonga fishermen.

*If you want to know how strange this land is, how charming,
then ask those who have lived in it for so many years. They
know how to behave themselves, how to talk with the ancestors
of Gotami, the humble chief. . . .*

*Your father stands on the edge of the field, on a hot moist day,
listening to the voices of the maize plants talking. He touches
the leaves of the plants and mumbles words about this life
measured in maize cobs. From each leaf he can feel the pulse of
the plant. The leaves shush to him, soothing his heart, whispering
to him the stories of wealth and plenty which he has told everyone
for so long. I wish everyone back home could see this, he thinks
aloud, the plants overhearing the yearnings of his flying soul.
Alone, he walks the fields, talking to the soil, hearing messages
from the plants, asking some plants why they should be thin
when all the others are fat. The man touches the soil in his
hands and with the soles of his bare feet. An outburst of joy
overpowers him like a man in a trance. All the time he whistles
a nameless tune, his passion afloat. The greenness seems to be
his own greenness, fresh and juicy. . . .*

*Did you watch your father walk among the cattle and the
sheep? No, not the goats. They don't please him. Personality.
They don't have personality. He hates them for that. He would
rather leave the goat business to the women, his wives. Your
father would listen to the cattle breathing, their sharp teeth
mowing the tall grass, grazing. He sits down to see them, his
eyes flaming. His heart too. Thanks to the ancestors for having
given me this wealth. He touches them and calls each by its
name. Every one of them born today or yesterday has a name
already. He knows them. They are his new children. Whenever
he calls them, they raise their heads to say, yes, we can hear
you, master. . . .*

*Your father talks with the calves too, as if to ask them what
they want to be when they grow up. Milk, do you like your new
milk? What is it like, jumping up in the sky, in this heaven of
grass and leaves? he asks them.*

*The cows, bulls and calves lick his fingers and palms, nodding
their heads with joy.*[6]

There are echoes here of the prophet Isaiah's vision of a new earth
where the lion will lie down with the lamb, and of biblical stories
where other species 'speak' directly to God's people in this way.[7]

Kwesi Dickson, a Methodist who has been described by James Cone as 'among the most important of the African theologians', tries to establish for African traditional religion some cultural continuity with the Bible. He claims that the African's belief in his 'kinship with Nature' is 'basically alien to the Westerner', but not necessarily inconsistent with biblical Christianity.

Theology of Nature

In both the Old Testament and the African languages best known to me there is no word corresponding to Nature. The Old Testament speaks of Creation, a word whose connotations are quite different from those usually associated with the word Nature, for the word 'creation' implies that the world has been created; in Genesis it is made clear the creation is the product of divine will, as well as being subordinate to man. Similarly in the Akan (Ghana) language, for example, the equivalent of what is meant by Nature is Nyame n'abodze (God's created things). Hence it is to be understood from the outset that we are here concerned with Nature which God has created.

African religion adumbrates, as essential to its understanding, a theology of Nature. It has already been observed that the African believes himself to share kinship with Nature, and relates to it in a way that is basically alien to the Westerner. The description of the gods of Africa as 'nature gods' is accurate only if it is understood to mean that various aspects of Nature are held to be the means whereby reality is experienced: the stone, the sea, the tree and generally the various elements in the human environment are meaningful to the African because they point to something beyond themselves. Man is in concert with Nature; not only is he subject to Nature's fierce wrath, but also he is sustained by Nature's bounty and shares kinship with the things that make up Nature. The African relies on the Supreme Being as well as the Earth Goddess.[8]

Dickson concludes that in both the Old Testament and the New, much can be found that is in accord with the African approach to religion.

A distinguished Ghanian theologian, Mercy Amba-Oduyoye of the University of Ibadan, also seeks to find continuity with the Bible. She sees Christian theology struggling with the question raised by C. H. Dodd: 'Is the God of our redemption the same as the God of our creation?' Relating the Genesis narrative to creation myths in West Africa, she calls for a new Christology to explain how our compassionate God suffers until the whole of Creation is liberated.

The Liberation of Creation

To read Genesis 1 is to call to mind the universal intuition that the universe, all in it, and all that happens in it has a Designer and Maker. 'Things' are not here by chance, and one expects an answer to the call 'is anyone in charge here?' In Genesis, God 'delivers' the universe from chaos, just as out of compassion God delivered the Habiru from Egypt. The narrative does not pretend to be a history of origins or a scientific explanation of what is. It is an attempt to say who God is, to affirm that chaos is contrary to the nature of God, and that the universe came into being out of the 'pain of God.' . . .

According to the elaborate creation myth of the Yoruba, Olodumare fashioned the earth and all that it contains through the use of agents, but closely supervised the process personally. By whatever process, when humans think of their earthly home, they perceive God at work. I do not know of any primal worldview of Africa that leaves our existence to chance. God is at work making a new thing out of the chaotic old. It is interesting to note that during the Habiru's days in the desert even the serpent was transformed into a salvific agent (Nm 21:9; Jn 3:14). . . .

In the creation narratives, one may trace the theme of redemption/liberation/salvation in Genesis 2-3. To correct the state of alone-ness and to create a community, God makes two sexes out of the Earth-Creature Adam.[9] Even when mistrust leads human beings to take their destiny into their own hands and to attempt to do without God, God still has compassion, cares and provides 'a covering' for the shame-evoking nakedness of the woman and the man. . . .

In Africa as elsewhere a literal reading of the creation narratives has stifled the theological content and buried the chance for real reflection. A rereading of Genesis 1-3 from the perspective of the liberated children of Israel conveys other messages. The narrative, far from sanctioning what is, is a judgment on the world as we run it. It exposes the sin in patriarchy as well as that in matriarchy.

Hierarchy that undermines community and ignores individuals' ability to contribute is condemned. The story exposes our refusal to observe limits set by the God who frees from chaos and who is the only lawgiver. We would gladly put limits on others if that made us feel fulfilled, and yet to have dominion over the earth involves being disciplined. The

*narrative shows our unbelief in our verbal acknowledgment
that God knows what we need. It calls us back to God in our
original shameless nakedness, vulnerability, and mutuality. It
calls for mutual respect, respect for the toughness and
tenderness that is latent or patent in both women and men.
Above all the narrative talks of the love of God for a recalcitrant
world.*[10]

In Kenya, Bernardo Bernardi found that in their story-telling elders
were spontaneously bringing together both traditional and missionary
teaching. Although he thinks the Meru are not rich in myths and
legends, their trend of thought being matter of fact rather than
speculative, yet story-telling is regarded as 'fitting to the wisdom of an
old man'.

The elders reckon it is a great honour to be offerred the chance to
narrate and they are always pleased when asked to do so. Of course,
the narration is not based on a formalized and accepted version of the
story as there is no writing to fix it, but it constitutes a creative process.
As this it varies with any individual. It may even become a true work
of art.[11]

In African thought Creation is diverse, with many species and many
kinds of people, all in need of salvation. Perhaps that is why Emmanuel
Milingo speaks of incarnations in the plural: the first at Creation when
man was made in God's image, the second when the Word became
flesh, and the third when he became food for us in the Eucharist. He
claims that God did not 'make a mistake' in creating him or his mother
African, although he admits that we all have to be transformed into
new creatures to achieve the innocence that was lost in the Garden of
Eden.

The Divinisation of Humanity

*What great incarnations God has made in order to be with us,
and to sustain us in our human goals. Let us now see what we
ourselves ought to do to 'divinise' ourselves into God.*

*To the measure that we become God, to that same measure
will we accept incarnation into other people. It is from God
that we understand what a fellow human is. 'Whatever you do
to the least of my brothers you do it unto me.' . . .*

*It is self-giving to those who are in need of one's services.
This self-giving must also include total love for others without
conditions to restrain its full outpouring. This battle against
self-indulgence is the hard part of man's divinisation. Failure
in this has the effects described by one of the bishops of*

> *Burundi: 'The Christianity which comes and goes in Africa reflects a foreign nature of its roots and methods. It also reflects the various national backgrounds of its missionary evangelisers, who use different methods of approach to the Apostolate.' These are the effects of the failure of the divinisation of humanity. God allows Himself to become everything, but never destroys the identity of the things in which He merges.*[12]

Consecrated Roman Catholic Archbishop of Lusaka in 1969, Milingo engaged in a ministry of healing and exorcism which led to his being deposed and subjected to intensive investigations in Rome in 1982. He was forced to resign his see, but his loyalty to the Pope never wavered, and the theologian Aylward Shorter is convinced that Milingo possesses 'God-given healing gifts.'[13] Bishop Kalilombe, who was at seminary with him, believes that Milingo has made an important contribution to the development of African theology expressed orally. Therefore, 'what one can read in his writings is but an inadequate expression of a truly theological praxis which has not yet found the kind of verbal form to give it the place it deserves in scientific circles'.[14] Mona Macmillan observes in her introduction to Milingo's book, 'The manifestation of African religion which most puzzles and alienates Europeans is spirit possession, and it was Milingo's frequent exorcism of those believed to be possessed which offended many of the white priests in Zambia'.[15] In his battle with evil spirits, Milingo gives thanks for the guardian angels who have been his most cherished friends and supporters and reflects on 'what was lost through Adam and Eve'.

The Company of Many Guardians

I am in the company of many guardians whose ranks I don't know. I am grateful to them all, for they have protected me on several occasions from the evil spirits and the spirits of revenge. They have been at my side as I travelled to distant places and lands. They are immediately at my side when I call upon them. They have lifted me up out of depressions and discouragements. They have been the most cherished friends to me. They have waged a harder war against the evil spirits than I have done, feeble human being as I am. . . . But to commune with God is not easy. While God as our creator continuously lavishes on us all the good we need, He does not force us to discover Him from within ourselves. For us to regain what we lost through Adam and Eve, it will be necessary to make our own personal efforts. 'Regaining' here does not mean just acquiring once again the goods we lost, but much more. We ourselves must

*once more be polished and become clean and innocent as we
were in Adam and Eve before they sinned. To come back to this
state, we have to be transformed into new creatures, even as
we lead this earthly life.*[16]

Milingo's healing gifts found enthusiastic followers amongst the laity
in Europe and America as much as in Africa, despite the reservations
of the Roman Catholic hierarchy. Kenneth Kaunda, the first President
of independent Zambia and a good Methodist, supported Milingo. He
also drew on the traditional wisdom of Africa to construct a national
philosophy, known as Zambian Humanism, based on an understanding
of mankind's relationship with the rest of creation.

Forces of Nature

*It is through co-operation with these forces that Man will
achieve all of which he is capable. Those people who are
dependent upon and live in closest relationship with Nature
are most conscious of the operation of these forces: the pulse
of their lives beats in harmony with the pulses of the Universe.
They may be simple and unlettered people and their physical
horizons may be strictly limited, yet I believe that they inhabit
a larger world than the sophisticated Westerner who has
magnified his physical senses through invented gadgets at the
price, all too often, of cutting out the dimension of the
spiritual.*[17]

Augustine Musopole suggests that,

> The current growing interest in spirituality with its own
> theological grounding as a budding discipline may be ill-
> conceived because it continues to separate what it should not.
> We need a theology that is spiritual and a spirituality that is
> theological because God is spirit.

He also recognizes that the 'Cartesian bifurcation of nature, which
separates salvific knowledge (wisdom or spirituality) from systematic
theology, has made the latter no more than a dry and arid academic
discipline'. Therefore, rejecting the Western dichotomy between
naturalism and supernaturalism, he takes up Jean-Marc Ela's demand
for an epistemological break.

Cosmic Consciousness

*In our creeds we confess the Holy Spirit as the giver of life.
This fact is very important for an epistemology arising from
an African view of reality in the cosmos. The inter-relatedness
of reality in the cosmos which I prefer to call ontological or*

life relationality, is foundation to the personal, communal, historical, and cosmic consciousness of the African peoples. . . .

To have no felt-kinship-relationship with God in Christ through the regenerating power of the Holy Spirit, God would remain a very distant deity or only a philosophical concept, logically deduced and very fuzzy. Unfortunately, this is the way God often has been treated. On the contrary, God is with humanity from the time of creation and it is out of this relationship that God acts specifically in history. The Biblical understanding of history presupposes his relationship. It is not the covenant that constitutes human beings into God's image, but God's image leads to covenantal relationship with the world. God does not intervene in history as an outsider. Whatever is referred to as God's intervention only presupposes and confirms the already-presence of God, God's permanent involvement and relationship with the world. God does not need to intervene in history because God is always involved with history, redirecting humanity from its own folly in the perennial struggle of life and death.

The reason we view God as an outsider, who must intervene from time to time, is that we have surrendered nature or creation to a false autonomy, that is, treating nature as if it were the be all and end all. Ultimacy is given to that which is not ultimate and God is restricted to the supernatural. The result is a struggle between naturalism and supernaturalism. From a Malawian understanding, I refuse to allow such a dichotomy. It distorts the reality of God on the one hand, and of humanity and nature on the other. This is a false struggle. It is the creation of our wrong headed intellectualism and the result of a Cartesian bifurcation of nature. The truly natural is what is under, in and with God. God is the most Natural Being there is. To be with, in, and under God is the most natural thing human beings can aspire to, while to be with humanity is the most natural thing that God does.

God's purpose in history is constant, and that is, to love humanity into fullness of life and freedom as at creation. It is to have a relationship with humanity that even death cannot dissolve. However, the question of humanity's attitude toward God is a different matter. While the With-Us-Ness of God does not historically begin with the bible, the Bible affirms for us that it goes back to the beginning of creation. The Bible and many myths of creation bear testimony to this fact.[18]

In South Africa under *apartheid,* theologians were reluctant to break with the accepted Western epistemology, yet differing views of creation were debated. On the one hand, most white Afrikaners saw themselves as God's chosen people, and their neo-Calvinist theology emphasized the Creator as the law-giver, who had established different races like separate species, each under the absolute sovereignty of the one Creator God. On the other hand, Black theology responded with a liberation theology of Creation that emphasized the unity and equality of men (if not, necessarily, of women!).[19] The Lutheran Bishop Manas Buthelezi's exposition of this more holistic approach unfortunately does not explicitly refer to other animal species, although it does cut 'man' down to size in relation to 'his' Creator.

God in Creation

The concept of the wholeness of life is important, not just because it happens to reflect a traditional African insight, but also because it is related to some of the modern concerns in theology. Here I have in mind the recurring themes of 'the solidarity between the Church and the world', and the whole question of the 'rediscovery of the secular'. The latter may also be termed the rediscovery of the doctrine of creation in contemporary theology.

According to the Bible to be a creature means to be related to God. Man's creaturely relationship is a given factor of his existence which even sin cannot annul. This relationship is on the basis not of what man does or has done, but of what God is doing and has done to man and in the world. For man, to come to be and to exist mean the same thing as to be a creature of God; so that creatureliness, which is the result of the positing of man in the world of existing things, is also descriptive of man's continuous dependence on God.

Thus understood, man's relationship to God is something given with his life, in as much as, for him, to live means to receive life from outside himself. To be sure, man may not be aware of this source outside himself, but that does not remove the fact of the matter. Here we are thinking not in terms of epistemological but creational categories. What is at the centre of our attention is the activity of God in creation, rather than the issue of man's conscious awareness of the nature of that activity.[20]

From an African viewpoint, not only is God present in Creation, but the natural world, including every animal species, awaits its redemption in Christ. Therefore C.M. Mwakamba argues that the missionary task is not simply a question of preaching to all peoples but to 'other living and non-living beings' who also have 'natural rights'.

Preaching to All Creation

The mission of the Church goes beyond preaching the Gospel to all nations; it encompasses the preaching to the whole creation (Mk. 16-15). If the human being is to preach the Gospel to all creation, this involves certain minimum presuppositions both socially and economically. The preaching cannot take place in a vacuum; it takes place in the created world. Therefore, it follows that the protection of the environment is the minimum guarantee of personal dignity and requirement for preaching the Gospel. The concentration of capital goods and other means of production amongst a few, the suppression and exploitation of many – an economic situation which allows many to die of hunger – the exploitative alliances of capital interests – all these are unworthy of humanity and mother nature. . . .

The respect for nature is deeply rooted in African traditions. These traditions are striking for their sense of the 'numinous in the created world'. The divine presence in nature is remarkable – to live in harmony with nature is to live in contact with the deep sources of divine life. . . .

The community of life binds together all creation. The human community, realizing the need to rediscover its position in the 'mother earth', has become conscious that it must recognise the rights of other living and non-living beings. Just as human dignity provides the source for human rights, so the dignity of creation is the God-given source of the natural rights of all other living things. The world community is harmed by the modern 'slavery' that dictates a differentiation between subject and object; a dualistic mentality, the dichotomy between humanity and nature, mind and matter. Such dichotomies hurt the symbiotic relationship which sustain human life on earth. The churches have a duty to rediscover the holistic world-view, propagate the gospel in accordance with this holistic vision.[21]

The holistic world-view that the churches have to rediscover may be found not only in oral traditions, often acted out with music and drama, but in other forms of art. Thomas Mukarobwa, an aged teacher of painting and sculpture, told Chenjerai Hove how important it is for him to record the stories and ancient wisdom of the ancestors in stone sculpture, because 'when the word dies, stone takes over. It is permanent'. He regards his art as 'holy' – inspired by the stone itself and also through dreams. Dreams are often a means by which God and the ancestors communicate their wisdom.

Carving Animals of Stone

I did not start with carving stone. At home, in the countryside, we were moulding mud into many forms of the life we lived. Frogs, lizards, cattle, sheep and goats, birds, lions, monkeys, all the animals that were part of the stories we were brought up on. We moulded them in mud. It is so when you grow up in the countryside, close to nature, talking with nature everyday and night. School was not that important in those days. I did not go to school much. My parents had died when I was a child. Uncles brought me up. My uncles only knew the school of the forest, nature. I was herding cattle, and that was the time I was moulding in mud all my experiences there. My uncles saw that as my type of education. . . .

Stone becomes story. We pass on the stories of our past through stone and word of mouth. When the word dies, stone takes over. It is permanent.

As an artist, I know that some of these things are gifts from God. My sculpture is from such inspiration. So, it is holy. When I carve stone, I search for the holiness of the stone in its former times. Whenever I touch a piece of stone, sometimes a vision of an artistic image appears with it. Before receiving that image, it is not possible to start carving. You wait until the image appears. Everything else appears with the picture. I don't carve from imitations of objects. The image must come from me, from my body, my heart and soul. If I end up carving a woman or man in worship, I first receive that image in my mind. It has to be a significant image. It is always complex to describe that moment of encountering the image. Words are too weak for that. Long back, when I walked in the forest, passing by a rock, I sometimes saw a human face on that rock. Sometimes I saw a river, or soil in that rock. Even animals appear on the face of that rock. Or birds in flight. You could see anything, surprising things in that rock.

If I take a piece of stone and look at it carefully, I see images as if they have already been carved. Raw stone talking to me, telling me what is in that stone. That is the voice of stone, the voice of the spirits of the land, giving me an image to carve from the raw stone. I sometimes see a stone, and my whole body shakes, my hair standing on end as if I am afraid. It can only

*mean there are eyes from within the stone which are seeing me.
I remember saying to myself: Let me lie down in the shade of
this rock. I had not willed it before. There are superhuman forces
from within the stone asking me to lie there, to rest. Admirers
within that rock are asking me to lie down so they can see me in
my dreams. The shadow of the stone gives me immense comfort.*

*Stone owns life. Stone gives life. Sometimes the stone tells
you to walk round and round it. I touch the stone and my heart
is soothed. It is because long back, all humans were mountain-
dwellers. Our people and stone are intimate friends. . . .*

*Dreams? I once dreamt seeing a person carried on the wings
of a flying bird. In most of my dreams I see myself descending
from the skies onto the earth. Sometimes I see lions, baboons,
many visions of sculpture appearing to me as dreams. When I
carved the dream of a python encircling a man, a woman and a
child, it was sculpture arising from dreams. I dream of images
for the sculpture I carve. I dream of paintings and then take my
tools to fulfil that dream.*[22]

The animals that such a sculptor sees in his dreams, and models in
stone, are spiritual creatures who may not bear much resemblance to
the wild animals Europeans once hunted almost to extinction and now
love to photograph in safari parks. Before the Europeans came, religious
restrictions on excessive hunting safeguarded wildlife. Hunters were
not allowed to kill indiscriminately. Baba Mhlanga describes the close
relationship, 'decreed by the Creator', that his people had with other
creatures, unlike the white people who 'come to hunt, killing many
animals at a time. We do not hunt like that.'

It is our Animal

*I was born here, in close proximity to the wild animals. I grew
up beside them, sharing my life with them. I cannot see us
surviving without them. Animals have always helped us, and
they still do so now.*

*Long back in our history, we used to hunt wild animals. A
hunter went out in the forest to kill just one animal for food.
They were our food. Even if they killed someone once in a
while, they have done that from time immemorial. They did
not kill all of us. Even now, it is not every day that they kill
someone. When wild animals kill a human being, we accept it.
Even the cattle that we keep with us, sometimes a bull charges
at you and kills you. When wild animals kill someone, we accept
and tell ourselves: Never mind, it is our animal. The fat beast*

has a shiny skin because it ate another beast. I am also healthy because I ate another animal. The wild animals and the tame ones are the same to us. We must live together with them harmoniously. Respect their life. They, too, respect our life. They have been doing so for many years.

The Creator of our life is also the Creator of the lives of the wild animals. The relationship we have with animals is decreed by the same Creator. Human beings share their life with both wild and tame animals.

Our ancestors listened to the roaring of the lions at night. If the lions roared in a special way, our ancestors knew they could go there in the morning, bow their heads in gratitude, and take the left-over meat from the lion's kill. Our ancestors continued like that, sharing their life with the life of wild animals. That is life. They gave this life to us. That is why we are alive today, thanking them for having known how to live well with both wild and tame animals.

There are people who do not understand or care about the life of wild animals. They come by night and kill our animals, sometimes illegally, sometimes with government licences. Killing animals, just taking the elephant tusks, and leaving the flesh to rot in the game park. That is not what we were taught by our ancestors. It is like killing your own bull, taking the horns, and leaving the meat to decay. Hunting was done carefully in the time of our fathers. Our customs and ways did not allow us to kill more than what you needed. A man with a large family could kill one or two impalas. No more.

To kill two animals took the hunter a day or two. You killed one animal, and the others ran for their life. If you followed them and killed the second one with your arrow, that was enough. For the second animal, whatever it was, you thanked your ancestors and the soil and left for your home.[23]

Not only do other species have natural rights, but some African prophets believe they need to be consulted and given a hearing. In Uganda, Heike Behrend found that there had been considerable adaptation of Acholi religious traditions by the prophetess Alice Auma, when she raised the 'Holy Spirit Mobile Forces' in the 1990s. Alice's father describes how in 1985 Alice was commanded by the Lakwena spirit to consult animals in the Paraa national game park. She told the animals that God had sent her to ask whether they bore responsibility for the bloodshed in Uganda. The animals denied blame. This prophetess adapted for her Holy Spirit soldiers a pre-Christian ritual of purification carried out before a killer could be cleansed and honoured after battle. Traditionally similar purification rituals were carried out for hunters who had killed big game like elephants, buffalo, or antelope.[24] As already noted, in many African societies, the killing of such an animal was regarded as almost equivalent to homicide.[25]

Purification Ritual

The Holy Spirit Movement also served to reintegrate and rehabilitate a large number of Acholi soldiers who, as internal strangers, had become liminal and impure. In a ritual that the Spirit invented while she was still in Kitgum, Alice purified the first 150 soldiers and made them holy.

Together with three technicians, ritual experts she brought with her from Opit, Alice set up a 'yard', a round site marked off on the ground with a line, with four entrances or exits pointing north, south, east and west. In the yard, the ritual centre of the camp, three charcoal stoves and a vessel filled with water were set up. After the soldiers had removed and burned all their magic charms (just as missionaries once burned 'pagan devil's works'), they were allowed to enter the yard. While the initiates walked around in a circle, the technicians sprinkled them with water. Then they sat down, prayed, and sang – mostly Catholic hymns. Later they had to spit in the mouth of a pig that absorbed all the evil into itself, just as, in the New Testament, Jesus exorcised the evil spirits and diverted them into swine. The pig, usually a boar, was then killed and burned. After this initiation, the soldiers were considered Holy Spirit soldiers.[26]

Thus some African rituals are being Christianized. In many ATRs it is believed that priests and prophets are taught, not only by animals, but also by spirits who live in pools. The prophetess Juliana, who is leader of an ecological movement that has recently swept across southern Zimbabwe, claims to have been taught by *njuzu* water spirits. She told Gurli Hansson how she became a *nyusa*, a messenger of the Matopos shrines, after being taken by the *njuzu* at the age of seven to live under water for four years.

Water Spirits

The Njuzu takes you under water and it stays with you. You live there just like crocodiles do. There is everything down there. The Njuzu trains and teaches you. . . . You are taught good manners, how to live well with other people and to be kindhearted. This is my job, to teach people to be humble with each other. . . . All the elders died – there is no-one to teach people. Nobody knows any more what the causes of all ills in our land are. . . . The Njuzu said: 'Go and teach the people, so they will live again according to law and order, so the rains will come again.'[27]

This prophetess blames the modernisers, who use explosives to build dams for making life intolerable for the water spirits. On 1 March 1998, the *Sunday Mail* reported Juliana addressing great crowds in Chivi, when she told them: 'Cease construction of dams. Stop the sinking of boreholes, otherwise there will never be rain in this area because the rain gods do not want to see anything which involves the use of cement'. Pilgrims and messengers journey barefoot to her rain shrine at Dzilo, bringing tribute. Juliana blows her ritual horn and speaks to the rock, from where the Voice of God may be heard endorsing her teaching. Although many AICs are taking up environmental issues, Juliana does not approve of their drumming on sacred mountains.[28]

AICs can find sufficient biblical references to justify the association of rain with holy mountains, so that when traditionalists in Zimbabwe 'climb the mountains' to communicate with tribal spirits, the 'Zionists and Apostles too ascend the hills to ask the Christian God for rain by means of prayer, fasting, preaching and prophecy'.[29] In 1991 the Association of African Earthkeeping Churches (AAEC) was established and is now affiliated to the Zimbabwean Institute of Religious Research and Ecological Conservation (ZIRRCON). Martinus Daneel, an anthropologist who was born on a Reformed Church mission station in Zimbabwe, thinks they are giving expression to what Moltman calls 'the messianic calling of human beings':

> It is to 'the Lamb' that rule over the world belongs. It would be wrong to seek the *dominium terrae*, not in the lordship of Christ but in other principalities and powers – in the power of the state or the power of science and technology.[30]

Daneel describes these African churches' extraordinary vision and his conversion to the movement, resulting in his own theological reorientation.[31]

The Holy Spirit as Earthkeeper

One salutary thing that grew out of my regular pilgrimages to Morgenster, the emotional drain, the anger and emptiness I experienced each time I saw those ravaged, fruitless slopes, was a kind of ecological conversion. I recognised myself to be one of the invaders who, in earlier years, had helped deplete the mountain's bird and rock rabbit population. Did I not notice some time ago that not a single rock rabbit was to be seen on the granite kopjes around World's View where I used to hunt them?

The recognition of my own ecological guilt . . . made me more alert to the land problems of my country – of which Morgenster's were but a symptom – and of our continent. My identification with the plight of the peasants and of nature itself in the communal lands grew. The Reformed missiologist could no longer focus his empirical research purely on religious beliefs and ceremonies; neither could he maintain the Western dualism of spiritual as opposed to physical reality. African holism became the hermeneutic for theological reorientation. Saving souls was important, I thought. But never at the expense of the salvation of all creation. In my situation conversion had little significance if it did not translate into full environmental stewardship. For the first time I really experienced myself as part of an abusing and abused creation which was reaching out for liberation, salvation. The biblical concept of a new heaven and a new earth no longer seemed merely a new dispensation to be ushered in by God, but a challenge to be realised in this existence. The myth of my childhood mountain fortress had to turn into a new myth. A myth born of vulnerability, but emerging from the unknown recesses of our common African unconscious. A myth which recognises Mwari in his African guise as the true murudzi venyika *(guardian of the land), calling all of us to heal the wounded land. . . .*

So the conviction grew among us independents that we had to do something about the environment. It was felt, for example, that – while still seeing the Holy Spirit as saviour, liberator and healer against the chimurenga *background – we had to move from a predominantly anthropocentric and therefore exploitive soteriology towards a more universal, cosmic and, by implication, altruistic approach which proclaims and promotes justice, peace and salvation for all creation. Such a broadened soteriology would entail a perception of the Holy Spirit as Earthkeeper and translate into a church praxis of ecological reform. . . .*

What is decidedly new in our movement, however, is the conviction that the same spiritual forces which were so decisive in the chimurenga *struggle are equally significant in the current ecological liberation/healing struggle, spurring on the masses*

to engage in sustained and meaningful environmental action.
Ours, therefore, is a conscious, innovative attempt to harness
the traditionalist and Christian religious heritage, specifically
in relation to the multifaceted concept of national liberation
and the historical struggle to achieve it. Accordingly our
emphasis is on the empowerment of religious key figures –
spirit mediums and church prophets in particular – through
funding, organisational structures, conscientisation and joint
ecological ventures, with a view to spreading the nascent
'greening-of-Africa' revolution beyond elitist circles to become
truly a people's movement.[32]

Daneel explains how, since White settler oppression in Zimbabwe was
defeated in 1980 after seven years of *Chimurenga*, traditionalists and
church leaders have been reunited in another battle. This one, in defence
of the environment, they call the 'battle of the trees'. He describes how in
1988 in Chief Negovano's area in Bikita district, a spirit medium knelt
next to the beer pots and seedlings, clad in black with a leopard skin
draped round her shoulders, and made a prayer, extolling the ancestor.

The Ancestors are the Land

Now that we come to address our ancestors we do so in the
knowledge that the ancestors are the land, the ancestors are
the water, the ancestors are the sadza *[stiff porridge] we eat,*
and the ancestors are the clothes we wear. Without the ancestors
we will be without water, without food, without clothes. All
*our wellbeing [*upenyu hwakanaka, *literally 'good life'] will*
be lost. So at this point we arrive at a moment of truth, one of
great importance. It is not a time to laugh derisively as some
of you do when you enter your churches.

Today we want to place our own spirits with those of our
ancestors, together with our activities in their land. We cannot
simply act on our own without informing them. If we do so, we
would be transgressing. Then all the trees we plant will die. We
will have worked to no purpose, without directing our action in
truth. Should we then later find that the trees of Negovano have
died, we will know that we have come here without purpose.[33]

Another initiative resulting from the *Chimurenga* war in Zimbabwe is
that of a remarkable old man, Zephania Phiri, who has become known
as the *Water Harvester*. A poor peasant farmer, struggling to preserve
the land he loves from degradation, he came into conflict with the
settler government during the guerilla war, when arms were found on

his land. He was tortured and kept in prison for three months without trial, only to be released in leg irons, which he had to wear at home for the next four and half years until Independence set him free. Since then he has pioneered systems of irrigation with the help of his two wives. The inspiration for his 'Phiri Pits', which have become a model not only for Zimbabwe but for other parts of Africa as well, came from both his affinity with the land and from the Bible.

Healing Water

I feel God created a human being and Earth the same because, in me, there is blood circulation. And yet in the soil, water also circulates. When you dig a deep hole into the soil, God's nature is going to send this circulation into that well, that hole. And the healing of that hole is mostly done by water. Gradually, water seeps into that broken area and then fills up. If you look at it properly, you will find that, within the system, some small elements can be seen. Very fine soil and some small stones fall within that pit.

To me, that shows it's a living system. Just as it happens to me if I break – if I get myself cut. My blood oozes through the broken part, then it clots. After the clotting, then is the healing, because God really does not want me to have a part of my body broken. Just in the same way, the soil. So, through that way, in my land I invite water to come for healing. . . .

One day I was reading from a book, from the Bible, Genesis, Chapter II, where Adam was offered a garden by God. The secret that touched me then was these rivers that ran across the Garden of Eden.

Now, to my knowledge, Adam did not know how to plant a tree or a vegetable. Or to use the water in the river; to take the water and to water the trees there. He didn't know about it. But God made it that Adam survived from the fruits in the garden.

So when I thought about the Tigris River, the Euphrates River, I picked up that the sole survival of these trees and Adam was because the rivers had water. Nature – God – made it that these trees survive from the moisture, from the seepage that came from the rivers. So it touched me.

I then thought, 'How can I also have this kind of water since in my area there is no river?' then I started. You know, when the rains fall, there is water pouring, the run-off water, from the ruware *near my house. So behind my house, I made a sand trap to catch the run-off soil and water. And I could watch water*

stopped by the trap. Then after some two, three weeks after the
rain, I could notice the crops near the sand trap still survived,
even though my other crops were getting drought. Dry!

Then I saw that this water was life.

I started making all these sand traps around here. I started a
reservoir. I watched the water that fell from the roof of my
house. Then I made a small tank so that I could harness the
run-off from my roof. So all these were the ideas of getting
survival for my family. When I did this, it really jerked me up,
because I got the chance. When other peoples' crops here failed,
my crops always proved a success, because of my water
harvesting. . . .

I call water life.

My trees around here seem to talk to me – 'Thank you, Phiri,
for harvesting all this water around here.' The frogs all sing
very lovely songs because when the reservoirs have water, they
all sing to enjoy. . . .

My joy is that I got the idea from the Book of God, and that
the rivers – that the secret people never come across, never
understand, is why the river, and why the Garden of Eden was
put there as a source of water. People do not think about it, but
I thought of it and practiced what it is. And today I have fish
at my home. Not at the river, but at my home pond – I have
fish! My children know how to hook just from my own fish
pond. So to me it's really a joy because I was given the energy
to do it by God.[34]

Apart from water, another important natural resource for improving
agriculture is compost, and African farmers are coming to realize that
what nature provides is, after all, preferable to the expensive chemical
fertilizers introduced by development agencies. Merfyn Temple, in his
report on a visit to Zambia, *A Dream of Donkeys,* extols the value of
donkeys in a country where most peasant farmers cannot afford a
tractor. As well as providing compost, donkeys are used for transport,
carrying water from the well or bags of maize to the grinding mill, and
children to and from school. As he says,

The price of hiring a tractor is equivalent to purchasing 400
donkeys, enough for the work of 100 farmers. To substitute
donkeys with a tractor would simply cause great unemploy-
ment. . . . Anyway, the tractor has to be fed daily on costly
diesel oil while donkeys can breed and feed themselves. One
male and half a dozen dams can increase the herd by 100% in

three years, and, what is more, a donkey's life span can be up to
40 years, while a tractor is lucky to last ten.[35]

Temple quotes a psalm composed by Ennias Michello, Agricultural
Director of the Roman Catholic Diocese of Monze in Zambia:

The Compost Makers

Zambia you are a land of forest
A land of sweeping savannahs.
Zambia you are the home of a multitude of animals.
Mighty elephants live here and tiny millipedes.
Animals as powerful as the buffaloes
And delicate as butterflies.
As they feed, elephants strip the bark and leaves from trees.
The elephants trample the grass of the savannah to the ground.
The elephant is Zambia's great compost maker,
But other animals are there to take on the work that he begins.
These are the little ones, millipedes and centipedes,
And ten thousand grubs and worms,
A billion busy ants work day and night
To build again the soil that rains have washed away.
We men and women, children too, must take great care
Great care of all our compost makers.
We must give respect to great and small
Even as we give respect to leaders and to chiefs.
Oh! Elephant and millipede, Oh! Buffalo and butterfly
You made the soil for all our ancestors.
You are making it now for our children and our children's
  children.
We sing a song of praise to you
And thank the God of all created things.[36]

African Christian preachers, like traditional story-tellers, make
imaginative use of animals, but their sermons are not often recorded.
One that was recorded by a missionary in the Cameroons reveals a
new understanding of the power of Jesus' blood to save the land and
all the creatures who live on it:

Blood Buys the Land

The Gbaya preacher Mbari Remy speaks about the meaning of
Jesus' death for his parishioners by reminding them about what
happens on a Gbaya hunt. Suppose Bouba invites Adamou's
family to join Bouba's family on a hunt, in an area that belongs
to Bouba's family. On that hunt, Adamou is gored by a buffalo

*and his blood is shed on Bouba's ground. Before anyone can
hunt in that area again, the hunter must call an elder from
Adamou's family to bless the land where blood was shed. Shed
blood and spoken blessing effect a change; now that land and
all the animals, birds, and fish therein no longer belong to
Bouba, but to Adamou and his family.*

*Remy explains to his congregation that 'something like that'
happened when God's only Son, Jesus, was sent to live on this
earth with us. His blood was shed right here on this land where
we walk, and God thereby blessed this earth and all who live
here. All of us who live on this earth now belong to God and to
God's Son, Jesus, says Remy, because Jesus shed his blood here.*

*With a wave of tongue-clicking and other affirmative noises,
the congregation indicates that it has understood the meaning of
Remy's analogy. The analogy relates a soteriological theme from
the Christian Bible with a soteriological theme from the traditional
Gbaya ritual. It makes the ordinary experience of the hunt a
parable for understanding the new ways of God in our midst.*[37]

Christian missionary teaching has led to new interpretations of blood
sacrifice and other traditional practices. Christian doctrines, such as
the Trinity, are also capable of being interpreted in surprising ways. In
Western Kenya a Christian prophet, Mango, appeared early in the
twentieth century. According to Cynthia Hoehler-Fatton, his followers
believe that his self-sacrificial death in 1934 'opened heaven to blacks
and ushered in the reign of the Holy Spirit in Africa.'[38] The church
known as *Roho* has no written doctrine, but its version of salvation
history is conveyed through hymns, prayers, and sermons. In explaining
the Holy Trinity their preachers make use of a metaphor that appears
in the O.T. prophet Zechariah's vision, and is well attested in the N.T.
by St. John the Divine.[39]

The Three Horses

*Preachers sometimes invoke the metaphor of 'the three horses'
when commenting on the uniqueness and superiority of the
Roho dispensation. In this allegorical image they depict the
Christian trinity sequentially, associating each divinity with
an increasingly advanced or more powerful stage (okang').
Daniel Otang'a of Yiro, a longtime member of the Ruwe Holy
Ghost church, gave the clearest exegesis of this 'horse trinity'.
He explained that there has been a succession of horses
occupying the throne in heaven. The first was a white horse
(ambuor ma rachar) who was God the Father. God the Father*

*was the God of the Europeans; when he had the throne, Europeans controlled the world. However, he was then superseded by the brown horse (*ambuor ma silwal*), God the Son, who was the lord of the Asians. The brown horse reigned for only a short time — Otang'a alluded to the influx of Indian laborers and merchants to Kisumu and Kakamega in the 1920s — before the rise of the black horse. The black horse (*ambuor ma rateng'*) is the Holy Spirit and the lord of the Africans. Odongo Mango's reception of the Holy Spirit marked the ascendancy of the black horse to the heavenly throne and the dawning of the final age on earth — an era in which Africans carry the Christian banner and are the keepers of the spiritual power.*[40]

The Holy Spirit plays a significant role in the growth of African churches and the development of their theological praxis. Having found biblical justification for the continuance of traditional blood sacrifices, according to James N. Amanze, some of them appeal to the inspiration of the Holy Spirit, regarding the particular animal to be offered.

Prophetic Choice of Animals

It is important to note that in most African Independent Churches the choice of the animal to be sacrificed is made through prophesy. In the Christ Apostolic Church the choice of the sacrificial animal is made according to the specifications of the prophet-healer at the inspiration of the Holy Spirit. In some cases the choice of the animal to be sacrificed is made according to the specification of the Bible. For example, in St Anna's Church when a sacrifice is made for the healing of the sick the Bible is opened by the patient. The chapter and verse chosen by the prophet is used to make a choice of what kind of animal needs to be sacrificed. . . .

Because of their importance and significance in the life of the new churches, sacrifices and offerings are made with proper ecclesiastical supervision requiring the presence of the Bishop of the church or his representatives such as pastors, healers or prophets. . . .

A number of African Independent churches are aware and recognize the fact that Christ put an end to animal sacrifices and that his own sacrifice on the cross was offered once and for all. It is however argued that present day sacrifices and offerings in their churches are not necessarily a repetition of Christ's sacrifice. They only actualize here and now the sacrifice offered by Christ nearly two thousand years ago. What is unique, however, is the involvement of the ancestors as intermediaries in order to enhance the efficacy of the sacrifices offered.[41]

The relationship between Christian and traditional ideas of sacrifice is beginning to be taken up by African students as the subject of theological research. Ezra Chitando at the University of Zimbabwe wrote an MA thesis about ideas of sacrifice amongst the Karanga people. He found that, although sacrifices are usually made to appease ancestors or clan spirits, a sacrifice is made to the creator God every New Year, because this is seen as 'an important turning point in the cosmic cycle'. The magnitude of the occasion seems to demand that they communicate directly 'with the highest power in the hierarchy of the invisible world'. He found that Musikavanhu, the Creator God, 'did not come with the arrival of Christianity in Zimbabwe'. He was already held to be 'the highest being in the spiritual hierarchy, the ultimate power before whom the ancestors bowed. As Samasimba (owner of all power) he was behind all the events in the universe'.[42]

African theologians are making serious attempts to bring traditional religious ideas into the Christian mainstream. A Christmas reflection by a Zairian theologian, Bénézet Bujo, sees the whole of creation groaning in the labour of childbirth, and humanity's role as one of a midwife, called 'to help so that everything goes well and so that the whole cosmos be the manifestation of the glory of God'.

The Creative Word

In the Negro-African tradition in general, although there are some exceptions, the company of elders and old persons is particularly sought, for these persons are supposed to possess wisdom. This wisdom which is communicated above all by the word makes individual and community life grow.

Thus people who biologically can no longer transmit life are in a position to perpetuate it by the word of wisdom. . . .

In such a context it is easy to understand that the word can have a capital role in healing. In a certain way the medicines administered by the traditional medicine-men receive a special effectiveness from the words that accompany them. Western medicine which is concerned before all with the technical and scientific side, without symbol, without a word that heals, remains finally a foreign reality to the traditional Negro-African conception. Medicines cannot produce all their beneficial effects if they are administered in silence. On the contrary they should be supported by a vivifying word, which can be drunk, digested and transformed together with the medicines and which is destined as well to restore health. . . .

In conclusion it may be said that the word is Creative *in Black Africa. This function concerns both good and evil. That explains why the good handling of the word is a work of long duration. What is in question is apprenticeship in the company of wise and experienced people; yes, a communitarian exercise where the living and the dead enter in communion. In other terms, the creative word is not limited uniquely to the terrestrial visible community, but it goes beyond death to include the words of all the persons of the community that precede us to the beyond. These words should also be continually recalled and* ruminated *by the community of living of this world. . . .*

All this goes to show that Black Africa is close, as has already been said, to the biblical mentality. . . .

If one reads the texts with the Negro-African sensitivity, what strikes even the reader with no theological or exegetical formation, is the role that the word plays, right from the first page of the Bible. Creation itself is already intimately linked to the effectiveness of the word:

Then God said, 'Let there be light', and there was light (Gen. 1:3; cf. Ps 33:6-9). . . .

The characteristics attributed to the word in the Old Testament are also attributed in the New Covenant where everything is going to concentrate on the person of Jesus. The power of the word spoken by Jesus recalls in a certain way the initial creative work. . . .

But if up till now it has been a question of the life of God in growth in each human person, which life should at all cost be encouraged, the incarnation of God is limited to humankind. Much more, it embraces the whole universe; it has a cosmic dimension.

It is important to say that at the time of ecological movements which more and more make us sensitive to the problems of God's creation, the insistence on our ecological responsibility is quite in the line of Negro-African thought. In Black Africa, the human being is not independent of the cosmos. The human person knows that he or she is influenced by the cosmos and vice versa.

To touch one is right away to touch the other. Here it is enough to think of sacred trees and woods, or sacred places, etc. Traditional medicine, for example, is unthinkable without this relation to nature, to plants, to animals. So many taboos have developed with regard to nature and it seems to me that we are wrong to condemn them indiscriminately in the name of the Christian faith, without studying the backdrop which often rests on the wisdom of the elders to save the indispensable elements in nature. . . . This is what St Paul reminds us with eagerness in the Letter to the Romans.

If the whole of creation groans in the labour of child-bearing, it belongs to us to help so that everything goes well and so that the whole cosmos be the manifestation of the glory of God. The birth that will come will be therefore that of Jesus to whom everything is submitted. To succeed in helping creation in this labour of delivery we must first liberate ourselves, in helping one another to bring forth this Child whose reign shall never end: Jesus Christ![43]

Excerpts presented in this Section illustrate the ways in which theologians from very different backgrounds are taking up the ancient wisdom of Africa and building on it creatively. They are increasingly aware of the unique role that their continent has to play, not only in liberating Christian theology from its Eurocentric traditions, but in understanding the way our Creator intends human beings to live in community and harmony with other creatures.

Conclusion

This book has been able to provide no more than a glimpse of the rich resources that are available in Africa for those seeking a theology of Creation that will give direction to current ecological concerns, particularly about wildlife and endangered species.

It is hoped that a new approach to Animal Theology will be found in the ancient wisdom of Africa, which until recently has been underappreciated by Western academics. Future theologians will no longer need to rely so exclusively on Christian resources, rich though these are, but will also find inspiration from African Judaism and African Islam, which have only been briefly illustrated in this book.

African Renaissance

It has not been easy for Africans to challenge the received wisdom of the Western world. But today Africa is enjoying something of a cultural renaissance, comparable with the European renaissance of the fifteenth and sixteenth centuries. Perhaps before economic and political development can take place in some of the poorest areas, African people must recover a sense of their own cultural identity, as Washington Okumu maintains:

> From the African standpoint, reference to the European experience is important because although the idea of an 'African Renaissance' will include economic renewal and political change, we must bear in mind that the preconditions and motivation for political and economic renewal derive from the same social forces that give rise to cultural renewal. However, it is vital not to equate the idea of Renaissance only with economics, for that is the Western materialist fallacy. . . .[1]

A francophone theologian, Kä Mana, argues that rediscovering the ancestors' world view should inculcate a sense of responsibility for the environment. He wants to take up once again the creative cultural abilities of ancient Africa, in order to integrate them into the world of today or more precisely, to rediscover the ancestors and their legacy as a starting point for planning the future. He seeks to rediscover the legacy of 'the Fathers and Mothers' of African culture,

> to encourage every African man and woman to develop a moral sense of their social responsibility, a conscience enriched by the faith which Africa has in itself, its history, its destiny, and in its ability to promote credible alternatives to political, economic, social and cultural crises of the contemporary world order.[2]

The traditional wisdom of Africa should be an inspiration, not only for Africans but for Christians everywhere, as Mercy Amba-Oduyoye told a Pan-African Conference of Third World Theologians in 1977:

> Utilizing African religious beliefs in Christian theology is not an attempt to assist Christianity to capture and domesticate the African spirit; rather it is an attempt to ensure that the African spirit revolutionizes Christianity to the benefit of all who adhere to it.[3]

There are now encouraging signs that Europeans are beginning to look to Africa for spiritual inspiration, and are even asking forgiveness for the sins of their ancestors. When the Catholic Bishops of Africa assembled for their Synod in Rome in 1994, some European Christians, including clergy, gathered to 'salute the entire church of Africa'. They asked forgiveness and healing for the wrongs inflicted on Africans by Europeans in the past, and affirmed their willingness to learn from the African church:

> We are ready to identify ourselves with the sins of our ancestors. We have begun to examine the ways in which we ourselves up to this day have taken part in the oppression of and contempt for your dignity and self-determination, politically, economically, ecologically, culturally, and even ecclesiologically. . . .
>
> Christians everywhere in the world are in need of the revelation God desires to make through the African church. We need and we want to learn from you because we are convinced that God's Spirit has entrusted you with new and wonderful gifts.[4]

Christians who desire to learn from this continent may be surprised to discover not only how many manuscripts were produced in North Africa in the formative years of the early Church, and how many have been preserved in Ethiopia, they may also be surprised to discover the role that animals played in early Christianity. Linzey and Cohn-Sherbok think that if Christians ignore this heritage and 'cut themselves off from their past, then their future will be deeply impoverished'.

Baptized lions, vegetarian leopards, creatures who can speak and praise their Creator surely, it will be protested, all this is too much. No wonder these works are deemed apocryphal, it may be said. But it is worth remembering that 'apocryphal' in this context is not synonymous with 'heretical'. There are undoubtedly gnostic traces in some of these works but they are clearly not gnostic works as such. What characterizes gnostic scriptures is their utter lack of interest in the world of creation, in the muddy and impure (to them) lives of other sentient creatures. In contrast, many of these apocryphal stories are uncompromisingly *this worldly*.[5]

African wisdom has in fact contributed long ago not only to the theology of European Christendom, but to the development of Judaism and Islam as we saw in Sections Three and Five. The folklore, myths and rituals of ATRs, illustrated in Section One, have much more to contribute to contemporary concerns, not only about ecology and mankind's exploitation of other species, but about other aspects of the spiritual universe which baffle scientific minds.

Because excerpts have been drawn from a huge variety of cultures all over the continent, tremendous differences, and even contradictions, will have been apparent. However, certain generalizations can be made. In addition to the conflicts with nineteenth and twentieth century missionaries over blood sacrifice, rain-making and healing, mentioned in our General Introduction, academic theologians need to give more serious consideration to three other themes which emerge as being particularly relevant to the life of other species, namely (a) *Angelic Powers;* (b) *Ancestral Spirits;* (c) *Language*.

Angelic Powers

A certain amount of confusion has arisen because early explorers and anthropologists referred to various spiritual powers venerated in Africa as 'gods'. This led to their rejection by Christian missionaries as pagan or diabolical and to their subsequent neglect by academic theologians. In Section One we saw how often ancestral and non-human spirits figure in ATRs, but these are not deities nor are they exactly what medieval Christendom defined as angels. In most ATRs there is only one supreme Creator god, and no concept of fallen angels. Multiple deities, or rival angelic powers, could be said to appear in the civilizations of the Nile Valley (Section Two), but it is only in African Judaism (Section Three) that angelic and satanic powers figure so largely. The creation of angels is well documented in the books of *Enoch, Jubilees* and other pseudepigrapha, but biblical scholars dispute whether such myths originated in Africa or in Mesopotamia. Angels figure in early African Christianity, largely as a carry-over from African Judaism, joining the saints in heaven round the throne of God, or appearing as important messengers, much as they do in African Islam. Ancient Egyptian deities were transformed into angels or devils in the folklore of medieval Europe. For instance, according to Regamey, the 'Gothic story of St Michael weighing the souls in a balance is not scriptural, but comes from the early days of ancient Egypt. Anubis held the balance, Cairis presided over the judgement'.[6]

Until the time of the Enlightenment in Europe, the power of angels was seldom doubted. Nor was it doubted that animals had immortal souls, but since the Protestant Reformation both animals and angels have been almost completely neglected in Western academic thought. Today, some theologians concerned about wildlife in Africa are returning to the biblical tradition. Like the charismatic Christians of the Fourth Century, who followed St Macarius into the desert, they turn for inspiration to the prophet Ezekiel and St John the Divine, who confirm that the Lord Almighty has at least four angelic animals worshipping before his throne, and the one with a human face appears in no way superior to the others:

> The first animal was like a lion, the second like a bull, the third animal had a human face, and the fourth animal was like a flying eagle.[7]

Angels figure largely in several pseudepigraphical texts, as we have seen in Section Three. Many of the early Christian manuscripts record the way angels were called upon for superhuman tasks. The *Testament of Solomon* describes how the king was able to command numerous 'demons' to work in building the temple; and in Ethiopia the rock churches of Lalibela are believed to have been built with the assistance of angels.[8] Using his authority over wicked demons and with the help of the good angels, Solomon was able to heal illness. Today Ethiopians regularly call upon angels for protection against all kinds of evil, including sickness ascribed to demonic powers. In a book brought to Ethiopia by his son Menelik, Solomon had drawn portraits of demons which are still used in making talismanic scrolls.

Ethiopian clerics, known as *däbtära*, have inherited a long tradition of talismanic art, including pharmaceutic knowledge, thought to have been bequeathed to Solomon by the angels. According to Mercier, the *däbtära* 'moves in the world before the Flood, when spirits revealed themselves to humans and showed them the secrets of the heavens'. The *däbtära* draws 'images with a reed pen on the parchment's inner side. There is usually an image at the top, one in the middle, and one at the bottom. Then he writes the prayers, inserting the recipient's baptismal name in red ink. Finally he makes a cylindrical case for the scroll in red leather'. The art of scroll-making is dependant on animal sacrifice, because until quite recently all Ethiopia's bound books were handwritten on parchment made from animal skin.[9]

As documented in Section Five, Muslims know that Solomon was able to communicate with animals, having derived his wisdom from *jinn*.[10] Jewish Midrashim and Swahili legends suggest that his wisdom was derived from the animals themselves. The teaching of African Islam, particularly that of Sufi mystics, reveals a vivid appreciation of the role of both living animals and angelic spirits in conveying wisdom to humankind. Moreover, we noted that according to Swahili legend, when Muhammed was conceived, all the female animals of the Kureshi clan became pregnant.[11] Perhaps this means that each species was blessed with its own prophet.

The Gospel of Luke reports that when Jesus was born a chorus of angels announced the good news to shepherds in the fields.[12] Perhaps this song was heard not only by the shepherds but by the sheep? Could it have been heard by all God's creatures everywhere and not just those who happened to be in the vicinity of Bethlehem? Was not this joyful song of the angels carried like a drumbeat across Africa?

In Section Six we saw that in Africa the world of the invisible is still quite wide, including 'first of all, the heavens where God resides. It also includes divinities and nature spirits'.[13] We learnt how a sculptor can talk about the spirits of the land which he sees in the rocks[14] and a prophetess claims to have been taught by the water spirits who live in pools.[15] Recently Kwame Bediako has taken up what he calls 'Primal Imagination', exemplified by two remarkable personalities. One is the Prophet Harris, an 'African Christian uncluttered by Western missionary controls', who was able to declare 'I am under God only through the intermediary of the Angel Gabriel'. The other is the Zambian Catholic Archbishop Milingo, who 'considers that the spiritual universe of the African primal world does offer valid perspectives for articulating Christian theological commitments'. Indeed, we saw in Section Six that Milingo relies heavily on the friendship of angelic powers.[16]

Ancestral Spirits

The Koran, like the Hebrew and Christian scriptures, claims the authority not only of angels, but of ancestors, particularly of Patriarchs such as Noah, Enoch, Abraham, and Solomon, for its revelations. In ATRs, ancestral spirits are equally revered, but assume different roles. They are the guardians of the land, and they play an important part in initiation ceremonies and the maintenance of law and order, sometimes requiring blood sacrifice if they are offended. Much as the ancient Hebrews did, African societies offer sacrifice to the supreme deity, the Creator, at the command of their ancestors and patriarchs. Like Moses, African patriarchs are the promulgators of divine laws, which have to be obeyed.

There is often a close relationship between animals and ancestors. Those creatures that live in the earth are believed to communicate with the dead, who may be buried there.[17] Brian Morris makes it clear that in Malawi, although ancestral spirits are associated with the earth and with the 'evergreen forests that clothe the mountains, with deep pools of rivers, and with the sky', they are not gods. They are created beings who once were, and in a very real sense still are, human:

Malawians recognize that when a person dies he or she becomes a spiritual being (*msimu*), who is immortal, and they therefore firmly maintain that there are no ancestral spirits that were not at one time or another existing in a living bodily personality.

The transformation of an individual person that takes place after death is compared with the metamorphosis of a caterpillar into a butterfly or a tadpole into a frog. A spiritual personality, 'whether or not malevolent', after death often manifests itself in the form of an animal. An ancestral spirit may appear as a human (a diviner or spirit medium) or as an animal in the woodland.[18]

According to Nyamiti, super-human powers are ascribed to the ancestors, and 'no one can be regarded as an ancestor unless he led a morally good life on earth', for an ancestor is also a model of behaviour for the living descendants. An honoured ancestor becomes 'a mediator between God and his earthly relatives':

When ancestors are neglected or forgotten by their living relatives they are said to be angry with them and to send them misfortunes as punishment. Their anger is usually appeased through prayers and rituals in the form of food or drinks. The ancestors long for contact with their earthly kinds; that is why they are supposed to visit often the latter through snakes, hyenas, caterpillars, and the like, or to have direct contact with them through possession.[19]

A plea for the recognition of African ancestors is made by the distinguished Francophone theologian Jean-Marc Ela, who asks for ancestors to be accepted by the Church into the Communion of Saints.

The ancestors cannot be totally withdrawn from the action of the Word which 'enlightens everyone that comes into the world'. We may thus include the ancestors among those Christians 'according to the Word', to use the words of St Justin the Apologist. But no serious reflection on whether or not they are saved is possible, unless we keep in mind not only the Word, but, above all, the one that is 'beyond the Word' – that is, the Holy Spirit at work in the universe. In this perspective, faith causes us to contemplate our pagan ancestors as part of that 'great multitude from every nation, from tribes and peoples and tongues' that no one can number (Rev. 7:9). Can we exclude the old sages of Africa from those in the world below, to whom the resurrected Jesus announced the good news of salvation (1 Peter 3:19-20)? African Christians must not be limited to invoking the 'saints', most of whom are unknown to them. Rather, based on our experience of communion with the ancestors, we must rethink the mystery of the church as a total communion with those ancestors who are not gods, but mediators of that life and those blessings that come from God alone.[20]

His plea has been taken up by a Professor of Theology at Fordham University, Elizabeth A Johnson:

In Africa the unseen but powerful presence of ancestors undergirds the sense of selfhood and is foundational for the whole social fabric including ethical values. Drawing on this genius of the African peoples for sensing a vital relationship between the living and the 'living dead,' various local communities and theologians are attempting to incorporate this ancient cult into veneration of the saints and Mary.[21]

African ancestors play a dominant role in conserving the environment, including wildlife.[22] Their guardianship is exercised in close cooperation with their living representatives, the chiefs, under the ultimate authority of one Creator God. According to Vincent Mulago, chiefs were traditionally regarded with the same kind of respect that is accorded to the ancestors:

The Bantu think of the chief as undergoing an ontic change, a profound transformation; he enters upon a new mode of being. This new mode of being modified or adapts the inner being so that it can live and act according to its new situation, that is to say, it can behave like the ancestors and be a worthy extension of their being. The investiture, by which an heir receives his predecessor's possessions is the rite intended to effect this inner change. . . . Indeed, before his nomination, before his investiture which consecrates and transforms him, the king is a mere mortal, a man like anyone else. When the finger of

God and the ancestors comes and designates him to take over
the government of his people, there occurs in him, through
this very nomination, which is consecrated by the investiture,
a total change, a change of *heart,* in the Hebrew sense of the
word.[23]

All natural resources come under the guardianship of the chief,
and Daneel points out that chiefly burial sites with their surrounding
tracts of sacred land – sometimes encompassing large mountain ranges
with thickly wooded slopes – become nature reserves safeguarded
by ancestral spirits and whatever guardian animals they choose to
use.[24]

This close association of ancestors with the animal kingdom enhances
an awareness of the wisdom that God's other creatures have to offer
to mankind. It is something not to be despised. The belief in animal
and ancestor spirits in Africa has been studied by ethnographers and
social anthropologists and it has inspired much contemporary sculpture
and literature;[25] yet until recently it has been sadly neglected by
academic theologians.

Language

We have noted the translation of Greek and Hebrew scriptures into
African languages at an early date.[26] Although the Koran was not
translated but almost everywhere preserved in its original language,
the Arabic script was widely used as a medium for the transmission of
African languages and culture. This often led to the adoption of Arabic
names and ideas by various African societies. Using Arabic Script,
Kiswahili has been a written language for at least five hundred years,
and the Ahmadiyya movement in East Africa even made a Swahili
translation of the Koran. As Mazrui points out, 'the great Swahili states
and culture were part of Africa's contribution to the wider civilization
of Islam'. Today Kiswahili has become an ecumenical and intercultural
language; the coastal people are only a small minority of the total
number of Kiswahili speakers, fifty million of whom Mazrui reckons
use it as a second language. As a result it has evolved into a medium of
worship and theology for Christianity and indigenous African religion,
as much as for Islam.

Both the Germans until 1918 and the British afterwards
contributed significantly to the triumph of Kiswahili as a region-
wide lingua franca. European missionaries generally promoted
Christianity and constrained the spread of Islam: ironically, they
often used the Afro-Islamic language of Kiswahili to spread
the Gospel of Jesus. British rule forced Kiswahili to give up

the Arabic script in favour of the Roman. And yet today Kiswahili is the most serious challenger to the English language itself in East Africa.[27]

The spread of languages in Africa has long been a subject of serious academic study in a number of disciplines. Today linguists are combining forces with archaeologists, anthropologists, zoologists, and ecologists (if not yet with theologians), to investigate African intuitions that human beings are not the only species with language. Not only traditionalists, but most African Muslims, Christians and Jews believe that at the time of Creation there was no language barrier, all God's creatures were able to communicate freely with each other and lived in harmony. Philo of Alexandria believed that other species shared not only speech but 'philosophical sight and hearing'.[28] Many today still hope and believe that this paradisial state of affairs will be restored, as prophesied in scripture.[29] Meanwhile, scientists are now beginning to decipher the hitherto unknown languages of various species on earth.

After the World Archeological Congress of 1986, discussions were held on the theme of 'Cultural Attitudes to Animals, including Birds, Fish and Invertebrates' which resulted in a book entitled *What is an Animal?* in which one of the contributors, Edward Reed, affirms that:

> The literature on animal communication is replete with studies showing that mammals and birds (at least) are aware of the animate environment in a social way, that they can and do share information about its affordances. Vervet monkeys, to mention one example, have an intricate system of alarm calls, distinguishing aerial from terrestrial predators, and distinguishing between several kinds of terrestrial predators as well. Perceptual learning is required to acquire this communicative skill.[30]

Marian Stamp Dawkins, who lectures in animal behaviour at Oxford University, also instances vervet monkeys among many species which communicate with each other in subtle ways. She reports on a long-term study made by Dorothy Cheney and Robert Seyfarth in Kenya, who recorded the vervets' low-pitched grunts or 'woofs'. When played back to other wild monkeys, the researchers discovered from their reactions that they were able to pick up subtleties that completely escape the human ear. Taking issue with those who think that animal consciousness is not capable of empirical proof and therefore not a proper subject for scientific study, Dawkins concludes that:

> What makes us reasonably certain that our fellow human beings are conscious is not confined to what they look like or how they live or even whether we can understand their language. Our near-certainty about shared experiences is based, amongst

other things, on a mixture of the complexity of their behaviour, their ability to 'think' intelligently and on their being able to demonstrate to us that they have a point of view in which what happens to them *matters* to them. We now know that these three attributes – complexity, thinking and minding about the world – are also present in other species. The conclusion that they, too, are consciously aware is therefore compelling. The balance of evidence (using Occam's razor to cut us down to the simplest hypothesis) is that they are and it seems positively unscientific to deny it.[31]

Dolphins, whales, elephants, chimpanzees and birds are now known to have their own languages, which modern technology has only recently made accessible to human ears. In her study of animal communication, Charlotte Uhlenbroek not only found that elephants may have as many as seventy different vocalisations, many of which are beyond our hearing range, she also observed their touching family relationships. Although there is much still to learn about the different calls of elephants, especially their long range contact rumbles, she thinks by far the greatest challenge will be to decipher the intimate, hidden dialogue between close family members.

In the great savannah lands of East Africa, a typical family herd of elephants comprises several females and their young, together with their grown-up daughters and grandchildren. These herds are led by a matriarch, usually the oldest female, whose job it is to protect and give leadership to the herd and make sure everyone sticks together. The very close social bonds between family members are immediately apparent when watching elephants. Their trunks are used not only in feeding and sensing the smells around them but are also wonderfully expressive, gently reaching out to touch and guide the young, to reassure or to greet one another after separation. Elephants also use many calls to keep in touch with each other and give warning if something is amiss.[32]

Ullenbroek mentions an extremely rare characteristic that elephants share with humans: the ability to live beyond the age that they can reproduce. The guidance of the matriarch is so essential to the herd that if anything happens to her – if she is shot by poachers, for example – the rest of the herd may put themselves through extraordinary danger rather than abandon her.[33]

Although academics are only now deciphering animal languages, Bushmen have long been able to understand them[34] and, according to scripture, King Solomon also had this gift. Theologians could begin to explore a possible connection between Solomon's gift and the gift of tongues experienced by people from every nation assembled in Jerusalem at Pentecost.[35] According to Cyril G. Williams, glossalalia or 'speaking in tongues' is nowadays recognized as either (1) inarticulate sounds or utterings; (2) articulate sounds or pseudo-language, alliterations and reiterations; (3) articulated and combined language-like sounds or fantasy language; or (4) automatic speech in a real language, which is termed xenolalia or xenoglossia.[36] It has been manifest in the last century in Pentecostal churches and charismatic prayer groups not only in Africa but in Europe and America, where it is sometimes described as the language of angels. At Azuza Street in Los Angeles it began with a black man, William Seymour, the son of African slaves and perhaps the inheritor of a 'subterranean stream' of Black religion. The Azuza Street congregation formed by the Revival was initially a remarkable inter-racial fellowship, worshipping under a black pastor on the basis of complete equality. Within a few years, however, controversy resulted in the emergence of separate white and black churches.[37]

Similarities between glossalalia and the language of animals or the song of birds has yet to be explored by academic linguists and theologians. However, without specifically mentioning glossalalia, at least one distinguished African philosopher at the University of Nairobi finds 'a common denominator between animal and human language'. In his study of *The Wisdom and Philosophy of the Gikuyu Proverbs*, he argues strongly that the language of animals is not only communicative, it is also symbolic:

> From this it follows that the distinction usually made between signal, when speaking about non-human communication, and symbol, when speaking about human language, does not appear to me to be valid. Signals can also be called symbols. In this respect, I would like to take issue with those theorists of language, especially evolutionary biologists, who teach that one of the differences between humans and the other animals is the possession of symbolic language by the former and its absence in the latter. My support, therefore, goes to those evolutionists who differ from this teaching and offer as an example of a symbolic language (communication) the dance which bees perform in order to indicate to other bees the whereabouts of the nectar and how far away it is.[38]

Connections could also be made, with the help of anthropologists, between the language of animals and the different voices used by spirit mediums in Africa. According to Gerrie ter Haar, the Institute of

Christian Leadership in Zambia has suggested that the Church is unable
to solve its problem with traditional Zambian beliefs because it has not
yet entered sufficiently into dialogue with modern scholarship, thereby
simply reinforcing traditional views.

> Scholars from different academic backgrounds have studied
> aspects of spirit possession. The most recent and important
> research concerns the neurophysiological changes that take
> place during possession. Those who have witnessed possession
> behaviour are struck by the radical changes which take place
> in people, depending on the identity of the spirit believed to
> have taken possession of them. For example, as Milingo found,
> possessed persons might speak with completely different voices
> from normal and generally behave in ways quite foreign to
> their usual natures.[39]

The connexion between spirit possession and healing has been widely
recognized in ATRs as it is now in the Christian charismatic revival.

The Way Forward

Clearly, academic theologians need to engage in dialogue with both
scientific scholarship and with African traditional beliefs. As was seen
in Section Six, ordinary Christian people are reflecting on the need to
preserve God's creation. Some have incorporated Christian symbols
into their traditional rituals, while others have expressed their Christian
faith in art, sculpture, music and dance.

The Ugandan cleric, Jean-Marie Waliggo has pointed out that Christianity
is meant for everyone, not only the élites or those who know how to read.
Therefore he favours the Catholic method of evangelisation based on
catechism rather than the Protestant reliance on scripture:

> The Bible, as a Book, is not the only method of knowing the
> word of God, and achieving real conversion, of becoming a
> committed Christian.
>
> The aim of Christianity is to make people know the liberative
> message of God and to live it. Certainly this message can be
> communicated in several ways. The Catholic evangelisation of
> Africa has been mainly based on the catechism and oral
> transmission. To base evangelisation on catechism has several
> advantages. It obliges the preacher to start from the known to
> the unknown. God's revelation is found in Africa long before
> Christian preachers arrived. This revelation can be given its
> due importance through the catechism.[40]

Laurenti Magessa suspects that mainline African Christianity has
been 'rather naive' in its use of the Bible:

The naivety in question involves in general the widespread assumption among Church leaders and general faithful alike that in biblical scholarship the results of interpretation are value-free, that is to say, neutral; that they are valid for Churches everywhere. . . .

For Catholicism and mainline Protestantism it seems to be taken as a matter of course that the findings of exegesis, historical or source criticism by scholars of international standing or repute need to adjustment in their application. If these scholars are western, for example, their findings are just as valid for Europe or America as well as for Africa. The so-called Independent Churches, or more correctly, the Indigenous African Christian Churches, are much less bound by such assumptions. Their interpretation of the Bible is usually not academic but pastoral; they interpret the Bible to suit particular pastoral situations in their areas.[41]

In 1996, African theologians held a conference at Mbabane, Swaziland, which resulted in the publication of a volume entitled *Theology Cooked in an African Pot*. They call for a theology that may not be to European or American taste, but is indigenous, and they bemoan the way that theology has lost sight of its original role in evangelism and, with the ascendancy of reason as the final epistemological court of appeal, it has become an end in itself. Augustine Musopole calls for a return to the inspiration of the Holy Spirit:

Theology in Africa has been cooked in western pots and, therefore, has had a western texture and taste. Our churches have inherited traditional denominational theologies also known as missionary theologies. These are the theologies that underlie the ecclesiastical practices of our churches up until now. They are theological relics with little to do with the realities of today. In reaction to these theologies, several attempts have been made to flavour these theologies with African spices through adaptation, but with little success. The taste proved to be less than African. . . .

Unless theology recaptures the dimension of salvific knowledge as a fundamental aspect to theological apprehension, its value as a Christian enterprise becomes greatly diminished. It faces the danger of becoming the cause of degenerative spirituality in the body of the community of faith. . . . The current growing interest in spirituality with its own theological grounding as a budding discipline may be ill-conceived because it continues to separate what it should not. We need a theology that is spiritual and a spirituality that is theological because God is spirit.[42]

If God's revelation could be found in Africa long before Christian preachers arrived, as Waliggo says, it may well have included a message concerning the salvation of animals and the whole of Creation. In Zimbabwe, as we have seen, AICs are getting together with traditionalists to initiate tree planting ceremonies to combat drought and environmental degradation. They are 'doing theology' in a very practical way while taking part in an ecumenical dialogue about Creation.[43] Practical co-operation between people of different faiths is manifest in other parts of Africa, too. Lamin Sanneh thinks that the inner vitality of African Islam is due to its willingness to enter into genuine dialogue with ATRs:

> In the encounter with traditional religions, African Muslims have delineated the situation in terms of what Islam permits (*halal*) and what it forbids (*haram*). In this way judgment is made on methods and forms of traditional religious worship and divination, not on the content and ideas. Ifa divination, for example, is assessed on the basis of whether it contravenes the religious code, not on whether it introduces people to ideas of the supernatural. African Christians, on the other hand, would seem to be attracted to those features of Ifa which prepared people for faith in the Creator and His Providence, considering as of less consequence the forms and methods of Ifa practice.[44]

Kwesi Dickson, who has been described by James Cone as 'among the most important of the African theologians', lays the foundations for a more ecumenical theology of Creation by comparing the sacred wells and mountains found all over Africa with references to similar sacred sites in the Bible. He points out that in most African languages there is no word corresponding to Nature. Like the Old Testament, they speak of Creation, 'a word whose connotations are quite different from those usually associated with the word Nature', because it implies that the world has been created. In Genesis it is made clear that Creation is the product of divine will, as well as being subordinate to man.

Dickson goes on to point out that from the evidence of the Old Testament, one has to recognize that Yahweh was sometimes represented as a Nature deity, who revealed himself to Moses in the Burning Bush and guided the Israelites through the desert by a pillar of fire and a pillar of cloud (Exod. 13:21). Thunder is Yahweh's voice. (Ps. 29:3-9). It was Elijah's purpose, in his challenge to the priests of Baal at Carmel, to assert that it was Yahweh alone who could send rain; the significance of this trial of strength is not merely that fire consumed Elijah's sacrifice, but that the prophetic act of pouring water issued in the coming down of rain to break the three-year drought.

> That Yahweh was conceived as a God of the wilderness, resident in a sacred mountain, revealing his power through storm and fire, is plainly true, but something more was present. It is just as wrong to deny that to ancient Israel Nature had some sacred significance as it is not to recognise that the essential characteristic of Israelite religion, and that which forms the basis of the New Testament faith, is the belief in a God who reveals himself through history.[45]

The Bible retains much that is in accord with African traditional religion, and the idea of animal rights and Animal Theology is to be found there. The western world, now more than at any other time, needs to emulate the respect and understanding which Africa has had and still has for its native wild animals. Scientists are pointing out that many species become extinct every year. This mass extinction, which threatens to remove much of the world's native wildlife from both land and sea within the next seventy-five years, is mainly due to western technologies and their destruction of habitats. There is often a conflict of interests, or of principles. As Aiden Teveera Manwa, custodian at Great Zimbabwe, told Chenjerai Hove:

> There is a conflict of wisdoms. The new wisdom is the wisdom of defeat, of conquering other wisdoms. The new wisdom fought to gain its space. The old wisdom does not fight for its space. It withdrew and looked forward to the day when it will be sought once more.[46]

Cyprian Nedewedzo believes that until the prophet, Johanna Masowe, was raised up in 1932, Africa had been neglected by God, because of the curse of Ham, and even Noah had refused to take them on board:

> Throughout the whole of Africa and among all African peoples, the light has not shone in Africa right from the time of Adam onwards and we never had a prophet of our own. When Noah came, he left Africans outside his ark. Our forefather, Ham, was cursed by Noah so that he might become the slave of slaves. . . . When Jesus came, he was asked why he had come and he said that he had come for the lost sheep of Israel. The race of Ham was neglected once again, and so, it did not obey the commandments. . . . In 1932 the word of God came and made it clear that it had come to the race of Ham. We received this word with great joy, because we knew that God had begun to visit the people of Africa.[47]

If twentieth-century Western technology has signally failed to provide answers that satisfy current environmental concerns, in the next century people of goodwill will no doubt increasingly turn to Africa for the Word of Wisdom, which is even more needed today than it was in 1958 when Bishop John V. Taylor wrote:

> The spiritual sickness of the West, which reveals itself in the divorce of the sacred from the secular, of the cerebral from the instinctive, and in the loneliness and homelessness of individualism may be healed through a recovery of the wisdom which Africa has not yet thrown away. The world Church awaits something new out of Africa.[48]

Remembering that African Christianity predates European Christianity, it is clear that African Christians have as much right to pass judgement on foreign churches and their theology as white missionaries ever had to disparage African traditional beliefs and practices. And Jesus warned us:

> On Judgement Day the Queen of Sheba will stand up and accuse the people of today, because she travelled all the way from her country to listen to King Solomon's wise teaching; and I tell you there is something here greater than Solomon.[49]

Afterword by Mercy Amba Oduyoye

I am fascinated by the naming of Africa as Sheba, a wise woman. One who judged Solomon to be wise can surely guide us to the habitation of wisdom. Though the image of the continent beyond her shores is often negative, the myths and legends of the continent sport many wise men and women, a proud people whose memory Mandela identifies as what asserts itself to give us hope. Africa's hope for life is being offered to the global community through this anthology. Myths and legends have preserved for us the memory of wise women who led their peoples out of troubles into life-enhancing situations.

The Word of Wisdom highlights the ecological aspects of the wisdom of Africa and brings to life Isaiah's saying that the stone the builders rejected has become the cornerstone. The moral values, spirituality and religion of Africa that were once disparaged as primitive paganism are being recognized as the core of ecological sanity. Being an anthology it challenges all to read about Africa and to do so from its beginnings found in the papyri and parchments of antiquity as well as told in oral literature.

Armed with perspicacity and wit, Shelagh Ranger has wandered through some fifty-eight books to select excerpts on animals and nature that capture African religious thought. The anthology introduces students of theology to Africa's traditional wisdom regarding God's creation and the relationship that human beings have, or should have with other animals. The variety is impressive, some are serious, some are playful, but all are deep and thought provoking. The myths, stories and legends provide a good example of learning through play as from tales. We learn of African Christianity which pre-dates European Christianity and of African Islam that predates its establishment in Mecca. The two are therefore no less religions of Africa than the primal Religions they have sought to transcend and to replace. The African Jewish heritage is acknowledged not only through Ethiopia, but in the fact that there have been Jewish settlements in Africa, that have left a mark, for example, in Elephantine.

We therefore have the benefit of the wisdom of African Judaism, Coptic and Ethiopian Christianity, Christianity of the African coast of the Mediterranean sea (North Africa), African Islam and the Cosmic Religions of Africa. All these contribute to the spinning of threads for theology that can be woven from nature, the earth, mountains, rivers, animals, plants as living entities and their interaction with human beings.

The book reads like other delightful animal stories with moral overtones for human beings. It is not easy to forget that 'the tameness of lion and tigers can never be trusted.' I love the story of the co-operation of the honey bird and human beings to 'steal' honey and wax from bees. The stories highlight the wisdom of animals in seeking only what is life-sustaining.

The author reminds us that the spirits among whom we live are but the other half of Eve's children hiding from being counted. These spirits and angelic powers as in Islam are concerned for the health of the ecology for the sake of all God's creatures on this planet. Hence both animals and the creatures of the spirit world convey wisdom to humanity.

Ancestral spirits, an aspect of African wisdom that has been most misunderstood, are clearly presented here. Ancestral spirits are the spirits of those who once lived on earth in bodies; they are still human. With them, whether they dwell in the forests, in ponds and rivers, or in the sky, a close relation is kept by all living beings. Indeed they can take the form of other beings in their attempt to communicate with the living. Ancestral spirits are not divinities. In African languages the supreme 'God' is a personal name and does not take the plural, 'gods'. These spirits are believed to have a passion for law and order, the protection of land and the maintenance of ecological harmony.

As we read what Africans have written about Africa, we are confronted with a theology of life, a theology bequeathed to us in the wisdom of Africa, a theology that calls for a re-reading of the anthropocentric, indeed androcentric theology that has passed for two thousand years as the norm in the Western world. Ranger challenges us to intensify our efforts at understanding other primal/cosmic religions and most urgently to learn to be humble about Western Christianity's contribution to the human quest and to seek the spirituality that will enable us to live in harmony with whom we share one eco-system.

Mercy Amba Oduyoye

GLOSSARY

Abuna: The metropolitan head of the Ethiopian Orthodox Church, who was appointed by the Patriarch of Alexandria from the fourth century until 1941 CE.

Abyssinia: (Arabic *Habesha*, mixed) The historic Christian kingdom of the highlands of **Ethiopia**, whose peoples used the **Semitic** languages, Tigrina, **Ge'ez** and **Amharic**.

Allah: Arabic name of God the Creator.

Amhara: The people of the **Ethiopian** highlands, who are both **Semitic** and Christian.

Amharic: The modern language of **Ethiopia**, originally a **Semitic** language introduced by the **Sabaeans**.

Amharisation: The attempt by the Emperor Haille Selassie to impose **Amharic** as the national language and **Orthodox** Christianity as the national religion of **Ethiopia**.

Anglicanism: Worldwide extension of the Church of England, owing a broad allegiance to the **Diocese** of Canterbury, and combining Catholic tradition and structure with some Protestant theology.

Anthropocentrism: (Gr. *anthropos*, man) The belief that humankind is the most important species on earth, with the right to rule over all others.

Anthropomorphic, Anthropomorphism: (Gr. *anthropos*, man, *morphe*, form) The attribution of human characteristics or behaviour to a god, animal, or object.

Apocalypse, Apocalyptic: (Gr. *apokálupsis,* uncover, disclose) A revelation of the workings of the cosmos, including the regions where sinners are punished and the righteous rewarded; **Israel**'s history down to the cataclysmic end-time, in which evil is finally destroyed. In the O.T. the most famous is the Book of Daniel, and in the N.T. the Revelation of St. John the Divine. Others in the **pseudepigraphia** are *Ethiopian Enoch, Apocalypse of Abraham,* and *Apocalypse of Zephaniah.*

Apocrypha: (Gr. *apokrupto*, hide away) The Apocrypha consists of works included in the **Septuagint** for which the Hebrew originals were lost, notably the *Odes, Psalms of Solomon,* and the books of *Esdras.* Works not included in the Hebrew Bible were regarded as apocryphal or were accepted as **deuterocanonical** by the Church. Early Christian gospels, acts and letters, not included in the **N.T. Canon** were regarded as apocryphal and with-held from general circulation.

Apostle: (Gr. *apostolos*, messenger) A missionary or pioneering supporter of an idea or cause. Jesus Christ chose twelve apostles, to whom he gave authority to lead the Church and, some believe, to appoint **bishops** as their successors. The apostolic succession is an essential teaching of the Roman Catholic Church denied by most Protestants.

Arian, Arianism: A Christian **heresy** preached by the Alexandrian presbyter Arius (died 336 CE), denying the full divinity of Jesus Christ and teaching that as 'Son of God' he was subordinate to God the Father, by whom he had been created before the beginning of time.

Ark: (Latin *arca,* box, chest) The floating vessel built by the **patriarch** Noah to rescue two of every species on earth at the time of the Flood (Gen. 6:14ff).

Ark of the Covenant: A rectangular chest built by Moses at God's command and plated with gold, in which the stone tablets of the Law (**Decalogue**) were carried from Mount Sinai to the land of Canaan, and later enshrined in the Temple of Solomon at Jerusalem. From thence Ethiopians believe it was transported to Aksum.

Aryan: A name once used by ethnographers and philologists for the parent stock of the Indo-European family of nations and languages, including Sanskrit, Zend, Latin, Greek, Celtic, Persian, Hindu, and most European languages. Used by the German **Nazi** party to denote any people or thing that was not **Semite**.

Assegai (Portuguese *azagaia,* a spear) A wooden spear or lance, usually pointed with iron, used in many parts of Africa.

Avatar: (Sanscrit word meaning descent) The **incarnation** of a deity in a visible form, which may be human or animal.

Babylon: An ancient city in Mesopotamia (located near Baghdad in present day Iraq), where the Tower of Babel is thought to have been built (*Gen.* 11:1-9). Nowadays amongst Rastafarians and others in the African **diaspora** the dominant white culture is so called.

Babylonian Captivity: The period (*ca.* 586 – 539 BCE) from the capture of Jerusalem by Nebuchadnezzar, when those deported became **exiles** in **Babylon,** until their return to Jerusalem after the conquest by Cyrus. During this **exile** the **rabbis** compiled the Babylonian **Talmud.**

Bantu: A term originally used to denote people of central and southern Africa whose languages are closely related yet distinctly different from those of West African **Negro** peoples or of the Central African **Pygmy**. The terms 'Bantu', 'Negro' and 'Pygmy' are now regarded as pejorative and no longer used by ethnographers.

Baqt: A treaty made in 652 CE following the Arab invasion of Christian Nubia, which lasted for 500 years, whereby the kingdom of Makuria undertook to deliver 360 slaves a year in return for Egyptian products.

Bilquis: Arabic name of the Queen of Sheba, known in **Ethiopia** as *Makeda.*

Bishop: (Gr. *episcopos,* overseer) The senior pastor within a Christian congregation: probably originally indistinguishable from an elder or presbyter (priest). Within the first hundred years of Christianity bishops emerged as the chief ministers to govern a **diocese** and to ordain other ministers.

Bull: (Latin *bulla,* seal) In Western **Christendom,** a solemn papal document or mandate announcing a binding decision made in Rome, and carrying the formal seal of a **Pope**.

Bushmen/Bushmenoid: Relating to the aboriginal peoples of southern Africa and their languages (nowadays usually referred to as San).

Byzantine: Another name for the Bezant, from Byzantium, the Greek city on the Bosphorous where Constantine established the new capital of the Roman empire in 330 CE, which then became known as Constantinople. The Byzantine Empire lasted from the separation of the eastern and western Roman Empires on the death of Theodosius in 395 CE until 1453 when Constantinople was captured by the Turks and renamed Istanbul.

Caliph: (Arabic *Khalifa*) The lieutenant of Muhammad and his successor; thus the head of all **Muslims**.

Caliphate: The office of **Caliph**.

Calvinist: A follower of John Calvin (1509-1564 CE), who taught the total depravity of mankind, the predestination of selected individuals for salvation through Christ, and the sole authority of Scripture.

Canon: (Gr. *kan ̄on*, rule) A rule of faith, particularly a collection or list of sacred books accepted as genuine.

Capuchin: (Italian *cappucino*, cowl or hood) A friar of the strict group of **Franciscans** that arose about 1520 CE, who wore the *capuce* or pointed cowl. The Capuchin became a separate order in the Roman Catholic Church *ca.* 1619 CE.

Cardinal: (Latin *cardo,* a hinge) At first any priest attached to a major church, later restricted to the parish clergy of Rome, local bishops and the district **Deacons** of Rome. Since 1179 CE cardinals have been the exclusive electors of a new Roman **Pontiff**.

Cartesian: The philosophical system of René Descartes (1596-1650 CE) based on the axiom *cogito ergo sum,* 'I think, therefore I am'. He taught that thought must proceed from the soul, and therefore human beings are not wholly material.

Caucasian: Properly a person who lives in the Caucasus. The white or European race was so called by Blumenfeld (1752-1840 CE).

Celt, Celtic: The peoples and languages of that branch of the **Aryan** family which includes the Irish, Manx, Welsh, Cornish, Breton, and Scottish Gaels. Applied by ancient Greeks and Romans to peoples of western Europe generally.

Chaceldonian: Relating to the General **Council** of Chalcedon, which in 451CE attempted to settle the dispute that had arisen after the Council of Ephesus (431CE) concerning the two natures of Christ, human and divine. Rome accepted the Chalcedonian teaching as the definitive expression of the Christian faith, but many Eastern Churches, who became known as **Monophysite**, persisted with a one-nature theology.

Cherub, pl. Cherubim: (Hebrew *krub,* pl. *krubim,* angel) One of the orders of the celestial hierarchy, gifted with knowledge, and often depicted in Christian art as a beautiful winged child. The word corresponds to the Babylonian *Karibu,* half-human, half-animal tutelary deities guarding temples and palaces. Moses was commanded by God to make two golden cherubim to guard the **Ark of the Covenant** (Gen. 25:18-22).

Chimurenga: A Shona word for the liberation war in Zimbabwe.

Christendom: All Christian countries generally; formerly also the state or condition of being a Christian.

Christology: The branch of theology relating to Jesus Christ.

Copt, Coptic: (Gr. *Aigyptos,* Arabic *Qibt*) Originally meaning the people and language of Egypt; nowadays the Christian **Monophysite** descendants of the ancient Egyptians whose **patriarchal see** of Alexandria also retained nominal jurisdiction over the Ethiopian Orthodox Church. Coptic had ceased to be a living language by the sixteenth century but is still used in the liturgy.

Council: A solemn assembly of **Bishops** called to determine doctrine or discipline for the Christian Church.

Creation: That which is created by God, animate or inanimate, human or non-human, anywhere in the universe. Thus all the natural world.

Crusades: (from Latin *crux,* a cross) A name derived from the cross which Crusaders wore on their dress, for wars undertaken by Christians in the late Middle Ages (between 1095 and 1272 CE) to secure the right of pilgrims to visit the Holy Sepulchre in Jerusalem and to recover the **Holy Land** from **Muslims** conquerors.

Cush (or Kush): Son of Ham and father of Nimrod (Gen. 10:6-12). Biblical name of an African nation, identified with **Ethiopia** or Nubia. (Isaiah 11:11, 18:1, Jeremiah 46:9). Cushitic (a branch of Afroasiatic) languages are spoken in Ethiopia.

Däbtära, Debeterea: (Ethiopic) A cantor in the Ethiopian Orthodox Church, believed to be descended from those who accompanied Menelik, the son of the King Solomon, when he returned to **Ethiopia**, carrying the Ark of the Covenant. Their hereditary role parallels that of a Levite in ancient **Israel**; as trained musicians and administrators, däbtäras are allowed to marry, occupying an intermediate position between ordained clergy and laymen.

Deacon: (Gr. *diakonia*, service, *diakonos*, a servant) An ordained Christian minister who is not (or not yet) a priest, originally appointed in the early church for a secular service such as distributing alms. (*Acts* 6: 2-6)

Decalogue: (Gr. *deka*, ten; *logos*, word) The Ten Commandments given to Moses.

Deist, Deism: (from Latin *deus,* god) One who acknowledges the existence of God the Creator and immutable laws of nature but rejects revealed religion.

Dervish : (Arabic *darwish,* Turkish *dervis,* Persian *darv + š,* poor) A Muslim mendicant ascetic; member of a Sufi religious fraternity.

Deuterocanonical: (from Gr. *deuteros,* second) Relating to a secondary **canon** of scripture, works included in the **Septuagint** but not found in the Hebrew Bible, such as *The Book of Wisdom* (Wisdom of Solomon), *Ecclesiasticus* (Wisdom of Sirach), *Baruch, Judith, Tobit* and parts of *Daniel.*

Diaspora: (Gr. *diaspeirein,* to disperse) The dispersion of the **Jews** beyond Israel or those in **exile** from Palestine. A term later applied to the dispersed people of African descent in the Americas and other parts of the world.

Diocese: (Gr. *diok–sis,* administration; Latin *diocesis,* governor's jurisdiction) District governed by a **Bishop**.

Ebionites: (Hebrew *ebion,* poor). In the early Church the name given to the ultra-**Jewish** Christians, many of whom rejected the Virgin Birth and who kept the **Jewish** sabbath as well as the Lord's Day (Sunday). From the second century, they called themselves the Poor Men.

Ecology: (Gr. *ökologie,* from *oikos,* house) Study of the relations of plants and animals within their habitat.

Eid El-Adha: (Arabic) **Muslims** celebration, re-enacting Abraham's offer to sacrifice his son, held as part of the **Hajj** pilgrimage.

Eid El-Fitr: (Arabic) **Muslims** celebration at the end of **Ramadan**.

Epistemology: (Gr. *epistém–,* knowledge) The theory of knowledge, especially with regard to its methods, validity and scope.

Ethiopia: Originally a wide area, including the source of the Nile, known to classical Greece as the 'land of the blacks'; a Christian empire formerly known as

Abyssinia, comprising a mosaic of languages and peoples; the modern state founded by Emperor Menelik II in the nineteenth century.

Ethiopic: The archaic **Ge'ez** (*GY'Yz*) language, still used in the **Ethiopian** Orthodox Church.

Exile: The state of being barred from one's native country. A term used to refer particularly to the **Babylonian Captivity.**

Falalsha:Ethiopian people of Agaw stock living to the north of Lake Tana, who are **Jews** but know no religious prescriptions outside the **Pentateuch.** The **Torah** they use is written not in **Hebrew** but in **Ge'ez** (*GY'Yz*), and their social life has much in common with that of their Christian neighbours.

Fatwa: (Arabic *fatw*) The formal opinion of a canon lawyer (*mufti*).

Franciscan: Follower of St Francis of Assisi (1182-1226). A religious order founded in 1209 CE, later divided into three: the Friars Minor, the Friars Minor Conventual and the Friars Minor **Capuchin.**

Ge'ez: (*GY'Yz*) The archaic language of **Ethiopia**, which has a Sabaean base with infusions of Greek, Syriac and Hebrew, otherwise known as **Ethiopic.**

Gemara: (Aramaic *gmr,* completion) A rabbinical commentary on the **Mishnah**, forming the second part of the **Talmud.**

Gentile: (Latin *gentilis,* of a family or nation) A term used in the Bible for nations other than **Israel**; thus **Pagan** or not **Jewish.**

Gnostic: (Gr. *gnosis*, knowledge of spiritual mysteries, from *gignoskeia*, to know) A term used from the second century onwards for those Christians who made a sharp distinction between spirit and matter, and claimed that only spirit can be redeemed.

Gospel: (Old English *godspel,* from *god,* good, *spel,* news, a story) The revelation of the life and teaching of Jesus Christ, as recorded in the first four books of the N.T.

Gregorian Calendar : A modification of the Julian calendar introduced in 1582 CE by Pope Gregory XIII. At first adopted only by Roman Catholic countries, it was not used in Great Britain until 1752 CE. The **Coptic** and **Ethiopian** Churches still retain their own calendars.

Hadith: (Arabic) Traditions of **Islam.**

Haggada: A genre of Jewish literature embracing whatever is excluded from the **Halakah**, appealing primarily to the conscience and the imagination, but unenforceable in a court of law.

Hajj (or Hadj): The annual **Muslim** pilgrimage to Mecca.

Hajji (or Hadji): Title given to one who has made the **Hajj.**

Halakah: The rules and rituals of **Judaism**; obligations and rights enforceable in civil society with appropriate sanctions.

Heathen: (Old English *haethen,* inhabiting open country, savage) A person lacking culture, a **Pagan** or infidel.

Hebrew: (Aramaic *'ibray,* Hebrew *'ibri,* one from the other side of the river; Arabic *habiru, 'apiru,* a nomad) Nomadic people of the Arabian peninsula, who eventually settled in Canaan, speaking a **Semitic** language akin to Arabic, which is today the liturgical language of **Judaism.**

Hebrew Bible: A compilation of sacred scriptures made by the Academy at Jimna fifty years after the destruction of the Temple in 70 CE, consisting of the **Pentateuch**, the Prophets and the Writings.

Hellenes: (Gr. *Hellenes*) From Hellen, son of Deucalion and Pyrrha, their legendary ancestor, the name has descended to the modern Greeks, whose sovereign is not 'King of Greece', but 'King of the Hellenes'. The ancient Greeks called their country *Hellas*; Romans called it *Graecia*. The name *Hellenes* was also used to refer to Greek speaking Jews, dwelling among the pagans, or to men of pagan origin converted to Judaism, but not circumcised. (*Jn.* 7:35; 12: 20; *Acts* 14: 1; 17: 4; 18: 4).

Hellenization: The influence of the Greek language and culture in North Africa and other parts of the Mediterranean from the time of Alexander the Great's conquest of Egypt (*ca.* 332 BCE).

Heresy: (Gr. *hairesis*, Latin *haeresis*, choice or thing chosen) A contrary opinion; the formal denial of **Orthodox** or Roman Catholic doctrine, formerly incurring severe legal penalties.

Hermetic Wisdom: The art or science of alchemy; so called from its hypothetical founder Hermes Trismegistus (the Thrice Greatest Hermes), the name given by the Neo-platonists to the Egyptian god Thoth. Forty-two books believed to have been written by Hermes Trismegistus, include propositions that the world was made out of fluid; that the soul is the union of light and life; that nothing is destructible; that the soul transmigrates; and that suffering is the result of motion.

Hieroglyphs: (Gr. *hieros*, holy; *glyph*, what is carved) The ancient Egyptian picture characters or symbols originally used in writing on stone.

Hijira (or Hegira): (Arabic *hijrah*, flight) The prophet's flight to Medina from Mecca. The Muhammadan era dates from this year, 622 CE.

Holy Land: Christians call Palestine the Holy Land, because it was the scene of Christ's birth, ministry, and death. **Muslims** call Mecca the Holy Land, because Mohammed was born there, and it is the site of the **Ka'ba**.

Holy Sepulchre: The cave in Jerusalem where Jesus Christ was entombed, said to have been found by St. Helena, mother of the emperor Constantine the Great.

Hyksos: Northern invaders of Egypt who ruled from 1640 until 1530 BCE, when they were overthrown by Thebans from the South and fled back to Canaan.

Ibn: (Arabic, son of) A term corresponding to Hebrew, *ben*.

Iconoclasm: (Gr. *eikōn*, image, *klân*, break). A term meaning 'image-breaking': applied especially to the reaction against religious images in the Eastern **Orthodox** Church in the seventh and eighth centuries CE.

Imam: (Arabic *imm*.leader) Leader of prayers in the mosque; the spiritual head of **Muslims**.

Incarnation: (Latin *carnis*, flesh) Embodiment of person, spirit, quality, etc. The Christian doctrine that in the man Jesus of Nazareth, the second person of the Trinity, God himself, took flesh and became a human being.

Indulgence: (Latin *indulgere*) A favour granted. In the Roman Catholic Church, the remission of the temporal punishment due for sins of which the guilt has been forgiven in the sacrament of Penance. An indulgence granted by the **Pope** may be plenary (i.e. entire, unqualified) or partial.

Injil: Arabic word for **Gospel** (from Greek, *evangel*, and Ethiopic, *Wangel*) in widespread use before Muhammad's time.

Islam: (Arabic *'islam* from *'aslama*, to submit, to surrender — i.e. to God). The **Muslim** religion that teaches that there is only one God and that Muhammad is his prophet; the **Muslim** world.

Israel: A nomadic tribe first recorded in the thirteenth century BCE. The **Patriarch** Jacob (father of Judah) was given this name by God after wrestling with an angel (Gen. 32:28-29). The northern kingdom of Israel split away from the kingdom of Judah after the death of Solomon in 931 BCE. An independent state created by **Zionists** in Palestine in 1948 CE took the name Israel.

Jacobite: Monophysite follower of Jacob Baradai, who rejected the 'orthodox' faith as defined at Chalcedon.

Jesuit: Member of the Roman Catholic Society of Jesus, founded by Ignatius Loyola (1491-1556 CE) to combat the Protestant Reformation and to propagate the Christian faith among the **Heathen**.

Jew, Jewish: A term first used during the **Babylonian Exile** to describe people of the southern kingdom of Judah. After the **Exile** it became the common name for the descendants of Jacob and for followers of the Mosaic religion.

Jewry: The **Jewish** people; a term applied to the **Jews'** quarter or ghetto in medieval European cities.

Jihad: (Arabic) A holy war proclaimed against unbelievers or the enemies of **Islam**.

Jinnee, pl. Jinn: (Arabic) Angels or demons of Arabian mythology, created two thousand years before Adam and Eve, who can assume the forms of animals or human beings. The evil *jinn* are hideously ugly, but the good are singularly beautiful.

Jubilee: (from Hebrew *Yobel*, a ram's horn trumpet; Latin *jubilare*, to shout for joy) According to the **Mosaic Law**, every seventh year is to be kept as a sabbath rest, and the land allowed to lie fallow. The fiftieth year after seven weeks of years (7 times 7 years) is celebrated as a jubilee, when everyone must return to their ancestral home (Lv. 25). In the Roman Catholic Church a year during which the **Pope** grants plenary **Indulgences**, when the Holy Door into St Peter's basilica is opened.

Judaism: The monotheistic religion of the **Jews**, based on the Old Testament and the **Talmud**.

Ka'ba, Kaaba: (Arabic *al-ka'ba*, the square house). The sacred building in Mecca, containing the black stone, believed to have been brought there by Adam from Paradise, which **Muslims** face when they pray, and the focus of the **Hajj**. It is believed to be the centre of the universe and the point on earth nearest to God.

Koran: (Arabic *Qur'an, kur'an*, recitation). The **Muslims'** sacred book, containing revelations communicated to the prophet by an angel. It was recited by the prophet to his followers and written down in Arabic after his death in the seventh century CE. It is divided into 114 chapters or **Surah**.

Kush: See **Cush**.

Logos: (Gr., *logos*, word or speech) The Word of God, believed by Christians to be the second person of the Trinity prior to the **incarnation** and the agent of **creation**. (Jn. 1:1)

Maghrib, Maghreb: Arabic name for the Western area of North Africa, which today includes Tunisia, Morocco and Algeria. *Maghreb al'aqsa* means the far West.

Mahdi: (Arabic word meaning Saviour or the Guided One) The hidden **Imam**, whom **Muslims** await to restore justice and righteousness in the world.

Makeda: The **Ethiopic** name of the Queen of Sheba (Saba), wife of King Solomon.

Maronites: Eastern Christians, mainly in Lebanon, who are in communion with Rome but retain their own liturgy, dating back to the seventh century. They were originally followers of Maro, an anchorite living near Antioch.

Maulidi: (Swahili from Arabic, *mawlid*) Poem recital in honour of the Prophet's birthday.

Mawlad El-Nabi: (Arabic *Mawlid an-Nabi*) The **Muslim** celebration of the prophet's birthday, when **Maulidi** and **Qasida** are sung.

Melchite (or Melkite): (Syrian, *malka*, king) Hellenized Greek-speaking **Copts** who accepted the Byzantine imperial **Orthodoxy** defined at Chalcedon, as opposed to **Jacobites** who adhered to the **Monophysite** doctrine.

Metaphysics: (Gr. *meta*, after, *phusis*, nature) A name posthumusly given to Aristotle's *First Philosophy*, which he wrote after his *Physics*. The science of metaphysics deals with the first principles of existence: the philosophy which establishes truth by abstract reason. At various times the whole range of philosophical inquiry has been classed as metaphysics, and the contrast between philosophy and science is comparatively modern.

Methodist: (Gr. *méthodos*, pursuit of knowledge) One who follows a certain method; member of the Holy Club established at Oxford in 1729; member of religious bodies originating in this. A Christian denomination originating in the 18th-century evangelistic movement of Charles and John Wesley.

Midrash, pl. **Midrashim:** (from Hebrew root *midhrs,* to investigate). Rabbinical commentary on, or exposition of, the Old Testament writings preached in synagogues. Midrashim often include popular folk tales.

Mishnah: (Hebrew *mišnh,* teaching by repetition) A collection of exegetical material written about 220 CE, embodying the oral tradition of Jewish law and forming part of the **Talmud.**

Monophysite: (Gr. *monos*, alone or single, *phusis*, nature) The doctrine that in Jesus Christ there is only one nature, which is divine, or an amalgam of divine and human exactly corresponding to neither. Since the Council of **Chanceldon**, Roman Catholic and **Orthodox** Christianity has maintained that Jesus Christ was a person composed of *two* natures, human and divine, in whom these two natures were united but not confused. The **Coptic** and **Ethiopian Orthodox** Churches adhere to the Monophysite doctrine.

Mosaic Law: The laws given to Moses and recorded in the **Pentateuch**, including the Ten Commandments.

Muslim (Moslem): (from Arabic *salama*, submit to God, *aslama*, to be safe, or at rest) A follower of the prophet Muhammad, whose words are recorded in the **Koran**.

Nazi: The shortened form of the German *National-Sozialist* party of Adolf Hitler.

Negro: (Latin *niger*, black). An African; in particular West African people distinguishable by their language from the **Bantu** or the **Pygmy**.

Nicene Creed: A statement of orthodox Christian beliefs issued in 325 CE by the Council of Nicaea, at which only the Western churches were represented. It added *Filioque* (and the Son) to the Creed, which was not accepted by the Eastern churches.

Nubia: An ancient African kingdom on the upper Nile (present day Sudan), supplying Egypt with slaves, mercenaries and gold. Its capital city, Kerma, later moved to Napata and finally Meroe, where pyramids bore inscriptions in the Meroitic language. There were Christian kingdoms in Nubia for over a thousand years.

Oracy: (from Latin *oris*, by mouth or speech) The ability to express oneself fluently and grammatically in speech, as opposed to literacy, the ability to read and write.

Original Sin: The sin of Adam and Eve in the Garden of Eden (Gen. 2). The Christian doctrine that all human beings inherit the guilt incurred by our first parents and therefore are, before baptism, essentially corrupt in nature.

Orthodox: (Gr. *orthos,* correct, *doxa,* opinion) Holding correct or accepted opinions, especially on religious doctrine, in harmony with what is authoritatively established. The Eastern autocephalous churches are referred to as Orthodox to distinguish them from the Roman Catholic Church, with which they are not in communion.

Pagan: (Latin *paganus,* civilian, rustic villager) A person holding religious beliefs other than those of the main world religions; a **Heathen** or non-Christian.

Papyrus, pl. Papyri: (Gr. *pápuros,* a reed or rush*)* The giant water reed from which the Egyptians manufactured a material for writing on. Hence the written scrolls of ancient Egyptians.

Paradise: The Greeks borrowed this word from the Persians, among whom it denotes the enclosed gardens and extensive parks of Persian kings. The **Septuagint** translators adopted it for the garden of Eden, and early Christian writers applied it to heaven, the abode of the blessed dead.

Patriarch: (Gr. *patria,* family; *archein,* to rule). The head of a tribe or family; a term applied to Abraham, Isaac and the twelve sons of Jacob. In the early Christian Church the chief **Bishops** were called Patriarchs, as they are today in the Eastern **Orthodox** churches.

Patriarchite: The area ruled over by a Christian **Patriarch**.

Pentateuch: (Gr. *penta,* five; *teuchos,* a tool, book) The first five books of the **Hebrew** Bible, attributed to Moses.

Pharoah: The 'great house' or ruler of ancient Egypt. The term was first used for the King of Egypt during the eighteenth dynasty with Akhnaton.

Platonism: The philosophy of Plato (*ca.* 428-348 BCE), pupil of Socrates, and founder of the Athenian Academy, characterized by the doctrine of pre-existing eternal ideas. Platonists teach the immortality of the soul, the dependence of virtue upon discipline, and the trustworthiness of cognition.

Pontiff: (Latin *pons, pontis,* a bridge) One who had charge of the bridges, under the care of the principal college of priests in ancient Rome. A term formerly applied to any Christian **Bishop** but now to the Bishop of Rome, who is known as the Supreme Pontiff.

Pope: (Gr. *pappas,* the infants' word for father). Originally the name for any **Bishop**, a usage continued in Eastern **Orthodox** churches where **Patriarchs** and even parish priests are so called; in the Roman Catholic Church now only used for the **Bishop** of Rome.

Prester John: In Medieval legend a Christian emperor of Asia, described in Marco Polo's *Travels* as lord of the **Tartars**. From the fourteenth century he was identified with the Emperor of **Abyssinia**.

Promised Land: Canaan on the eastern shore of the Mediterranean; so called because God promised Abraham, Isaac, Jacob and Moses that their descendants should possess it. (Gen. 12:1-7; Deut. 1:8 and 4:37-38)

Protoevangelism: (Gr. *protos,* first, *euaggélion,* good news) The first proclamation of the Gospel of Jesus Christ, prior to the writings of the four Evangelists, Matthew, Mark, Luke and John.

Pseudepigraphia: (Gr. *pseudes,* false, *graphein,* to write) Old Testament manuscripts that were included in neither the **Hebrew** Bible nor in the Christian Bible and **Apocrypha.** Amongst them are **Apocalypses,** testaments (the last words of a prophet or patriarch), psalms, prayers, narratives and philosophical writings.

Pygmy: (Gr. *pugme,* length from elbow to knuckles, also the fist). Small people in Central Africa, distinct from the **Negro** and the **Bantu.**

Qasida: The ancient praise poems from Mali, Nigeria, Sudan, Tanzania and Ethiopia, composed by **Sufi** brotherhoods and chanted at **Mawlad El-Nabi.**

Qolle: (*GY'Yz*) The spirits of particular places in Ethiopia.

Qur'an: See **Koran.**

Rabbi: (Hebrew *rabbi,* my master) **Jewish** doctor of the law, particularly one authorized by ordination to perform ritual and other functions.

Rabbinical: Pertaining to the **Judaism** that developed in the **diaspora** after the destruction of the second Temple (70 CE), when the synagogue became the centre of worship.

Ramadan: (Arabic *ramadn,* hot month) The annual thirty-day fast held in the ninth month of the **Muslim** lunar calendar.

Rastafarians: Jamaican religious sect named after Ras Tafari, the Emperor Hailé Selassie (b. 1892 CE); they regard themselves as the true **Jew**s, whose original home is Ethiopia, the **Promised Land** to which they hope to return.

Rasul: (Arabic) Messenger or apostle. A term used in the **Koran** to refer to Jesus as well as to Muhammad.

Renaissance: (Latin *renascere,* rebirth) A term originally applied to the revival of learning in fourtheenth and fifteenth-century Europe, marked by a rediscovery of the classics, the questioning of religious dogmas, scientific discoveries, developments in art and literature, and the emancipation of the human intellect. More recently, a term applied to post-colonial African societies' rediscovery of their past culture.

Saba: A royal city in Africa, later named Meroe, according to Josephus.

Sabaean: Relating to: the descendants of Cush's son, Seba (*Gen.* 10:7); the kingdom of Saba (Sheba); the ancient **Semitic** language and culture of South West Arabia and East Africa.

Saracens: (Gr. *Sarakenos,* possibly from Arabic *sharqui,* an 'oriental'). The name given by the Greeks and Romans to the nomadic tribes of the Syro-Arabian desert; applied by mediaeval writers to all infidel nations who opposed the **Crusades.**

Scholastic, Scholasticism: (Latin *scholasticus,* learned, studious) The philosophy and doctrines of mediaeval Schoolmen, concerned with applying Aristotelian logic to Christian theology.

See: (Latin *sedes*) The seat or throne of a **Bishop,** hence the town where the bishop's cathedral is located and from which he takes his title; to be distinguished from **Diocese,** the territory over which he has jurisdiction.

Semite, Semitic: Pertaining to the descendants of Shem, the eldest son of Noah (Gen. 10: 22-32). Among Semitic languages are Aramaic, Syriac, Arabic, **Hebrew,** Samaritan, **Sabaean, Ethiopic,** and old Phoenician.

Septuagint: (Lat. *septuaginta,* seventy) The most important Greek version of the Old Testament and **apocrypha,** believed to have been translated from **Hebrew**

Scriptures in the third century BCE by 72 learned **Jews** who completed the task in 72 days. It is more probably the work of Jewish scholars at Alexandria working over a long period of time. Septuagint is commonly abbreviated as LXX.

Shaman: (German *shamane,* Russian *shaman,* from Tungus *šaman*) Originally a Slavonic word for the priest of a Siberian cult, who propitiates the good and evil spirits by which the world is governed. A term now widely used by ethnographers in Africa for anyone who practices sorcery.

Shari'ah: Arabic word for the law of **Islam,** which governs all human activities and recognizes no distinction between the sacred and the profane.

Shia: (Arabic *Shi'ah*) **Muslims** who revere the descendants of Muhammad's daughter, Fatima, and her husband, Ali, as the true heirs to the **caliphate.** They believe that there is an infallible **imam** in every age to whom God entrusts guidance of the faithful. He possesses superhuman qualities which descend to him from the first prophet, Adam, through the last prophet, Mohammed. Shia await the coming of the **mahdi.**

Stella, pl. Stelae: (from Gr. *stele,* standing block) An upright slab or pillar of stone bearing a sculptured design or inscription. Those at Aksum in **Ethiopia** are nearly two thousand years old.

Stoic: (Gr. *stoa,* a porch) The school of philosophers founded by Zeno (*c.* 308 BCE) who gave his lectures in the *Stoa poikile* (painted colonnade) in the agora of Athens. Stoics taught that virtue is the highest good, and that the passions and carnal appetites should be rigidly subdued.

Sufi: (Arabic *sufi,* woollen, *suf,* wool). A **Muslim** philosopher and mystic is so called from the rough woollen garment associated with ascetics. Sufis follow a non-violent gnostic Path to ascend to God.

Sunni: (Arabic *sunna,* custom, divine law) **Muslim**s who follow one of four *madhhib* (schools or 'ways'): Hanifite, Mlikite, Shfi'ite and Hanbalite. Sunni elect their **imam** and are thought to be more democratic than the authoritarian **Shia.**

Sura, Surah: (Arabic *skrah*) A chapter or section of the **Koran.**

Swastika: (Sanskrit *svasti,* good fortune) A cross-shaped design used to ward off evil. A reversed version was adopted by Adolph Hitler as the **Nazi** party emblem.

Synagogue: (Gr. *sunagogé,* assembly or place of assembly) **Jewish** institution for worship, social life and the study of Judaism, which had its origins at the time of the **Babylonian Captivity.** Its symbols include the **Ark,** in which scrolls of the **Torah** are kept, the ever-burning lamp, and the Reading Desk.

Synod: (Latin *synodus,* Gr. *sunodos,* meeting, council) A local assembly of clergy under their bishop, or of a number of local bishops, possessing less authority than a General **Council.**

Tabernacle: (Latin *tabernaculum,* small tent) Tent containing the **Ark of the Covenant** carried by Moses and his followers in the wilderness. In the Roman Catholic Church a receptacle in which the Blessed Sacrament is reserved.

Tabot, pl. Tabotat: (GY'Yz *tabot, tabotat,* from Aramaic *t–bkt,* Hebrew *t–bh,* Ark) Noah's **Ark;** the Tablets of the Law, brought from Jerusalem in the **Ark of the Covenant** and now preserved at Aksum. Replicas, known as *tabotat,* are venerated in every Ethiopian church, much as the scrolls of the **Torah** are in a Jewish **synagogue.**

Talisman: (Arabic *cilsam,* Gr. *télesma,* mystery) A charm or magical figure or word, supposed to communicate to the wearer spiritual influence and protection.

Talmud: (Hebrew *talmûdh,* instruction) An abbreviation of Talmud **Torah**, the collection of Jewish civil and religious law, moral doctrine, and ritual founded on Scripture. It consists of the **Mishnah** with its commentary, the **Gemara**. There are two recensions: the Palestinian, or Jerusalem Talmud, produced in the fourth century CE; and the much longer Babylonian Talmud, completed at the end of the fifth century CE.

Targums: (Aramaic *targkm,* interpretation) Aramaic (Chaldean) translations of the Old Testament, made in Babylon and Palestine when **Hebrew** was ceasing to be the everyday speech of the **Jews**. They were transmitted orally; the oldest written Targum, that of Oneklos on the **Pentateuch**, is probably second century CE.

Torah: (Hebrew *tôrh,* instruction, doctrine, law). The **Pentateuch** which contains the **Mosaic Law**. The revealed will of God as contained in the **Hebrew** Bible.

Vatican: (Latin *Mons Vaticanus,* the hill of the *vaticinatores,* soothsayers) The centre of the Roman Catholic Church, recognized as a separate sovereign state with its own coinage in a Concordat made with Italy and signed by Mussolini in 1929 CE.

Vulgate: (Latin *editio vulgata,* public or common edition) The Latin translation of the Old and New Testament, made about 384-404 CE by St. Jerome. The first printed edition was the Mazarin Bible in 1456 CE.

Zion: (Hebrew *Tsiyon,* a hill). The holy hill of ancient Jerusalem; figuratively, the **Hebrew** theocracy; the chosen people; the Christian Church; the Heavenly Jerusalem or the kingdom of heaven. Ethiopians believe it is Aksum, where the **Ark of the Covenant** resides.

Zionism, Zionist: A movement for the establishment of a 'national home' for **Jews** in Palestine, as a result of which the independent state of **Israel** was established in 1948 CE.

Footnotes

Introduction and Historical Background

1. Darwin (1871/1891).
2. When John William Colenso, Anglican bishop of Natal, was persuaded by an African convert that the time-scale in Genesis could not be taken literally; in 1863 he was castigated as a heretic. See Guy (1983).
3. Midgley (1994), 129.
4. Campbell, (1988), 86.
5. Such as the Masowe Apostles, referred to in Section Six, Outside the Ark. See Dillon-Malone (1978).
6. Frye (1982), xviii.
7. Hall (1996), 213-215; and Deacon (1994), 249.
8. Rahner (1978), 163-4.
9. Midgley (1994), 117.
10. Tindal, *Christianity as Old as the Creation*, 11, 13. Cited in Pailin (1984), 41.
11. Baxter, *The Reasons of the Christian Religion* (London: R. White for Fran. Titon, 1667) cited in Pailin (1984) 154.
12. Idowu (1969), 9.
13. Kinoti (1997), 115-117.
14. Amba-Oduyoye (2001) 12.
15. Casson (1975), 122.
16. Iliffe (1995), 23.
17. See Lion of the South in Section Two.
18. Iliffe (1995), 27-28.
19. Asante (1990/1992), 77.
20. Iliffe (1995), 24.
21. Davidson (1994), 20.
22. Davidson (1994), 21-22.
23. Breasted [1912] (1959), xiii, xvii, 4, 88.
24. Bernal (1987), 130-134.
25. Mazrui (1986), 48.
26. Davidson (1994), 20.
27. Davidson (1994), 323-4.
28. Asante (1990/1992), 104.
29. Copenhaver (1992/1994/1995/1997), xiii-xv.
30. Mazrui (1986), 46.
31. Bernal (1987), 219-220.

32. Davies (1988), 99.
33. Gen. 47:11.
34. Hays (2003), 66. Also see Porter (2001), 62-65.
35. Gen. 49: 25-26; and Gen. 50.
36. Guillaume (1954) 2.
37. Exod. 2:19; Acts 7:22.
38. Freud (1939).
39. Exod. 12: 37-51.
40. Num. 12:1. Both the LXX and the Vulgate translate 'Cushite' as 'Ethiopian'.
    See Hays (2003), 73.
41. Hays (2003), 68, 82. See *Exod.* 6: 25 and *Num.* 25: 7-11.
42. Romer (1988), 55-56.
43. Barnavi (1992- 1998), 24.
44. See Louis F. Hartman, 'Daniel' in The *Jerome Biblical Commentary* (London
    & Dublin: Geoffrey Chapman, 1969/1970), 446-7.
45. Grierson and Munro-Hay (2000), 101-105.
46. Beckwith, Fisher and Hancock (1990), 49-52
47. Barnavi (1992-1998), 93, 259. He estimates that as many as 230,000 emigrated
    to the new state of Israel from Morocco alone.
48. Oded (2003).
49. Schultz and Meyer (2000).
50. 1 King*s* 10:1-13; 2 *Chron.* 9: 1-12.
51. Grierson & Munro Hay (1999), 196.
52. Surah 27 'The Ant' in Dawood (1956), 82-83.
53. Ibn' Arabi (1989/1991), 74.
54. E.g. Nicholas Clapp at the British Museum's Queen of Sheba Study Day, June
    2002.
55. Grierson & Munro-Hay (1999), 195 ff.
56. Alvares (1961), 462-463.
57. Mercier (1997)
58. Greenfield (1965) 41-43. Grierson & Munro-Hay (1999) 1-2, 223.
59. Hastings (1994) 17-21.
60. Baur (1994) 22.
61. Armstrong (1983), 159-163.
62. Porter (2001), 8.
63. Hastings (1994), 6-7.
64. Baur (1994) 24.
65. Acts 8:27-39.
66. Iliffe (1995) 40-42. See Christian Kingdoms below.
67. As delegates reported to the World Council of Churches meeting in Harare,
    December 1998.
68. O'Mahony (1994), 298-303.
69. Isichei (1995), 43. Talal (1998), 86-87.
70. Dalmais (1960), 25.
71. Hastings (1994), 7.
72. St Sophronius (1885), 562-563.
73. Cited in Snowden (1970), 211; and in Levine (1974), 6.
74. Hastings (1994), 9
75. Haile (1995), 40.

76. Mitchell (1977), 58-59.
77. Mercier (1997), 115.
78. McEvedy, (1980/1995), 30. The elephants the Carthaginians used were a local North African breed, hunted to extinction during the Roman period.
79. Baur (1994), 27 notes, 'Typically the two were the most legally minded pontiffs in antiquity'.
80. Frend (1982/1985), 75.
81. Mommsen, Theodor *Das Romische Imperium* (Berlin, 1941), 491, 492, quoted in Hoornaert (1989), 61.
82. King (1986), 78-81.
83. Hoornaert (1989), 66.
84. Synod of Bishops (1990), 5.
85. Mandela (1994), 253-255.
86. Baur (1994), 33.
87. Hastings (1994), 69.
88. Hays (2003), 176-177. See *Acts* 13:1.
89. Elliott (1993), 530-531.
90. Levine (1974), 70.
91. Iliffe (1995), 56-57.
92. Beckwith, Fisher, and Hancock (1990), Greenfield (1965), 33-36.
93. Berhane-Selassie (1994), 157.
94. Baur (1994) 37.
95. Levine (1974) 73.
96. Hastings (1994) 4.
97. Grierson and Munro-Hay (1999/2000), 264.
98. O'Hanlon (1946), 62-63.
99. Hastings (1994/1996), 74.
100. Alvares (1961), 455-456.
101. Grierson & Munro-Hay (1999), 240-241.
102. Greenfield (1965), 287.
103. Beckingham and Huntingford (1954), xxii.
104. Beckwith, Fisher and Hancock (1990), 49-52. See page 16 above.
105. *Tewahedo* means 'made one'. See Chaillot and Belopopsky (1996), 25-26.
106. Hastings (1994), 17.
107. Baur (1994), 17.
108. Hastings (1994/1996), 82.
109. Frye (1982), 3.
110. Introduction to Ecclesiasticus in the *Jerusalem Bible* (1966) 1034-1035.
111. O'Hanlon (1946) 19, 33. See Hastings (1994) 5- 6, 9..
112. Porter (2001), 6.
113. Neuman (1950), vii-xi.
114. Urban (1995), 23.
115. Cameron (1982), 23.
116. Pagels (1979/1981), xiv-xvi.
117. Isenberg (1990), 141.
118. Morrice (1997), 154.
119. Elliott (1993), 48.
120. Cameron (1982), 107.
121. Chadwick (1995/ 1997), 47-51.

122. Talal (1998), 36-37.
123. Hastings (1994/1996), 9.
124. Baur (1994), 123, 349-350.
125. Oded (2004); Twaddle (1993); see ref. to Abuyudaya in Section Three below.
126. Romer (1988), 62; Casson (1965/1968), 132.
127. 2 Chron. 2:17-18.
128. Hastings (1994/1996), 56-57.
129. Davidson (1961/1970/1980), 40-41.
130. Augustine, *De Civitate Dei,* 19, 15, quoted in Pagels (1990), 114.
131. Aristotle, *Pol.* I.5, 1254b 20-4, quoted in Sorabji (1993), 135.
132. Mudimbe (1994), 37.
133. Vogel (1988), 13 –20; see also Hastings (1994/1996), 74.
134. Davidson (1994), 29.
135. Miller (1988), 271.
136. Synod of Bishops Special Assembly for Africa (1990), 5.
137. Message of Pope Paul VI, *Africae Terrarum* (29 October 1967), 3: *AAS* 59 (1967), 1074-1075.
138. Pope John Paul II (1994/1996), 241-242.
139. Glassé (1989/1991), 21.
140. Guillaume (1954), 24. Arberry (1950/1970), 15-16.
141. Grierson & Munro-Hay (1999) 157-158.
142. Iliffe (1995) 55.
143. Nyang (1990) 41.
144. Hastings (1994/1996) 70.
145. Ibn Tumart in Hilliard (1998), 198- 201
146. Levine (1974), 71.
147. Nyang (1990), 16- 23.
148. McEvedy (1980/1995), 44, 46.
149. See *Mali, ancient* in Appiah & Gates (1998).
150. Mazrui (1986), 150.
151. Nyang (1986),.
152. Cragg (1992), 57.
153. Padwick (1961), 123-124, cited in Cragg (1992), 60-64.
154. Finnegan (1970/1976), 52.
155. Finnegan (1970/1976), 171-175. For instance, she mentions one *utenzi* praising Julius Nyerere, recited at his inauguration as President in 1965.
156. Finnegan (1970/1976), 48-51. She draws attention to 'the now obsolete *tifinagh* script of the Berbers of North Africa'.
157. Frye (1982), 122.
158. Sumner (1986), 49.
159. Budge (1933), xxvi-xxix.
160. Sumner (1986), 29.
161. Werner [1933] (1995), 25 and 252.
162. See Section One, *The Cruelty of Fire.*
163. Paris (1995) 21-22.
164. Paris (1995) 46-48.
165. Alice Walker, in Gates and Appiah (1993), 51.
166. Kalilombe (1981), 65, quoted in Kalilombe (1999), 119-120; See Section Six.
167. John Philip (1828), quoted in de Kock (1996), 40.

168. Livingstone (1874), entry for 18th August 1870, made at Bambarre.
169. M. Hennell (1958/2003), *John Venn and the Clapham Sect* (London: Lutterworth Press), quoted in Bediako (1995/1997), 198.
170. Darwin (1871/1891), 180, 188; Thomas (1983), 187-188.
171. Schweitzer [1922] (1956/1970), 110-112. This entry is dated July 1916. Schweitzer received the Nobel Peace Prize in 1952.
172. Shorter (1985), 196.
173. Muller Albert S.J. (1927), *Princiers chretiens et colonization* (Brusselles: Editions de la Cite Chretienne), 17, 20, cited by Kanyandago (1994), 41, 42.
174. *Maximum Illud: Apostolic Letter on the Propagation of the Faith throughout the World* (1919). See Dachs and Rea (1979) 132-133.
175. Hebga (1988) 321-322.
176. Livingstone, 'Conversations on Rain-making' (1858), 22-27. Cited in Grinker & Steiner (1997), 301.
177. Anderson (1981), 51, 56, 174.
178. Schoffeleers (1979), 2.
179. 1 Kings 18; See Dickson (1984), and excerpt *Cultural Continuity with the Bible* in Section Six.
180. Mbedzi, Smith, a 'political activist', quoted in Ranger (1999), 283.
181. Ranger (1992), 241-268.
182. Feierman, Steven, 'The Social Origins of Health and Healing in Africa' MS., (1984), 66, quoted in Ranger (1992), 249-250.
183. Shorter (1985), 171-2. Also see Sundkler and Steed (2000), 1033.
184. Mwaura (1994), 62, 67, 69-70.
185. Shorter (1985), 3-4.
186. Shorter (1985), 26.
187. Kinoti (1997), 114. See page 7 above.
188. A. Mbembe (1986), 20, quoted in Isichei (1995) 1.
189. Linzey and Cohn-Sherbok (1997), 117. Also see Linzey (1994).

Section One: Traditional Religions South of the Sahara

1. Horton (1993), 223-224.
2. Mbiti (1970), 39.
3. Smart & Hecht (1992), 348.
4. However, the Jewish tradition recorded in the Talmud and other writings, has more to say about animals. See Section Three.
5. Alex Chima, 'Story and African Theology', in *African Ecclesial Review (AFER)*, 26, 1-2 (February-April, 1984), 56, quoted in Healey & Sybertz, (1996), 63.
6. James (1988), 31-36.
7. Beier (1966), 7.
8. Kipury (1983/1993), 4.
9. Kipury (1983/1993), 30-31.
10. Morris (2000), 177-178.
11. Schoffeleers (1997), 10-11.
12. Edouard Foà, *La traversée de l'Afrique* (Paris, 1900), 40; transl. Matthew Schoffeleers (1997), 12.
13. Imasogie (1982/1985)
14. Kalilombe (1981), 40.

15. Morris (2000), 196-197.
16. Robert Tredgold, ed. (1956), *The Matopos* (Federal Department of Printing, Salisbury,) 85, quoted in Ranger (1999), 20.
17. Ranger (1999), 283, and 23.
18. Aschwanden (1990), 31, 217. Cited in Ranger (1999), 22.
19. Zvabva, 'Nyachiranga Regional Cult', BA Honours thesis, Religious Studies, University of Zimbabwe, November 1988.
20. Gen. 3:9 ff.; Exodus 33:22; 1 Kings 19:8-9.
21. Knappert (1990), 137.
22. Werner [1933] (1995), 305-306.
23. Fisher (1998).
24. Hodza (1979).
25. Bernardi (1959).
26. Bhebe (1979), 13-14.
27. Garlake (1995), 115.
28. Mutwa (1996), 13.
29. Mutwa (1996), 216-217.
30. Uhlenbroek (2002) 47. See *Language* in Conclusion.

Section Two: Early Civilizations of Egypt

1. Breasted [1912] (1959), 85-88.
2. See Introduction and Historical Background, *Early Civilizations in the Nile Valley,* above and Davidson (1994), 20.
3. Apuleius, quoted by Murray (1935), 406.
4. Murray (1935), 407.
5. King (1986), 75-77.
6. O'Hanlon (1946), 62-63. Such talismanic scrolls were also worn by the living. See Mercier (1997).
7. E.A. Wallis Budge, *Osiris and the Egyptian Resurrection,* 2 (London & New York, 1912), 387-88, quoted in Schama (1995), 257.
8. Schama (1995), 255.
9. Murray (1935) 402-4.
10. Janssen (1989), 8.
11. Asante (1990/1992), 54-56.
12. Janssen (1989), 7.
13. *The instruction of a king,* quoted by Lesko, in Seltzer (1987/1989), 40-1.
14. Janssen (1989), 23, 51ff.
15. Wente (1976), 19-31.
16. Ikhnaton's Hymn, trans. Leonard Lesko, 'Egyptian Religion', in Seltzer (1987/1989), 43.
17. *Ezek.* 29: 3-6.
18. Bratton (1961), 184-186.
19. Particularly Psalm 104. For another biblical comparison see *Amos* 9:5.
20. This translation is based on that of Bratton (1961), 117-120, 125-126.
21. Wente (1976), 19-31.
22. Larue (1991/1993/1995), 33-35.
23. Mazrui (1986) 45.
24. Janssen (1989) 36, 62.
25. *Address to the Gods,* from *The Book of the Dead,* quoted in Engels (1999/

2000) 120.
26. Engels (1999/2000), 28, 42.
27. O'Connor (1993), 79.
28. Zabkar (1975).
29. *Prayer to the Lion-God Apedemak* by Priests of Meroe, in Shinnie (1967), 143.
30. *The Lion in Search of Man,* Leiden Demotic Papyrus, I, 384. Translation based on that of C.A. Blackshire-Belay in Asante & Abarry (1996), 340-341.
31. Frye (1982), 22.
32. Janssen (1989), 47.
33. Copenhaver (1997), xiv-xv.
34. From the *Poimander* of Hermes Trismegistos. Text: Nock, trans., Festugiere, ed. *Corpus Hermeticum* Vol. 1, 1-19, 30-31, in Doria and Lenowitz (1976), 28-30.
35. Introduction to the Wisdom Books in *The Jerusalem Bible* (1966), 723.
36. Porter (2001), 118-119.
37. *The Words of Ahiqar* in Charlesworth (1985), Vol.2, 499.
38. Sorabji (1993).

Section Three: African Judaism

1. Barnavi (1992/1998), 24.
2. Oded (2003), and Twaddle (1993). See *African Jewry* in General Introduction above.
3. *Yalkut Shimoni* on *Joshua* 24:22 in Toperoff (1995), 8.
4. Jellinek, Adolf, *Beth Hamidrash,* vol.5 (Vienna, 1878), 22, quoted in Toperoff (1995), 8-9.
5. Recorded in the *Targum Yerushalmi* on the Book of *Esther,* chapter 1, and in the Koran, Surah 27. See *Wisdom of Sheba* in General Introduction above.
6. Toperoff (1995), 118-119.
7. Grierson and Munro-Hay (1999/2000), 340-342. See *Wisdom of Sheba* in General Introduction and Historical Background above.
8. Beckwith, Fisher and Hancock (1990), 49-52.
9. Ullendorff [1968] (1997), 115-118.
10. Flad (1869), 29.
11. Flad (1869), 14.
12. Flad (1869), 48-49.
13. Cohn (1993), 176. See *Sacred Scriptures* in General Introduction above.
14. *Jude* 14-15.
15. Haile (1995), 41.
16. The blind Alexandrian Christian scholar, Didymus, referred to it by this name in the 4th century, as did Jerome in the 5th.
17. Porter (2001), 28.
18. Cohn (1993), 180-181.
19. *Jubilees 3:26 – 4:9* in Charlesworth (1985), Vol. 2, 60.
20. Cohn (1993), 177.
21. Compare *Gen.* 9:12-17 with *Jubilees* VI:15-20..
22. Porter (2001), 126.
23. *Jubilees* VII:27-32.
24. *Jubilees* VII:34-38.

25. *The Apocalypse of Adam* in Robinson (1978/1988/1990), 279-280; *Gen.* 7:23; *Luke* 17:27.
26. Cohen [1949](1975), 96.
27. *Book of the Penitence of Adam* in Dimier (1964), 50-52, 56-60.
28. Porter (2001), 16-17.
29. *The Book of the Conflict of Adam* in Dimier (1964), 31-32.
30. *Jubilees 4:17.*
31. Dimier (1964), 21.
32. Genesis 6:1.2.; 1 Enoch LXXXVI.
33. 1 Enoch 6-7 transl. Charlesworth (1985), Vol. 1, 15-16.
34. 1 Enoch CVI – CVII in Sparks (1984), 314-317.
35. Allen, 'Philosophy', in Hastings (2000), 535.
36. See *Hellenization* in General Introduction and Historical Background above.
37. Philo of Alexandria, quoted by Murray (1990), 425-432.
38. Boccaccini (1991), 195.
39. Philo of Alexandria quoted in Boccaccini (1991), 195-6.
40. See Section Four, *Maxims of Skendes,* where the philosopher Secundus (known in Ethiopia as *Skendes)* gives a slightly different answer.
41. Philo of Alexandria, *Philo Supplement I: Questions and Answers on Genesis,* transl. Marcus (1953), 19.
42. See Uhlenbroek (2002), and *Language* in Conclusion below.
43. Friedlander (1956), xvi-xxv. Also see Maimonides (1963/1974), in which Leo Straus states in his introduction: 'The *Guide* contains a public teaching and a secret teaching. The public teaching is addressed to every Jew including the vulgar; the secret teaching is addressed to the elite'. xvii.
44. Maimonides (1952/1956), Chapter LXXIII, 130, and Chapter XLVIII, 371-372.

Section Four: Early African Christianity

1. Hastings (1994), 5-6, 9.
2. Helmut Koestler, *Foreword* in Cameron (1982), 9.
3. Porter (2001), 110.
4. *Odes of Solomon*, Ode 19, quoted in Porter (2001), 113, transl. Charlesworth (1983).
5. Linzey and Cohn-Sherbok (1997), 66, 69. They question from 'a doctrinal standpoint how biblical scholars can be so sure about the dividing line between apocryphal and canonical development . . . all doctrine is, in one sense, development even, and especially, from meagre statements in the canonical gospels'. 87, note 32. Also see Linzey and Yamamoto (1998), 38-39, and *Cruelty to Animals* in Section Three above.
6. From a *Coptic Bible*, Dunkerley (1957), 143-4.
7. *The History of James,* in Schneemelcher Vol. I (1991/1992), 421.
8. Elliott (1993), 84.
9. Elliott (1993), 68- 72.
10 *The account of Thomas the Israelite philosopher concerning the childhood of the Lord* in Schneemelcher (1992), Vol 1, 444.
11. Schneemelcher (1992), Vol. 1, 456. The Infancy stories may have reached India in this form.
12 *The Arabic Infancy Gospel* in Schneemelcher (1992), Vol. 1, 461, *cf.* also E. A.W. Budge, *History of the Virgin*, 1899.

13. Ullendorff [1968] (1997), 18-19.
14. Elliott (1993), 512, 513.
15 *The Acts of Philip* in Elliott (1993), 515-6.
16. Schneemelcher (1992), Vol. II, 442-443.
17. *Acts of Thomas* in Schneemelcher (1991/1992), Vol. II, 464-465.
18. *Acts of Thomas* in Schneemelcher (1991/1992), Vol. II, 480-481.
19. *Acts of Paul* in Schneemelcher (1991/1992), Vol. II, 351. Also see *Acts of Peter, ibid.* 275.
20. *Acts of Paul* in Schneemelcher (1991/1992), Vol. II, 362-363.
21. *Acts of Paul, ibid.* 388-389.
22. Elliott (1993), 379.
23. Tilley (1994), 104-5.
24. Porter (2001), 158.
25. Baur (1994), 23.
26. Clement of Alexandria in Zeiller (1960), 128-130.
27. Pettersen (1995), 194.
28. Jerome (1885), 34-46.
29. Kelly (1975), 60-61; Also see Waddell (1974), 42-48.
30. St Sophronius, Patriarch of Jerusalem, in *The Lives of the Fathers of the Eastern Deserts* (1885), 410-412.
31. Pearson (1975), vii-viii. Also see *The Lives of The Fathers of the Eastern Deserts* (1885), 125.
32. Hastings (1994).
33. *Ezek.* 1:5-25.
34. St Macarius, *Homily* I, in Maloney (1978), 27-28.
35. St Macarius, *Homily* 12 in Maloney (1978), 83-86.
36. Maloney (1978), 6-7, 16.
37. Kadloubovsky and Palmer (1954), 182; also see Murray (1992), 147.
38. *The Ascetical Homilies of St Isaac the Syrian*: Homily Seventy-Seven, in Belopopsky and Oikonomou (1996), 79.
39. White (1954/1960), 231-2.
40. Sumner (1986),. 25-28.
41. *The Physiologue* in Sumner (1986), 83- 88.
42. Cited in Lloyd (1971), 113.
43. Sumner (1985), 166.
44. *Maxims of Skendes* in Sumner (1985), 214, 218, 219.
45. Ullendorff [1968] (1997), 74.
46. Budge (1932). See *Wisdom of Sheba* in Introduction above.
47. Cited in Levine (1974), 102.
48. Ullendorff [1968] (1997), 9. Psalm 68:31.
49. *Kebra Nagast* ('The Book of the Glory of Kings'), in Budge (1932), 17-25.
50. Hastings (1994), 17-21.
51. See *Christian Kingdoms* in Introduction and Historical Background above.
52. Sumner (1986), 37.
53. Sumner (1978), and (1986), 21-25.
54. Zera Yacob's *Treatise* Chapter X, in Sumner (1986), 134-135.
55. Walda Heywat, in Sumner (1978), 59, 131, 280, 281.
56. *The Treatise of Walda Heywat* in Sumner (1986), 141-142.
57. Berhane-Selassie (1994), 155-167.

Section Five: African Islam

1. 1 Kings 10:1-13, 2 *Chronicles* 9:1-12. *Targum Yerushalmi* on the Book of Esther, chapter 1. See *The Wisdom of Sheba* in General Introduction above.
2. *The Koran, Surah* 27, ' The Ant', transl. Dawood [1956] (1993), 265. Dawood's later revised translation has different page numbers; one or the other edition has been used, as indicated.
3. Knappert (1992), 58-59.
4. Knappert (1992), 60.
5. Sura 21, *The Koran*, Dawood (1993), 232.
6. Knappert (1992), 61-62. See Mutwa (1996) and *Dolphin the Redeemer* in Section One.
7. Mercier (1997). See *The Wisdom of Sheba* in General Introduction above.
8. *The Maulidi Cycle* in Knappert (1992), 67-68.
9. Knappert (1992), 69.
10. Grierson & Munro-Hay (1999/2000), 153.
11. Surah 19 in Dawood (1956), 33.
12. Guillaume (1954), 13-14. See *African Islam* in General Introduction above.
13. *Sura 105* in Dawood (1993), 432.
14. Guillaume (1954), 22.
15. Guillaume (1954), 33-34. See *African Islam* in General Introduction above.
16. Glassé (1991), 74.
17. Ryan (1978), 1-2.; Hilliard (1998) 311.
18. Mapanje and White (1983), 16.
19. Dhu 'l-Nûn the Egyptian in Arberry (1950/1970), 52-53.
20. Alhaji Abubakar Imam, *Magana Jari Ce,* volume i, in Johnston (1966), 85-87.
21. *Gen.* 9: 18-28.
22. Incidentally, the *griot* claims that this hero established a democratic government long before the Europeans came. Thomas A. Hale in Johnson, Hale, and Belcher (1997), 201.
23. This excerpt is based on a version of the *Epic* recorded in 1990 in Rosso, Senegal, transl. Diop (1995).
24. *Gen.* 8: 20; 9: 3.
25. *Surah* 22: 25-37. Cragg (1988/1993), 291-292.
26. David Conrad, *The Epic of Fa-Jigi* in Johnson, Hale & Belcher (1997), 23.
27. *The Epic of Fa-Jigi* as narrated by Seydou Camara in Johnson, Hale & Belcher (1997), 28-29.
28. Koran Sura 49: 11-13. Transl. Nanji (1991/1993/1995), 108.
29. Ibn'Arabi (1989/1991), 21.
30. Ibn' Arabi (1989/1991), 167-168.
31. Glassé (1989/1991), 235.
32. Brenner (1984), 1 ff.
33. Cerno Bokar, in Brenner (1984), 180-182.
34. Amadou Hampaté Bâ and Marcel Cardaire, (1957, revised 1980), *Tierno Bokar: le Sage de Bandiagara* (Paris), quoted in Soyinka (1976/1990), 78.
35. Soyinka (1976/1990), 79.
36. Kane (1972) quoted in Soyinka (1976/1990), 79.
37. Stamer (1995/1996), 112.

Section Six: African Theology Today

1. Gitau (2000), 17.
2. Kalilombe (1999), 224-226.
3. Elà (1993), 29-36.
4. Kahari (1988), 57- 62. At the time of writing his *Critique,* Kahari was Professor of African Languages and Literature at the University of Zimbabwe.
5. Chitepo (1958).
6. Hove (1996), 37-39, 77-79.
7. *Isaiah* 11:6-9; *Numbers* 22:22-35 and 2 *Peter* 2:15-16.
8. Dickson (1984), 158-159.
9. *Adam,* from *adamah,* 'earth-soil', leads to this rendition of the first human being (*adam*) as a sexually undifferentiated being.
10. Amba-Oduyoye (1986, 1991), 90-96.
11. Bernardi (1989), 52.
12. Milingo (1984/1985), 104-105.
13. Shorter (1985), 197.
14. Kalilombe (1999), 153.
15. Mona Macmillan's introduction inMilingo (1984/1985). See *Angelic Powers* in the conclusion above.
16. Milingo (1984/1985), 74, 118-121.
17. Kaunda (1966), 19-20, quoted in Meebelo (1973), 16.
18. Musopole (1996/1997/1998), 7, 11, 15, 26-27.
19. Also see Klaaren (1997).
20. Buthelezi (1987/1991), 96.
21. Mwikamba (1993), 28, 29.
22. Thomas Mukarobwa, in Hove & Trojanow (1996), 89-96.
23. Baba Mhlanga in Hove & Trojanow (1996)
24. F.K. Girling, *The Acholi of Uganda* (London, 1960), cited in Behrend (1999), 42.
25. See Section One, *Man and Elephant in the Garden* and *Why do you Kill?*
26. Behrend (1999), 43-44.
27. Mbuya Juliana, interviewed by Gurli Hansson in 1993, quoted in Ranger (1999), 285.
28. Ranger (1999), 284-286.
29. Daneel (1987/1991), 17, 235.
30. Moltmann (1985), 227. quoted in Daneel (1994).
31. Daneel (1998), 17.
32. Daneel (1998), 17-18, 75, 77-78, 256-7.
33. Spirit medium vaZarira speaking in December 1998, trans in Daneel (1998), 131.
34. Zephaniah Phiri in Witoshynsky (2000), 9, 11-12, 37, 41, 46-47.
35. Temple (1999),14-15.
36. Ennias Michello in Temple (1999) 22.
37 Christensen (1990), 3.
38. Hoehler-Fatton (1996), 120-122.
39. Zech. 1:8; 6:1-6; Rev. 4: 6-11; 5:13-16; 6:1-8.
40. Hoehler-Fatton (1996), 120-122.
41. Amanze (1998) 190-192.
42. Chitando (1993) 49, 93.
43. Bujo (1995), 20, 21, 22, 23, 77, 78.

Conclusion

1. Okumu (2002), 18-20. Also see *Carthage* in General Introduction above, and Mandela (1994,) 253-255.
2. Mana (2002) 8.
3. Amba-Oduyoye (1986) 247.
4. 'Admission of Guilt' by Northern Theologians in Browne (1994/1996) 71.
5. Linzey and Cohn-Sherbok (1997), 68.
6. Regamey (1960), 124.
7. Ezek. 1:5-25, and Rev. 4: 7. See *Four Spiritual Animals* in Section Four above.
8. *The Testament of Solomon* in Sparks (1984), 746-748. Re Lalibela see Beckwith, Fisher, and Hancock (1990). Also see *Christian Kingdoms (b) Abyssinia* in General Introduction & Historical Background above.
9. Mercier (1997), 46-50.
10. Koran, Surah 27, *The Ant*.
11. *The Maulidi Cycle*, in Knappert (1992), 67-68. See Section Five above, *The Light of Paradise*.
12. Luke 2: 8-14.
13. Kalilombe (1999), 224-226. See *The Invisible Forces of Nature*, in Section Six above.
14. Thomas Mukarobwa, quoted in Hove & Trojanow (1996), 89-96. See *Carving Animals of Stone*, above.
15. Ranger (1999), 285-286. See *Water Spirits*, in Section Six above.
16. Bediako (2000), 85-86. See *In the Company of Many Guardians* in Section Six above.
17. See *Anansi the Spider* and *Ancestral Snakes* in Section One above.
18. Morris (2000), 223, 226. See excerpt in Section One, *The Mother and the Serpent*, above.
19. Nyamiti (1984), 15-16.
20. Ela (1993), 21 ff.
21. Johnson (1998), 14.
22. See *It is Our Animal*, in Section Six above.
23. Mulago (1969/1972), 146.
24. Daneel (1998), 195-6. See Section Six, *The Holy Spirit as Earthkeeper*.
25. See Section Six: *Gotami's Strange Land, Carving Animals of Stone* and *The Ancestors are the Land*.
26. See *Hellenization and the Coptic Church* and *Sacred Scriptures*, in General Introduction & Historical Background above.
27. Mazrui (1998), 170-171.
28. See Section Three *Animals share in Speech* and *The Garden of Eden*. Also see Section One, *Animals are People* and *Dolphin the Redeemer*; Section Four, *Language*; and Section Five, *A Secret Language*.
29. *Isaiah* 11:6-8; 65:25.
30. Reed (1988), 120.
31. Dawkins (1993), 22-23, 176-177.
32. Uhlenbroek (2002), 37.
33. Uhlenbroek (2002), 33.
34. See *Animals are People* and *Dolphin the Redeemer* in Section One above.

35. Acts 2: 4-5.
36. Williams (1981), 17.
37. Wilkinson (1993), 56.
38. Wanjohi (1997), 57.
39. Ter Haar (1992), 120.
40. Waliggo (1997), 179-180.
41. Magessa (1997), 25.
42. Musopole (1998), 7,11,15.
43. See *The Holy Spirit as Earthkeeper* and *Ancestors are the Land* in Section Six above.
44. Sanneh (1983/1992) 236.
45. Dickson (1984), 158-164.
46. Hove and Trojanow (1996), 84.
47. Cyprian Nedewedzo, quoted in Dillon-Malone (1978), 60-61. Today the Masowe Apostles form one of the largest and fastest growing AICs.
48. Taylor (1958), 259.
49. Luke 11:29-31.

Select Bibliography

Alvares, Francisco (1961), in C.F. Beckingham and G.W. Huntingford *Prester John of the Indies: A true Relation of the Lands of Prester John*, trans. Lord Stanley of Alderley (1881) (Cambridge: the Hakluyt Society at the University Press)

Amanze, James N. (1998), *African Christianity in Botswana: The Case of African Independent Churches* (Gweru, Zimbabwe: Mambo)

Amba-Oduyoye, Mercy (1986), 'The value of African Religious Beliefs and Practices' in Deane W. Ferm (ed.), *Third World Liberation Theologies* (Maryknoll, NY: Orbis)

Amba-Oduyoye, Mercy (1986/1991), *Hearing and Knowing: Theological Reflections on Christianity in Africa* (Maryknoll NY: Orbis).

Amba-Oduyoye, Mercy (2001), *Introducing African Women's Theology* (Sheffield Academic Press).

Anderson, W. B. (1981), *The Church in East Africa 1840-1974* (Dodoma, Tanzania: Central Tanganyika Press).

Appiah, Kwame Anthony, & Henry Louis Gates Jr., (eds.) (1998), *The Dictionary of Global Culture* (Penguin Books).

Arberry, A.J. (1950/1970), *Sufism: An Account of the Mystics of Islam* (Routledge & Kegan Paul)

Armstrong, A.H. (1983), *An Introduction to Ancient Philosophy*, (Totowa, NJ: Rowman & Allanheld).

Asante, Molefi Kete (1990/1992), *Kemet, Afrocentricity and Knowledge* (Trenton, NJ: Africa World Press).

Asante, Molefi Kete, & Abu S. Abarry (eds.) (1996), *African Intellectual Heritage: A Book of Sources*, (Philadelphia: Temple University Press).

Aschwanden, Herbert (1990), *Karanga Mythology* (Gweru, Zimbabwe: Mambo).

Balasuriya, Tissa (1984), *Planetary Theology* (London: SCM)

Barnarvi, Eli (ed.) (1992-1998), *A Historical Atlas of the Jewish People: From the Time of the Patriarchs to the Present* (London: Hutchinson and Kuperard).

Baur, John (1994), *2000 Years of Christianity in Africa: An African History 60-1992* (Nairobi: Paulines).

Beckingham, C.F. & G.W.B. Huntingford (eds. & trans.) (1954), *Some Records of Ethiopia 1593-1646: Being Extracts from the History of High Ethiopia or Abassia by Manoel de Almeida together with Bahrey's History of the Galla*, (London: Hakluyt Society).

Beckwith, Carol, with Angela Fisher & Graham Hancock (1990), *African Ark: People and Ancient Cultures of Ethiopia and the Horn of Africa* (London: Collins; and New York: Harry N. Abrams).

Bediako, Kwame (1995/1997), *Christianity in Africa: The Renewal of a Non-Western Religion* (Edinburgh: Edinburgh University Press; and Maryknoll NY: Orbis).

Bediako, Kwame (2000), *Jesus in Africa: The Christian Gospel in African History and Experience* (Regnum Africa and Editions Clé, with Paternoster).

Behrend, Heike (1999), *Alice Lakwena & The Holy Spirits: War in Northern Uganda 1986-97* (Oxford: James Currey; Kampala: Fountain; Nairobi: East African Educational Publishers; and Ohio University Press).

Beier, Ulli (ed.) (1966), *The Origin of Life & Death: African Creation Myths* (London: Heinemann).

Belopopsky, Alexander, & Dimitri Oikonomou (eds.) (1996), *Orthodoxy and Ecology: Resource Book* (Bialystok, Poland: Orthdruk for SYNDESMOS, the World Fellowship of Orthodox Youth)

Berhane-Selassie, Tsehai (1994), 'Ecology and Ethiopian Orthodox Theology' in David G. Hallman (ed.), *Ecotheology: Voices from South and North* (Geneva: World Council of Churches; and Maryknoll, NY: Orbis).

Bernal, Martin (1987), *Black Athena: The Afroasiatic Roots of Classical Civilization Vol. 1: The Fabrication of Ancient Greece 1785-1985* (New Brunswick NJ: Rutgers University Press).

Bernardi, Bernardo (1959), *The Mugwe. A Failing Prophet: A study of a religious and public dignitary of the Meru of Kenya* (Oxford: OUP).

Bhebe, Ngwabi (1979), *Christianity and Traditional Religion in Western Zimbabwe 1859-1923* (Harlow, Essex: Longman).

Birch, Charles & Lukas Vischer (1997), *Living with the Animals: The Community of God's Creatures* (Geneva: WCC Risk).

Blackshire-Belay, C. A. (trans.) (1994), *The Lion in Search of Man* (Twenty-First Dynasty, 1070-945 B.C., Kemet), from the Leiden Demotic Papyrus, I, 384. Translated into German by W. Erichsen, *Demotische Lesestucke* (Leipzig, 1937), and from the German into English.

Boccaccini, Gabriele (1991), *Middle Judaism: Jewish Thought, 300 BCE to 200 CE* (Minneapolis: Augsburg Fortress).

Bradlow, Frank R. & Margaret Cairns (1978), *The Early Cape Muslims: A study of their mosques, genealogy and origins* (Cape Town: A.A. Balkema).

Bratton, Fred Gladstone (1961), *The First Heretic: The Life and Times of Ikhnaton the King* (Boston: Beacon Press).

Breasted, James Henry (1959), *Development of Religion and Thought in Ancient Egypt* [1912] (New York and Evanston: Harper & Row).

Brenner, Louis (1984), *West African Sufi. The Religious Heritage and Spiritual Search of Cerno Bokar Saalif Taal* (Berkeley and Los Angeles: University of California Press, Berkeley and Los Angeles).

Browne, Maura, SND (ed.) (1994/1996), *The African Synod: Documents, Reflections, Perspectives* (Maryknoll, NY: Orbis Africa Faith & Justice Network).

Budge, Ernest A. Wallis (1932), *The Queen of Sheba and Her Only Son Menyelek* (London).

Budge, Ernest A. Wallis (1933), *The Alexander Book in Ethiopia: The Ethiopic Versions of Pseudo-Callisthenes, the Chronicle of Almakin, the Narrative of Joseph Ben Gorion, and a Christian Romance of Alexander,* translated into English from MSS. in the British Museum and Bibliotheque Nationale (London: Oxford University Press).

Bujo, Bénézet (1995), *Christmas: God Becomes Man in Black Africa* (Nairobi: Paulines).

Buthelezi, Manas (1987/1991), 'Salvation as Wholeness' in John Parratt (ed.) *A Reader in African Christian Theology* (London: SPCK).

Cameron, Ron (ed.) (1982), *The Other Gospels: Non-Canonical Gospel Texts* (Casmbridge: Lutterworth Press).

Campbell, Joseph (1988), *The Power of Myth* (with Bill Moyers, ed. by Betty Sue Flowers) (New York: Doubleday).

Casson, Lionel (1975), *Daily Life in Ancient Egypt* (American Heritage Publishing Co., McGraw Hill).

Chadwick, Owen (1995/1997), *A History of Christianity* (London: Weidenfeld & Nicolson; and Phoenix).

Chaillot, Christine & Alexander Belopopsky (eds.) (1996), *Towards Unity: Theological Dialogue between the Orthodox Church and the Oriental Orthodox Churches* (Geneva: Inter-Orthodox Dialogue).

Charlesworth, James H. (1983/1985), *The Old Testament Pseudepigrapha*, 2 vols. (London: Darton, Longman and Todd).

Chitando, Ezra (1993), *Sacrifice as a Type. An Application to Karanga Religion* Unpublished MA thesis, Department of Religious Studies, Classics and Philosophy of the University of Zimbabwe.

Chitepo, Herbert W. (1958), *Soko Risina Musoro: The Tale without a Head* (Cape Town: Oxford University Press for SOAS).

Christensen, Thomas G. (1990), *An African Tree of Life* (Maryknoll, NY: Orbis).

Cohen, A. [1949] (1975), *Everyman's Talmud* with Intro. by Boaz Cohen (New York: Schocken Books).

Cohn, Norman (1993), *Cosmos, Chaos and the World to Come: The Ancient Roots of Apocalyptic Faith* (Newhaven and London: Yale University Press).

Copenhaver, Brian P. (1992/1994/1995/1997), *Hermetica: The Greek Corpus Hermeticum and the Latin Asclepius in a new English translation, with notes and introduction* (Cambridge University Press).

Cragg, Kenneth (1988/1993), *Readings in the Qur'an* (London: Collins).

Cragg, Kenneth (1992), *Troubled by Truth: Life-Studies in Inter-Faith Concern* (Edinburgh, Cambridge, Durham: Pentland Press).

Dachs, A.J., & W.F. Rea (1979), *The Catholic Church and Zimbabwe, 1879-1979* (Gweru, Zimbabwe: Mambo Press).

Dalmais, Irenée-Henri (1960), *Eastern Liturgies*, translated from French by Donald Attwater (New York: Twentieth Century Encyclopaedia of Catholicism, Hawthorn Books).

Daneel, M.L. (1987/1991), *Quest for Belonging: Introduction to a study of African Independent Churches* (Gweru and Harare, Zimbabwe: Mambo Press).

Daneel, M.L. (1994), 'African Independent Churches Face the Challenge of Environmental Ethics' in David G. Hallman (ed.), *Ecotheology: Voices from South and North* (Geneva: World Council of Churches; and Maryknoll NY: Orbis).

Daneel, M.L. (1998), *African Earthkeepers: Volume 1. Interfaith mission in earth-care* (Pretoria: Unisa Press).

Darwin, Charles (1871/1891), *The Descent of Man* (London: John Murray).

Davidson, Basil (1961/1970/1980), *The African Slave Trade* (Boston and Toronto: Little, Brown, & Co.).

Davies, Alan (1988), *Infected Christianity: A Study of Modern Racism* (Kingston and Montreal: McGill-Queen's University Press).

Dawkins, Marian Stamp (1993), *Through Our Eyes Only? The search for animal consciousness* (Oxford and New York: W.H. Freeman; Heidelberg: Spektrum).

Dawood, N. J. (trans.) (1956 and revised ed.1993),*The Koran* (Penguin).

Deacon, Janette (1994), 'Rock Engravings and the Folklore of Bleek and Lloyd's / Xam San Informants' in Thomas A. Dowson & David Lewis-Williams (eds.),*Contested Images: diversity in Southern African rock art research* (Johannesburg: Witwatersrand University Press.

de Kock, Leon (1996), *Civilising Barbarians: Missionary Narrative and African Textual Response in Nineteenth Century South Africa* (Johannesburg: Witwatersrand University Press).

Dickson, Kwesi A. (1984), *Theology in Africa* (Maryknoll NY: Orbis; London: Darton, Longman & Todd).

Dillon-Malone, Clive M. (1978), *The Korsten Basketmakers, A Study of the Masowe Apostles, An Indigenous African Religious Movement* (Manchester University Press for the University of Zambia).

Dimier, Catherine (1964), *The Old Testament Apocrypha,* translated by S.J. Tester, Vol.71, Section VI, of Twentieth Century Encyclopaedia of Catholicism (New York: Hawthorn Books).

Diop, Samba (1995), in *The Oral History and Literature of the Wolof People of Waalo, Northern Senegal: The Master of the Word (Griot) in the Wolof Tradition* (Lewiston: Mellen Press).

Doria, Charles, & Harris Lenowitz (eds.) (1976), *Origins: Creation Texts from the Ancient Mediterranean* (Garden City, NY: Anchor Books).

Dunkerley, Roderick (1957), *Beyond the Gospels* (London: Penguin).

Ela, Jean-Marc (1993), *My Faith as an African,* trans. John P. Brown & Susan Perry (Maryknoll NY: Orbis).

Elliott, J.K. (ed.) (1993), *The Apocryphal New Testament: a Collection of Apocryphal Christian Literature in an English Translation based on M.R. James* (Oxford: Clarendon).

Engels, Donald (1999/2000), *Classical Cats: The rise and fall of the sacred cat* (London and New York: Routledge).

Finnegan, Ruth (1970/1976), *Oral Literature in Africa* (Oxford, Nairobi, Dar es Salaam: Oxford University Press).

Fisher, Robert B. (1998), *West African Religious Traditions: Focus on the Akan of Ghana* (Orbis)

Flad, J. M. (1869), *The Falashas (Jews) of Abyssinia* (London: William Macintosh).

Fortune, G. (ed. & trans.) (1979), *Shona Praise Poetry*, compiled by A. C. Hodza (Oxford: Clarendon).

Frend, W.H.C. (1982/1985), *The Early Church* [1965] (Philadelphia: Fortress).

Friedlander, M. (transl.) (1956), *The Guide for the Perplexed* by Moses Maimonides [1881] (New York: Routledge & Kegan Paul and Dover).

Freud, Sigmund (1939), *Moses and Monotheism* (New York: Random House).

Frye, Northrop (1982), *The Great Code: The Bible and Literature* (London, Melbourne & Henley: Routledge & Kegan Paul).

Garlake, Peter (1995), *The Hunter's Vision: The Prehistoric Art of Zimbabwe* (Harare: Zimbabwe Publishing House; London: British Museum Press).

Gates, Henry Louis, & Appiah, KA. (eds.) (1993), *Alice Walker: Critical Perspectives Past and Present* (New York: Amistad).

Gilbert, Katharine Stoddert, with Joan K. Holt & Sara Hudson (eds.) (1976), *Treasures of Tutankhamun* (New York: Metropolitan Museum of Art).

Gitau, Samson K. (2000), *The Environmental Crisis: A Challenge for African Christianity* (Nairobi: Acton).

Glassé, Cyril (1989/1991), *The Concise Encyclopaedia of Islam* (London: Stacey International).

Greenfield, Richard (1965), *Ethiopia: A New Political History* (London: Pall Mall Press).

Grierson, Roderick, & Stuart Munro-Hay (1999/2000), *The Ark of the Covenant* (London: Weidenfeld & Nicolson and Phoenix/Orion).

Grinker, Roy Richard, & Christopher B. Steiner (eds.) (1997), *Perspectives on Africa: A Reader in Culture, History and Representation* (Oxford: Blackwell).

Groves, Charles Pelham (1948-1958/2002), *The Planting of Christianity in Africa* (London: Lutterworth Press; Cambridge: James Clarke & Co)

Guillaume, Alfred (1954), *Islam* (Harmondsworth: Penguin).

Guy, Jeff (1983), *The Heretic* (Pietermaritzburg: University of Natal Press; Johannesburg: Ravan Press).

Haile, Getatche (1995), 'Highlighting Ethiopian Traditional Literature' in Taddesse Adera and Ali Jimale Ahmed (eds.), *Silence is Not Golden: A Critical Anthology of Ethiopian Literature* (Laurenceville, New Jersey: Red Sea).

Hall, Martin (1996), *Archaeology in Africa* (London: James Currey; Cape Town: David Philip).

Hastings, Adrian (1994/1996), *The Church in Africa 1450-1950* (Oxford: Clarendon).

Hastings, Adrian, with A. Mason & H. Piper (eds.) (2000), *The Oxford Companion to Christian Thought* (Oxford University Press).

Hays, J. Daniel (2003), *From every People and Nation: A biblical theology of Race* (Leicester: Apollos, Inter-Varsity Press).

Healey, Joseph, and Donald Sybertz (1996), *Towards an African Narrative Theology* (Nairobi: Paulines).

Hebga, Meinrad (1988), 'The Evolution of Catholicism in Western Africa: The Case of Cameroon' in T. M. Gannn (ed.), *World Catholicism in Transition* (London/ New York: Macmillan).

Hennecke, E. (1965), *New Testament Apocrypha, Vol. II,* ed. W. Schneemelcher *q.v.* Originally published as E. Hennecke, *Neutestamentliche Apokryphen* (J.C.B. Mohr, Tubingen, Germany, 1964). English translation edited by R. McL. Wilson (Lutterworth Press; Guilford) See Schneemelcher (revised edition).

Hilliard, Constance B. (ed.) (1998), *Intellectual Traditions of Pre-Colonial Africa* (McGraw-Hill).

Hodza, A.C. (1979), *Shona Praise Poetry,* ed. and trans. G. Fortune (Oxford: Clarendon).

Hoehler-Fatton, Cynthia (1996), *Women of Fire and Spirit: History, Faith, and Gender in Roho Religion in Western Kenya* (Oxford University Press).

Hoornaert, Eduardo (1989), *The Memory of the Christian People,* trans. from Portuguese by Robert R. Barr (Tunbridge Wells: Burns & Oates).

Horton, Robin (1993), *Patterns of thought in Africa and the West: Essays on magic, religion and science* (Cambridge University Press).

Hove, Chenjerai (1996), *Ancestors* (Harare: College Press; London: Macmillan).

Hove, Chenjerai, & Trojanow, Ilija (1996), *Guardians of the Soil: Meeting*

Zimbabwe's Elders (Munich: Frederking & Thaler Verlag; and Harare, Zimbabwe, Boabab).

Ibn'Arabi, Muhyi-D-Din (1989/1991), *Tarjuman al-Ashwaq*, in Cyril Glassé, *The Concise Encyclopaedia of Islam* (London: Stacey International) 21.

Idowu, E. Bolaji (1969), 'Introduction', in Kwesi Dickson and Paul Ellingworth (eds.) *Biblical Revelation and African Beliefs* (London: Lutterworth).

Iliffe, John (1995), *Africans: The History of a Continent* (Cambridge U.P.).

Imasogie, O. (1982/1985), *African Traditional Religion* (Ibadan: University Press).

Ingold, T. (1988), *What is an Animal?* (London, Boston, Sydney, Wellington: Unwin Hyman/Allen & Unwin).

Isenberg, Wesley W. (1990), in *The Nag Hammadi Library in English* (Harper Collins).

Isichei, Elizabeth (1995), *A History of Christianity in Africa: From Antiquity to the Present* (London: SPCK; Lawrenceville, N.J: Africa World Press; Grand Rapids: Eerdmans).

James, Wendy (1988), *The Listening Ebony: Moral Knowledge, Religion, and Power Among the Uduk of Sudan* (Oxford: Clarendon).

Janssen, Rosalind and Jack (1989), *Egyptian Household Animals* (Princess Risborough: Shire Publications)

Jerome, Saint (1885), *'St. Paul the First Hermit'* abridged from his *Life* in *The Lives of the Fathers of the Eastern Deserts; or the Wonders of God in the Wilderness* (New York: D. and J. Sadlier & Co.).

Johnson, Elizabeth A. (1998), *Friends of God and Prophets: A Feminist Theological Reading of the Communion of Saints* (London: SCM).

Johnson, John William, with Thomas A. Hale, & Stephen Belcher (eds.) (1997), *Oral Epics from Africa: Vibrant Voices from a Vast Continent* (Bloomington & Indianapolis: Indiana University Press).

Johnston, H.A.S. (1966), *A Selection of Hausa Stories* (Oxford: Clarendon).

Kadloubovsky, E., & G.E.H. Palmer (eds. & trans.) (1954), *Early Fathers from the Philokalia: together with some writings of St Abba Dorotheus, St Isaac of Syria and St Gregory Palamas* (London: Faber & Faber).

Kahari, George P. (1988), *Herbert W. Chitepo's Epic Poem: Soko Risina Musoro, The Tale without a Head – A Critique* (Harare: Longman Zimbabwe).

Kalilombe, Patrick A. (1981), 'The Salvific Value of African Religions' in Gerald H. Anderson & Thomas F. Stransky (eds.) *Faith Meets Faith* (New York: Paulist Press; Grand Rapids: Eerdmans).

Kalilombe, Patrick A. (1998/1999), *Doing Theology at the Grassroots: Theological Essays from Malawi* (Gweru, Zimbabwe: Mambo Press for Kachere).

Kane, Cheik Hamidou (1972), *Ambiguous Adventure* (London: Heinemann).

Kanyandago, Peter (1994), 'Violence in Africa: Pastoral Response from a Historical Perspective', in D.W. Waruta & H.W. Kinoti (eds.), *Pastoral Care in African Christianity: Challenging Essays in Pastoral Theology* (Nairobi: Acton).

Kanyandago, Peter (1997), 'The Cross and Suffering in the Bible and the African Experience', in H.W. Kinoti and J.M. Waliggo (eds.), *The Bible in African Christianity* (Nairobi: Acton).

Kaunda, Kenneth D. (1966), *A Humanist in Africa* (London: Longmans).

Kelly, J.N.D. (1975), *Jerome: His Life, Writings, and Controversies* (Harper & Row).

King, Noel Q. (1986), *African Cosmos: An Introduction to Religion in Africa* (Belmont, CA: Wadsworth).

Kinoti, Hannah W. (1997), 'Well-being in African Society and the Bible' in H.W. Kinoti and J.M. Waliggo (eds.), *The Bible in African Christianity* (Nairobi: Acton).

Kipury, Naomi (1983/1993), *Oral Literature of the Maasai* (Nairobi: East African Publishers).

Klaaren, Eugene M. (1997), 'Creation and Apartheid: South African Theology since 1948' in R. Elphick and R. Davenport (eds.), *Christianity in South Africa: A Political, Social and Cultural History* (Oxford: James Currey; Cape Town: David Philip).

Knappert, Jan (1990), *The Aquarian Guide to African Mythology,* Illus. Elizabeth Knappert (Wellingborough: The Aquarian Press).

Knappert, Jan (1979/1992), *Myths and Legends of the Swahili* (Kenya: Heinemann).

Larue, Gerald A. (1991/1993/1995), 'Ancient ethics' in Peter Singer (ed.), *A Companion to Ethics* (Oxford: Blackwell)

Lesko, Leonard H. (1987/1989), 'Egyptian Religion' in Robert M. Seltzer (ed.), *Religions of Antiquity* (New York: Macmillan).

Levine, Donald N. (1974), *Greater Ethiopia: The Evolution of a Multi-ethnic Society* (University of Chicago Press).

Linzey, Andrew (1994), *Animal Theology* (London: SCM; Illinois University Press).

Linzey, Andrew & Dan Cohn-Sherbok (1997), *After Noah: Animals and the Liberation of Theology* (London: Mowbray).

Linzey, Andrew, & Dorothy Yamatoto (1998), *Animals on the Agenda: Questions about Animals for Theology and Ethics* (London: SCM).

Livingstone, David (1857), *Missionary Researches and Travels in South Africa* (London: John Murray).

Livingstone, David (1874), *The Last Journals of David Livingstone, in Central Africa, from 1865 to his death, continued by a narrative of his last moments and sufferings obtained from his faithful servants Chuma and Susi by Horace Waller, F.R.G.S.,*Vol.II, (London: John Murray).

Lloyd, Joan Barclay (1971), *African Animals in Renaissance Literature* (Oxford: Clarendon).

Macmillan, Mona (1985), Introduction to E. Milingo, *The World in Between: Christian Healing and the Struggle for Spiritual Survival* (London: Hurst; Maryknoll NY: Orbis; Gweru, Zimbabwe: Mambo).

Magessa, Laurenti (1997), 'From Privatized to Popular Biblical Hermeneutics in Africa', in Hannah W. Kinoti & John M. Waliggo (eds.), *The Bible in African Christianity* (Nairobi: Acton).

Maimonides, Moses [1881] (1956), *The Guide for the Perplexed,* trans. M. Friedlander (New York: Dover with Routledge & Kegan Paul).

Maimonides, Moses (1963/1974), *The Guide of the Perplexed,* trans. Shlomo Pines, 2 vols. (Chicago and London: University of Chicago Press).

Maloney, George A. (1978), *Intoxicated with God: The Fifty Spiritual Homilies of Macarius* (Denville, NJ: Dimension Books).

Mana, Kä (2002), *Christians and Churches of Africa envisioning the Future: Salvation in Jesus Christ and the building of a new African society* (Editions Clé and Regnum Africa).

Mandela, Nelson (1994), 'African Renaissance' a speech given at the Organization of African Unity meeting of heads of state on 13 June 1994, in *Granta 48 Africa,* Summer 1994 (distributed by Penguin Books).

Mapanje, Jack, and Landeg White (eds) (1983), *Oral Poetry from Africa* (London: Longman).

Marcus, Ralph (trans.) (1953), *Philo Supplement: Questions and Answers on Genesis* (London: Heinemann; Cambridge, Mass: Harvard University Press).

Mazrui, Ali (1986), *The Africans: A Triple Heritage* (Boston & Toronto: Little, Brown).

Mazrui, Ali (1998), *The Power of Babel: Language and Governance in the African Experience* (Oxford: James Currey; Nairobi: E.A.E.P.; Kampala: Fountain; Cape Town: David Philip; and University of Chicago Press).

Mbembe, A. (1986), 'Rome and the African Churches', *Pro Mundi Vita*, Africa Dossier 37-8. 20.

Mbiti, John S. (1970), *Concepts of God in Africa* (New York: Praeger; London: SPCK).

Mbiti, John S. (1986), *Bible & Theology in African Christianity* (Nairobi: Oxford U.P.).

McEvedy, Colin (1980/1995), *The Penguin Atlas of African History* (London: Penguin).

Meebelo, Henry S. (1973), *Main Currents of Zambian Humanist Thought* (Lusaka: Oxford University Press).

Mercier, Jacques (1997), *The Art that Heals: the Image as Medicine in Ethiopia* (Munich: Prestel-Verlag; New York: Museum for African Art).

Meredith, Martin (2001/2002), *Africa's Elephant: A Biography* (London: Hodder & Stoughton; Anstey: Thorpe Charnwood).

Midgley, Mary (1994), *The Ethical Primate: Humans, Freedom and Morality* (London and New York: Routledge).

Milingo, Emmanuel (1984/1985), *The World in Between: Christian Healing and the Struggle for Spiritual Survival*, ed. and intro. Mona Macmillan (London: Hurst; Maryknoll NY: Orbis; and Gweru, Zimbabwe: Mambo Press).

Miller, Joseph C. (1988), *Way of Death: Merchant Capitalism and the Angolan Slave Trade 1730-1830* (Madison: University of Wisconsin Press).

Mitchell, G. Frank (1977), 'Foreign Influences and the Beginnings of Christian Art' in Polly Cone (ed.), *Treasures of Early Irish Art 1500 BC to 1500 AD* (Metropolitan Museum of Art).

Morrice, William (1997), *Hidden Sayings of Jesus: Words attributed to Jesus outside the Four Gospels* (London: SPCK).

Morris, Brian (2000), *Animals and Ancestors: An Ethnography* (Oxford and New York: Berg).

Mudimbe, V.Y. (1994), *The Idea of Africa* (Oxford: James Currey; Bloomington & Indianapolis: Indiana U.P.).

Mulago, Vincent (1969/1972), 'Vital Participation' in Kwesi Dickson & Paul Ellingworth (eds.), *Biblical Revelation and African Beliefs* (London: Lutterworth)

Murray, Alexander S. (1935), *Manual of Mythology: Greek and Roman, Norse and Old German, Hindoo and Egyptian Mythology* (New York: Tudor Publishing Co.).

Murray, Robert (1990), 'The relationship of creatures within the Cosmic Covenant', *The Month,* November 1990, 425-432.

Murray, Robert (1992), *The Cosmic Covenant: Biblical Themes of Justice, Peace and the Integrity of Creation* (London: Sheed & Ward).

Musopole, Augustine C. (1996/1997/1998), in Klaus Fiedler, Paul Gundani, Hilary Mijoga (eds.), *Theology Cooked in an African Pot* (Special Issue of ATISCA Bulletin nos. 5 & 6, 1996/1997) (Zomba, Malawi: Association of Theological Institutions in Southern and Central Africa).

Mutwa, Credo (1996), *Isilwane The Animal: Tales and Fables of Africa* (Cape Town: Struik).

Mwaura, Philomena Njeri (1994), 'Healing as a Pastoral Concern' in D.W. Waruta and H.W. Kinoti (eds.), *Pastoral Care in African Christianity: Challenging Essays in Pastoral Theology* (Nairobi: Acton Publishers).

Mwikamba, C.M. (1993), 'Shifts in Mission: An Ecological Theology in Africa', in A. Nasimiyu-Wasika & D.W. Waruta (eds.), *Mission in African Christianity: Critical Essays in Missiology* (Nairobi: Uzima Press).

Nanji, Azim (1991/1993/1995), 'Islamic ethics' in Peter Singer (ed.) *A Companion to Ethics* (Oxford: Blackwell)

Neuman, Abraham A. (1950), 'Foreword' to Sidney Tedesche (trans.), *The First Book of Maccabees* (New York: Harper & Bros. for the Dropsie College for Hebrew and Cognate Learning).

Nyamiti, Charles (1984), *Christ as Our Ancestor: Christology from an African Perspective* (Gweru: Mambo Press).

Nyang, Sulayman S. (1984/1990), *Islam, Christianity, and African Identity* (Brattleboro, Vermont: Aman Books).

Nyang, Sulayman S. (1986), 'History of Muslims in North America', *Al-Ittihad* (September): 39-47.

O'Connor, David (1993), *Ancient Nubia: Egypt's Rival in Africa* (Philadelphia: University of Pennsylvania).

Oded, Arye (1995), *Religion and Politics in Uganda* (Nairobi: East African Educational Publishers).

Oded, Arye (2003), *Judaism in Africa: the Abuyudaya Jews of Uganda* (Jerusalem: The Israel-Africa Friendship Association).

Oduyoye, Mercy see Amba-Oduyoye

O'Hanlon, Douglas (1946), *Features of the Abyssinian Church* (London: SPCK).

Okumu, Washington A.J. (2002), *The African Renaissance: History, Significance & Strategy* (Trenton N.J. and Asmara, Eritrea: Africa World Press).

O'Mahony, Anthony (1994), 'From survival to revival: the Copts of Egypt' in *The Month*, August 1994.

Padwick, Constance (1961), *Muslim Devotions: A Study of Prayer Manuals in Common Use* (Oxford: One World Publications).

Pagels, Elaine (1979/1981), *The Gnostic Gospels* (New York: Random House and Vintage Books paperback).

Pagels, Elaine (1990), *Adam, Eve and The Serpent* (Weidenfeld and Penguin).

Pailin, David A. (1984), *Attitudes to Other Religions: Comparative religion in seventeenth and eighteenth-century Britain* (Manchester University Press).

Pankhurst, Richard (1990), *A Social History of Ethiopia* (University of Addis Ababa, Ethiopia).

Paris, Peter J. (1995), *The Spirituality of African Peoples: The Search for a Common Moral Discourse* (Minneapolis: Fortress Press).

Pearson, Birger A. (1975), Introduction to *The Life of Pachomius (Vita Prima Graeca)*, trans. Apostolos N. Athanassakis (Missoula, Montana: Scholars Press for Society of Biblical Literature).

Pettersen, Alvyn (1995), *Athanasius* (Geoffrey Chapman and Morehouse).

Pope John Paul II (1994/1996), 'Post-Synodal Apostolic Exhortation' in Africa Faith & Justice Network, *The African Synod: Documents, Reflections, Perspectives* (Maryknoll NY: Orbis).

Porter, J.R. (2001), *The Lost Bible: Forgotten Scriptures Revealed* (London: Duncan Baird).

Rahner, Karl (1978), *Foundations of Christian Faith: An Introduction to the Idea of Christianity* trans. William V. Dych (New York: Seabury).

Ranger, Terence (1992), 'Plagues of beasts and men: prophetic responses to epidemic in eastern and southern Africa' in T. Ranger & Paul Slack (eds.), *Epidemics and Ideas: Essays on the historical perception of pestilence* (Cambridge University Press).

Ranger, Terence (1999), *Voices from the Rocks: Nature, Culture & History in the Matopos Hills of Zimbabwe* (Harare: Baobab; Oxford: James Currey; Indiana U.P.).

Reed, Edward S. (1988), 'The affordances of the animate environment: social science from the ecological point of view' in T. Ingold (ed.), *What is an Animal?* (London, Boston, Sydney, Wellington: Unwin Hyman).

Regamey, Pie-Raymond, O.P. (1960), *What is an Angel?* trans. Dom Mark Pontifex (New York: Hawthorn Books).

Robinson, James M. (1978/1988/1990), *The Nag Hamadi Library in English: the definitive new translation of the Gnostic scriptures, complete in one volume* (Leiden: Brill; London: Harper Collins Paperback).

Romer, John (1988), *Testament: The Bible & History* (London: Michael O'Mara).

Ryan, Patrick J. (1978), *Imale: Yoruba Participation in Muslim Tradition: A Study of Clerical Piety* (Missoula, Montana: Scholars Press, Harvard Dissertations in Religion).

Sanneh, Lamin (1983/1992), *West African Christianity: The Religious Impact* (London: Hurst; Maryknoll NY: Orbis).

Sawyerr, Harry (1969/1972), 'Sacrifice' in Kwesi Dickson & P. Ellingworth (eds.), *Biblical Revelation and African Beliefs* (London: Lutterworth).

Schama, Simon (1995), *Landscape and Memory* (London: Fontana HarperCollins).

Schneemelcher, Wilhelm (ed.) [1965] (1991) (ed.), *New Testament Apocrypha* 2 vols. (London: Lutterworth Press; Cambridge: James Clarke).

Schoffeleers, J. Matthew (ed.) (1979), *Guardians of the Land: Essays on Central African Territorial Cults* (Gwelo, Zimbabwe: Mambo).

Schoffeleers, J. Matthew (1997), *Religion and the Dramatization of Life: Spirit Beliefs and Rituals in Southern and Central Malawi* (Blantyre, Malawi: CLAIM; Bonn: Culture & Science).

Schultz, Kenneth, & Matthew Meyer (2000), 'Reunited with Our Ancient Faith: Practicing Judaism in Uganda' in *Judaism*, Fall, 2000.

Schweitzer, Albert [1922](1956/1970), *On the Edge of the Primeval Forest: The Experiences and Observations of a Doctor in Equatorial Africa* [A. & C. Black] (London: Collins Fontana).

Seltzer, Robert M. (ed.) (1987/1989), *Religions of Antiquity. Religion, History, and Culture. Selections from the Encyclopedia of Religion* (New York: Macmillan).

Shinnie, P.L. (1967), *Meroe: A Civilization of the Sudan* (New York: Frederick A. Praeger).

Shorter, Aylward (1985), *Jesus and the Witchdoctor: an approach to healing and wholeness* (London: Geoffrey Chapman; Maryknoll, NY: Orbis).

Smart, Ninian, and Richard D. Hecht (eds.) (1992), *Sacred Texts of the World: A Universal Anthology* (New York: Crossroad).

Snowden, Frank M. Jr. (1970), *Blacks in Antiquity: Ethiopians in the Greco-Roman Experience* (Cambridge, Mass: Harvard University Press).

Sophronius, St (1885), 'St Mary of Egypt' in *The Lives of the Fathers of the Eastern Deserts: or the Wonders of God in the Wilderneess* (New York: D. & J. Sadlier & Co.).

Sorabji, Richard (1993/1995), *Animal Minds & Human Morals: The Origins of the Western Debate* (Ithaca NY: Cornell University Press).

Soyinka, Wole (1976/1990), *Myth, Literature and The African World* (Cambridge University Press).

Sparks, H.F.D. (ed.) (1984), *The Apocryphal Old Testament* (Oxford: Clarendon).

Stamer, P. Joseph (1995/1996), *Islam in Sub-Saharan Africa* (Konigstein, Germany: Aide a l'Eglise en Detresse; Estella, Spain: Editorial Verbo Divino).

Sumner, Claude (1978), *Ethiopian Philosophy Volume III: The Treatise of Zar'a Ya'eqob and of Walda Heywat. An Analysis* (Addis Ababa University).

Sumner, Claude (1985), *Classical Ethiopian Philosophy* (Addis Ababa University).

Sumner, Claude (1986), *The Source of African Philosophy: The Ethiopian Philosophy of Man [Aethiopistiche Forschungen]* (Stuttgart: Franz Steiner Verlag GMBH).

Sundkler, Bengt, & Christopher Steed (2000), *A History of the Church in Africa* (Cambridge University Press).

Synod of Bishops Special Assembly for Africa (1990), *The Church in Africa and Her Evangelizing Mission towards the Year 2000, 'You shall be my witnesses'* (Acts 1:8): *Liniamenta,* (Vatican City: General Secretarial of the Synod of Bishops and Libreria Editrice Vaticana).

Talal, El Hassan Bin (1998), *Christianity in the Arab World* (New York: Continuum).

Taylor, John V. (1958), *The Growth of the Church in Buganda* (London: SCM).

Temple, Merfyn (1999), *A Dream of Donkeys* (Pangbourne privately published report)

Ter Haar, Gerrie (1992), *Spirit of Africa: The Healing Ministry of Archbishop Milingo of Zambia* (London: Hurst).

Thomas, Keith (1983), *Man and the Natural World: Changing Attitudes in England, 1500-1800* (Oxford University Press).

Tilley, Maureen A. (1994), 'Martyrs, monks, Insects and Animals' in Michael Barnes (ed.), *An Ecology of the Spirit: Religious Reflection and Environmental Consciousness* (Lanham, NY, and London, England: University Press of America).

Toperoff, Shlomo Pesach (1995), *The Animal Kingdom in Jewish Thought* (Northvale, NJ, and London, England: Jason Aronson).

Trimingham, J. Spencer (1952), *Islam in Ethiopia* (Oxford University Press).

Tumart, Ibn, (1998), *The Muslim Creed*, in Constance B. Hilliard, *Intellectual Traditions of Pre-Colonial Africa* (McGraw-Hill) 201.

Twaddle, Michael (1993), *Kakungulu & the Creation of Uganda 1868-1928* (London: James Currey; and Ohio University Press).

Uhlenbroek, Charlotte (2002), *Talking with Animals* (London: Hodder & Stoughton).

Ullendorff, Edward [1968] (1997), *Ethiopia and the Bible: The Schweich Lectures of the British Academy, 1967* (Oxford University Press for the British Academy).

Urban, Linwood (1995), *A Short History of Christian Thought. Revised and Expanded Edition* (New York and Oxford: Oxford University Press).

Vogel, Susan (1988), 'Introduction' to Ezio Bassani and William B. Fagg, *Africa and the Renaissance: Art in Ivory* (New York: The Center for African Art and Prestel-Verlag).

Waddell, Helen (ed.) [1936] (1974), *The Desert Fathers* (London: Constable).

Waliggo, J.M. (1997), in Hannah W. Kinoti & John M. Waliggo (eds.), *The Bible in African Christianity: Essays in Biblical Theology* (Nairobi: Acrton).

Wanjohi, Gerald Joseph (1997), *The Wisdom and Philosophy of the Gikuyu Proverbs: The Kihooto World-View* (Nairobi: Paulines).

Wente, Edward F. (1976), in Katharine Stoddert Gilbert et al (eds.), *Treasures of Tutankhamun* (New York: Metropolitan Museum of Art).

Werner, Alice [1933] (1995), *Africa – Myths & Legends* (London: Senate Studio).

White, T.H. (1954/1960), *The Bestiary: A Book of Beasts* (New York: Putnam and Capricorn).

Wilkinson, John L. (1993), *Church in Black and White. The Black Christian Tradition in 'Mainstream' Churches in England: A White Response and Testimony* (Bonn: Pahl-Rugenstein; Edinburgh: St Andrews Press).

Williams, Cyril G. (1981), *Tongues of the Spirit: A Study of Pentecostal Glossolalia and related phenomena* (Cardiff: University of Wales).

Willis, Roy (1974/1975), *Man & Beast* (Hart-Davis, MacGibbon Ltd.; and St. Albans: Paladin).

Witoshynsky, Mary (2000), *The Water Harvester: Episodes from the Inspired Life of Zephaniah Phiri* (Harare: Weaver).

Young, Frances M. (1979), *The Use of Sacrificial Ideas in Greek Christian Writers from the New Testament to John Chrysostom* (Cambridge, Mass.: The Philadelphia Patristic Foundation).

Zabkar, L.V. (1975), *Apedemak: Lion God of Meroe* (Warminster: Aris & Phillips).

Zeiller, Jacques (1960), 'Clement of Alexandria' in *Christian Beginnings* (trans. P. J. Hepburne-Scott) (New York: Hawthorn).

Zvabva, Oliver (1988), 'Nyachiranga Regional Cult', *unpublished* BA Hons thesis in Religious Studies, University of Zimbabwe, November 1988.

The Holy Qur'an (1991), Arabic text, English translation and commentary by Maulana Muhammad Ali, published by Ahmadiyyah Anjuman Isha'at Islam, Lahore, Inc. U.S.A. [1917] Revised Ed.1991.

The Jerusalem Bible (1966), (Garden City, NY: Doubleday & Co.).

The Oxford Annotated Bible with the Apocrypha (1965), Revised Standard Version (Oxford University Press).

The Lives of the Fathers of the Eastern Deserts: or the Wonders of God in the Wilderness (1885), (New York: D. and J. Sadlier).

Index

Printed in the United States
88740LV00001B/37-44/A